Alain Badiou

C000063197

Modern European Thinkers

Series Editor: Professor Keith Reader,
University of Newcastle upon Tyne

The Modern European Thinkers series offers low-priced
introductions for students and other readers to the ideas and
work of key cultural and political thinkers of the post-war era.

Jean Baudrillard
Mike Gane

Edgar Morin
Myron Kofman

Pierre Bourdieu
Jeremy F. Lane

Walter Benjamin
Esther Leslie

André Gorz
Conrad Lodziak and Jeremy Tatman

Gilles Deleuze
John Marks

Guy Hocquenghem
Bill Marshall

Georges Bataille
Benjamin Noys

Régis Debray
Keith Reader

Julia Kristeva
Anne-Marie Smith

Alain Badiou

A Critical Introduction

Jason Barker

Pluto Press

LONDON • STERLING, VIRGINIA

First published 2002 by Pluto Press
345 Archway Road, London N6 5AA
and 22883 Quicksilver Drive, Sterling, VA 20166–2012, USA

www.plutobooks.com

Copyright © Jason Barker 2002

The right of Jason Barker to be identified as the author of this work has been
asserted by him in accordance with the Copyright, Designs and Patents Act
1988.

British Library Cataloguing in Publication Data
A catalogue record for this book is available from the British Library

ISBN   0 7453 1801 0 hardback
ISBN   0 7453 1800 2 paperback

Library of Congress Cataloging-in-Publication Data

Barker, Jason.
Alain Badiou : a critical introduction / Jason Barker.
p. cm. — (Modern European thinkers)
Includes bibliographical references and index.
ISBN 0–7453–1801–0 (hard) — ISBN 0–7453–1800–2 (pbk.)
1. Badiou, Alain. 2. Political scientists—Biography. 3. Political
science—Philosophy. 4. Philosophy, French—20th century. I. Title.
II. Series.
JC229.B33 B37 2002
320'.092—dc21
2001003499

11   10   09   08   07   06   05   04   03   02
 9   8   7   6   5   4   3   2   1

Designed and produced for Pluto Press by
Chase Publishing Services, Fortescue, Sidmouth EX10 9QG
Typeset in Stone from disk by Gawcott Typesetting Services
Printed in the European Union by TJ International, Padstow, England

Contents

Acknowledgements

I would like to thank Christopher Norris for his expert comments and guidance throughout the researching and writing of this book, particularly the many discussions which were a regular source of inspiration. My sincerest thanks are also due to Martin Jenkins for his support and belief in this project right from the very beginning. Special thanks to Jean-Jacques Lecercle for kindly agreeing to read one of several draft versions of the manuscript, and to Peter Hallward for sending me extracts of his own work in progress. I am grateful to Andy Goffey and the equally talented Benoit Létourneau for – quite unbeknown to them I'm sure – setting my thoughts on the right track. I should also like to thank Alain Badiou for his generous invitation to participate in the colloquium on his work, held at Bordeaux in October 1999, and for providing me with the appropriate biographical details. I must express my appreciation to the staff and acknowledge the excellent facilities at Cardiff University, and thank Gary Winterbottom for his first-rate hospitality on my numerous visits to Cardiff. Thanks to the staff at Pluto Press, particularly Melanie Patrick, Robert Webb and Anne Beech, and to Veronique Serafinowicz for her editorial comments. Needless to say any lingering inconsistencies in my use of Badiou's terminology are solely down to me.

Abbreviations

I refer the reader to my bibliography for full details of the following works. All references relate solely to the French editions with one exception.* In this case corresponding page numbers of the English edition are provided in italics.

CM   *The Concept of Model*
TC   *Theory of Contradiction*
I   *Of Ideology*
NR   *The Rational Kernel of the Hegelian Dialectic*
TS   *Theory of the Subject*
PP   *Can Politics Be Thought?*
EE   *Being and the Event*
MP   *Manifesto for Philosophy*
C   *Conditions*
E   *Ethics*
D   **Deleuze. The Clamour of Being*
AM   *Summary of Metapolitics*
CT   *Short Treatise on Transitional Ontology*
PMI   *Light Inaesthetic Manual*
DO   *An Obscure Disaster*

Introduction: The Unnameable

It is 5 a.m. Paris awakens to barricades, trees strewn in the streets. The protest is, according to General de Gaulle, difficult to grasp. Unforeseeable, it profoundly shakes the government. A radical protest is sweeping France and provoking the most important social movement the country has ever known: ten million strikers. A shock.[1]

The philosophy of Alain Badiou is an impossible wager. Arguably the most ambitious speculative thinker since Hegel and the most materialist since Lucretius, Badiou defies the liberal diplomacy of the linguistic turn and the crisis of Western metaphysics in a heroic effort to rescue philosophy from its time in exile. His intervention in philosophy today forces us to interrogate most if not all of our post-modern beliefs: from the death of Marxism and the deconstruction of the subject to the revival of neo-Kantianism and scientific pragmatism, Badiou pierces the common sense of each and every one in order to reveal, against a backdrop of conventional wisdom, philosophy as a militant discourse on truth.

But who is Badiou? And what are we to make of a 'militant' philosopher so conspicuously deprived of latter-day philosophical allies?

Born in Rabat, Morocco in 1937, Badiou studied at the École Normale Supérieure in Paris between 1956 and 1961, obtaining his *licence* and *maîtrise* from the Sorbonne. In 1958 he helped to found the PSU (United Socialist Party), an offshoot of the French Socialist Party strongly opposed to the French Algerian War. Like many young political activists of his generation, Badiou's anti-imperialist consciousness would prove paramount in dictating the future path of his intellectual life. He wrote the first of several novels – *Almagestes* (1964) – and in 1967 began participating in a Spinoza research group created by the Marxist philosopher Louis Althusser. The same year he was invited to join Althusser's 'Philosophy Course

1

for Scientists'[2] and in 1968, invigorated by the events of May, he began investing his political energies in the setting up of a break-away Maoist organisation, the UCFML (Group for the Foundation of the Union of Marxist-Leninist Communists of France).[3]

It was a major turning point. By now a professor at the University of Vincennes, a modernist enclave and bastion of the Far Left, Badiou joined the struggle for political hegemony of the philosophy department, eventually provoking Gilles Deleuze to denounce his 'Bolshevism' (D, 8; 2). An acolyte of Jacques Lacan, whose unbridled reign over the department of psychoanalysis would prompt a petition from Deleuze and Lyotard against 'Stalinisation',[4] Badiou continued to distance himself from all forms of 'progressive' thinking. Responding to Althusser's *Essays in Self-Criticism* he ridiculed the 'arrogance' of his former master in abandoning the masses under the pretence of 'autocritique', and exposed the errors of Althusser's 'imaginary' theory of the subject (I, 22). He branded Deleuze an 'ideologist' and, at the height of the French renaissance in metaphysics, wrote an uncompromising series of political essays on Maoism – *Theory of Contradiction* (1975), *Of Ideology* (1976) and *The Rational Kernel of the Hegelian Dialectic* (1978). The 1970s also witnessed the rise of another political adversary in the form of the *nouveaux philosophes*, or 'new philosophers', whose self-aggrandising antics would at least serve to underscore the integrity of Badiou's militant exercise. Comprising ex-Maoists like André Glucksmann and Bernard-Henri Lévy, this loose band of philosophical entrepreneurs had no philosophy to speak of, and their only political agenda involved securing a media platform for launching opportunist assaults on the Left.[5] Drowned out by the deluge of the *nouvelle philosophie*, Badiou appeared to be politically out of step as Maoism, in France and China, stood on the brink of ideological collapse. However, as Badiou would come to accept some years later, politics always lags behind events.

In *Theory of the Subject* (1982) Badiou took his lead from Lacan ('our Hegel') in undertaking a detailed analysis of the universal logic of the subject and its endurance of its own historical destruction. Badiou's reliance on Lacanian psychoanalysis was strongly at odds with the Deleuzo-Guattarian construction of a political unconscious. Unlike the anti-psychiatrist Félix Guattari, Badiou never underwent analysis with Lacan, and so crucially had no axe to grind with the institutional arrangements of Lacan's École Freudienne. For Badiou, power was not – and has never been – the issue, and his interest in

Lacan would only ever amount to confirming the status of the latter, along with Mallarmé, as one of 'The two great modern French dialecticians' (TS, 12). Badiou's outright refusal to enter into more open dialogue with Spinozism and the landmark studies of Macherey, Deleuze and Matheron,[6] coupled with his uncritical acceptance of the orthodox Hegelian interpretation of 'Substance', remained a dialectical sticking point. Also at odds with Derridian deconstruction, for Badiou the subject would remain the means of 'propping up' historical contradictions (TS, 40–3).

Badiou shifted his approach, if not his position, in *Can Politics Be Thought?* (1985), adding his voice to the discourse on the death of Marxism while continuing to maintain the symptomatic significance of the resulting crisis for politics. The crisis of Marxism still demanded a subject to *think it* – a subject *of* the crisis – even if Marxism was no longer sufficiently qualified as a doctrine, or credible as a grand narrative, to do so. Moreover, the fact that the Marxist vocabulary, with its sacred talk of States and revolutions, was now completely sterile made no difference to the 'heterogeneous political capacity' of Marxism to explore new ways of doing politics (PP, 53). Here, then, Badiou had risen to the challenge of postmodernism by liberating Marxism from academicism on the one hand, and distancing it from the dogmatism of the party on the other, while at the same time managing to avoid postmodernism's more dubious political side-effects (nihilism, historical relativism).

Badiou's work is polarised by a further crisis often associated with the collapse of grand narratives: namely, the crisis of metaphysics, long since accepted as the lingua franca of postmodern critique. What the crisis induces in the work of Heidegger, Wittgenstein and Lyotard, to name three of its key protagonists, is the anxiety over the question of truth. In the hermeneutic tradition especially, what philosophy is said to think – assuming it thinks at all – is the nostalgia for a time when it – philosophy – was still able to provide answers to the fundamental questions of human existence (Does God exist?[7] What is knowledge? How can a human being live a good life?). The crisis itself, which stretches back as far as Kant, is widely regarded by postmodernists as the sign of something *incurable* in the philosophy and history of the West. When Jacques Derrida writes that Western cultural values 'describe the styles of an historical movement which was meaningful – like the concept of history itself – only within a logocentric epoch',[8] we take him to mean that philosophy no longer exerts the ethical authority that it once had and is destined to remain trapped within a (textual) history of its own making. The fact that 'there is nothing outside the text' hangs a question mark over the universal vocation of philosophy, its ability to tolerate difference, and its disregard for what lies at the margins of sense. Need we recall Plato's repressive decision to expel the poets from the Republic, since their art allegedly dealt with appearances and not truth, as evidence of the *violence* of metaphysics?

The problem of separating truth from mere appearances has indeed been accompanied by an aesthetic orientation in philosophy. 'The moderns, and even more the postmoderns, readily advance the wound that will inflict on philosophy the proper mode whereby poetry, literature, and art in general, attest to our modernity' (C, 101). However, the modern or postmodern 'age of the poets' does not require the prohibition of art as recommended by Plato in the *Republic* in order to safeguard the status of truth, thereby preventing the uncertainty which sometimes hinders our ability to separate fact from fiction. For Badiou, this can only lead to political disaster. Nor at the other extreme does it require a post-classical theory of truth in order to *accommodate* the controversies which nowadays regularly surround scientific interpretation. Badiou would certainly have nothing to do with the logical revisionism of Hilary Putnam *et al.* which regards some of the momentous discoveries of modern physics (e.g. his theory of quantum mechanics) as significant enough to warrant a thorough reappraisal of logic itself.[9] For after all, why should the scientists themselves have a monopoly on truth?

Being and the Event (1988) is Badiou's defiant riposte to the post-modern condition, a condition which claims that philosophy has exhausted its universal history.[10] For Badiou no amount of poetic nostalgia, scientific revisionism or political scepticism is enough to alter what philosophy itself is. *Philosophy is the means of seizing truths.* Truth has no interest in interpretation; instead, truth exposes the gaps in our understanding. What is more, bearing in mind that we have known since Plato that truth is eternal, it is irrelevant to high-light the apparent crises of the regional disciplines (in the arts, politics and science) as evidence of the end of philosophy. The task of philosophy is not to lament its own demise, but to think through the 'conditions'[11] of its renewal, and to prepare the ground for its possible return. The philosopher remains somewhat aloof and disengaged from the normal pressures of the everyday world, all the better to respond, perhaps, to the event of the unexpected. However, the professional philosopher does not inhabit some ideal or imaginary community, but is the architect of a possible, although no less real, realm of experience.

For Badiou access to the real is governed by ontology which he defines as the 'science of being-as-being', a science which is unmistakably Platonist in its founding assumptions about the nature of reality. As we discover in Plato's *Republic*, 'any given plurality of things which have a single name constitutes a single specific type'.[12] Let us consider Plato's example of a table. While the craftsman is only at liberty to manufacture a table based on his own practical expertise, and the artist can only create a mere semblance of the thing (a painting or poetic description), it falls to the philosopher to reveal what the table, as a pure 'type', actually is. The philosopher presents us with the true idea of the table – the essence of 'tableness' so to speak – in which all worldly tables 'participate'. For Badiou the mathematical set theory of Cantor is today the only discourse which can think this idea of plurality directly without resorting to interpretation. A mathematical truth is purely tautological, stripped of all meaning, even to the point of its own deductive consistency, although it is here that the potential difficulties arise. For if a true idea ('pure multiple' in Badiou's jargon) is nothing in particular, then how can it even be said to exist?

The problem of determining the nature of a unique element originates in the thought of the pre-Socratics. According to Parmenides, the void – or what would eventually become the mathematical zero – is 'the negativity of the infinite'.[13] The fact that the void is infinitely multiple while at the same time remaining essentially unchanged provides us with one of the founding principles of ontology, since it permits us to posit an element in terms of what can be subtracted from it. For the mathematician, $0 = n - n$. For example, the number 10 takes its place in the system of decimal notation by virtue of the 0 which makes it a multiple of 5. The void is what *bounds the inconceivable*, and thereby forecloses itself from any other relation, including its self-identity. It is startling that Badiou discovers in the bare concept of the void 'all' the resources for a science of being as being, where being is conceived as pure multiplicity. It is no less ingenious that this science is then used as the conceptual apparatus for an axiomatic reexamination of the history of philosophy itself: 'The *Parmenides* of Plato on the one and difference, Spinoza on excess, Hegel on the infinite, Pascal on the decision, Rousseau on the being of truths, etc.' (CT, 56). Suddenly these familiar categories exhibit all the theoretical consistency ordinarily reserved for the theory of sets.

The void – which adopts the mathematical symbol ϕ – has a supplementary association besides its founding importance for set theory. As well as foreclosing relations the void is also that which annihilates being, and appears (or disappears) into (or out of) existence. Badiou dictates that as far as mathematical ontology is concerned the void should not be mistaken for an 'empirical' or 'astrophysical' phenomenon (EE, 156), although as far as philosophy is concerned the void always implies the existence of something which cannot be rationally accounted for, or 'counted as one'. Mathematics cannot totalise philosophy completely, and occasionally something happens which escapes thought. Badiou names this unforeseen happening the 'event'.

In *Being and the Event* Badiou adds amorous, scientific and artistic events to the politics of his Maoist past. The event is what changes a situation. Quite what the event will turn out to have been after the event, however, is a question of time, or what Badiou calls the 'interval [*écart*] of two events' (EE, 232). That *an* event can only be established by means of its relation to another one, and therefore by means of the event's immanent time-lag, is a brilliant intuition which Badiou retrieves from the dialectical materialist tradition. Unlike Deleuze for whom the event as *Aion*[14] is the '*pure empty form of time*' – 'Always already passed and eternally yet to come'[15] – for Badiou the event marks a definite break in the situation and heralds a true phase in history. The incalculable occurs, and the philosopher is plunged into the process of raising the event above the level of a mere natural phenomenon. Here, then, we gather the sense of Badiou's assertion that his is a philosophy of time.[16]

This philosophy has no object. Following Althusser's lead in *Lenin and Philosophy*, Badiou draws a 'dividing line' between philosophy as the realm of the 'unnameable' – 'the *Kampfplatz* [battlefield] that Kant discussed'[17] – and science as the realm of encyclopaedic knowledge. For Althusser the incision is a militant act which requires an 'intervention' in philosophy, although the 'tendency' of any historical struggle is a 'process without a subject'. For Badiou, by slight but significant contrast, the intervention – akin to a Pascalian wager on truth – sets in motion a 'generic fidelity procedure' during the course of which a subject must *find its name*. In much the same way as the event is always undecidable, the subject's militant integrity is forever being put in question, and beyond doubt only at the expense of imposing – 'forcing' – a linguistic norm on a community. At this ecstatic threshold of the future–past the subject is seized by the impression that something extraordinary did in fact take place (the Russian Revolution, set theory, serialism ...). This post-eventmental fidelity procedure is therefore where philosophy *as* politics, science, art, and love explores its spontaneous capacity for self-expression without becoming a philosophy *of* politics, science, art and love – and therefore without being captured by an already named discourse (which would be associated with the representation of the State or, adopting Badiou's terminology, the 'state of the situation').

The undoubted strength of Badiou's position in *Being and the Event* lies in the *positive uncertainty* – although some might say 'nothingness' – which he adds to our sense of history. The rational juridical foundation of the State merely qualifies the state of nature, and is no more historically final than any other infinite point in time. Philosophy gives us pause to assess, and to inhabit, a limitless horizon of possibilities. And yet despite his assurances to the contrary[18] there is still an unmistakably heroic attitude to Badiou's project – an ascetic heroism at that – which confines the event to four 'purely'[19] generic procedures. Why, we might ask, in an age when the 'law' of the global market provides sufficient grounds for Western State intervention in the internal affairs of developing nations, is there no such thing as an economic event for Badiou? The absence of economics as one of Badiou's favoured practices is not surprising in a period when 'Capital seems to triumph from within its own weakness, and what is ... miserably fuses with what can be' (AM, 115). However, Badiou's insistence that politics must be absolutely subtracted from capital-parliamentary norms is problematic, since it appears to count for its combative force on a blind voluntarism where resistance, rather than a politics aimed at concrete transformation, is the only viable option. In the eyes of neo-Gramscians like Ernesto Laclau and Chantal Mouffe, capitalism provides the civil platform, not for the renunciation of liberal-democratic ideology, but for its expansion 'in the direction of a radical and plural democracy' capable of building solidarity between minority groups.[20] However, this type of socialist strategy – 'communitarianism' – is scathingly criticised, even caricatured by Badiou, for whom 'The peaceful co-existence of cultural, religious, national, etc. "communities", the refusal of "exclusion", is its grand ideal' (E, 26).

As far as the non-reductive theories of difference as advanced by Derrida, Lyotard, and Deleuze are concerned, Badiou remains equally unmoved. 'For the real question, extraordinarily difficult, is much rather that of *the recognition of the Same*.' The blanket deployment of the various concepts of difference can only lead to cultural relativism – 'the genuine fascination of the tourist for the diversity of morals, customs and beliefs'. On Badiou's reading any such 'difference' is nothing of the kind, and only amounts to the '[infinite] banality of every situation' (E, 25–6). It is a wise insight – although perhaps one which only a mathematician could make convincingly – that in order for there to be difference there must first be a measure of sameness which enables comparison between two things.

In *Deleuze: The Clamour of Being* (1997) Badiou embarked on his most controversial project to date by subjecting his former adversary to a scholastic cross-examination. Deleuze is the unrivalled inspiration behind Badiou's presentation of multiplicity, and in *Deleuze* Badiou reopens the file on their unfinished correspondence. The joint author of *Anti-Oedipus: Capitalism and Schizophrenia* is sidelined by Badiou on the grounds that this most celebrated of Deleuze's works belongs to a superseded political conjuncture. Moreover, 'contrary to the common image (Deleuze as liberation of the anarchic multiple of desires and errant flows) ... it is the occurrence of the One, renamed by Deleuze the One-all' (D, 19; *11*) which provides the grounds for debate. Rather than enlisting the support of a potential ally Badiou's study marks not only an intervention in Deleuze scholarship, but also an attempted takeover which, true to Badiou's preferred method, aims to drive a wedge between their respective 'positions': Badiou's 'Platonism of the multiple' versus Deleuze's 'Platonism of the virtual' (D, 69; *46*). Badiou's approach certainly flies in the face of 'standard' Deleuzianism, although as I argue in Chapter 5, whether Deleuze can really be judged by dialectical or scientific criteria is highly questionable. Whether or not Badiou has provided us with a true impression of Deleuze, perhaps only time will tell.

Badiou is above all – although not only – a mathematical philosopher, and no serious introduction to his work could bypass its scientific foundations. He is, on my reading at least, an epistemological and ontological anti-realist, although crucially the terminology is somewhat perilous here due mainly to the influence of Lacan, who makes the virtually polar opposition in the *Écrits* between 'real' and 'reality'.[21] It should also be noted with caution that 'anti-realism' is a term which does not appear anywhere in Badiou's work. My reason for using it here is no more than instrumental in seeking to identify Badiou's scientific method for the benefit of an English-speaking audience who may be unfamiliar with the discourse of French metaphysics. Firstly, an epistemological anti-realist is one who denies that there could ever be adequate correspondence between independently existing objects and our knowledge of them. Secondly, an ontological anti-realist is one who denies the very existence of an objective, mind-independent universe of objects. For Badiou there is nothing outside thought, and questions of objective knowledge and/or existence must be posed solely in terms of what is and what is not thinkable – accepting the aphorism of Parmenides that thought and being are identical[22] – for the subject.[23] Far from guaranteeing any degree of external rapport between subject and object, ontology so defined confronts the immanent possibility of the subject's hypothetical existence. Nothing can be taken for granted as far as the subject is concerned, and it lies beyond the scope of science to verify with any level of empirical assurance that any such thing has ever existed.

Badiou draws on three 'orientations' of set theory in *Being and the Event*, which sometimes complicates the priority he accords to each of them at different stages in the book. Georg Cantor is the originator of set theory's so-called continuum problem, which poses the question: how many sets of integers exist? Traditionally, before the work of Cantor and his fellow mathematician Dedekind in the nineteenth century, the standard response to this question would have been to assert that, since every integer can be increased indefinitely, there is no limit to how many sets of integers can exist. Their number would be infinite, although infinite only in the sense of a virtual and unattainable limit. For example, when counting from 0 the set of ordinal numbers 1, 2, 3, ... we cannot actually *reach* infinity since no matter how far we progress towards it there will always be a number which is 'larger' than the point at which we finish counting. The revolutionary advance of Cantor, however, is to turn the problem completely around. For him, any set of integers which can, in principle, be counted to infinity *is* infinite. According to Cantor's logic the idea, attributable to Aristotle, that we must somehow *physically arrive* at infinity by means of a laborious counting process which – it is already decided in advance! – can always be infinitely extended anyway, is a sophistic mode of reasoning. Such an idea merely chains the infinite to a finite law of indefinite expansion. Cantor's reasoning dictates that in order for there to be an *actual* infinite number it is enough to prove that however many sets of integers exist in the universe (and since we assume that they are infinite it hardly matters how many) their infinity *is countable*.

In Cantor's hands the question of how many infinite sets exist becomes the question of whether infinite sets can be made to correspond with one another and, therefore, be counted. Where a one-to-one correspondence between the elements of one set and those of another can be established we say that these sets share the same cardinal number. Moreover, since the correspondence in question concerns the relations between infinite sets it follows that any difference in quantity between them will amount to an infinite number. Assuming we are able to establish *this* difference then the counting of infinity can commence. However, Cantor's continuum hypothesis turns out to be something of a paradox – not least because the very notion of 'correspondence' between infinite sets soon leads to disputes between mathematicians regarding the consistency of the axioms employed in finding its proof. The 'axiomatisation' of set theory, devised by Ernst Zermelo and eventually named Zermelo-Fraenkel set theory (ZF), introduces a standard system of axioms for the investigation of the continuum hypothesis (CH). An infinite number can only be counted, after all, on condition that any counting operation is consistent with the axioms of extensionality, infinity, the null set, etc. which (purport to) define 'set theory' itself.[24] For Kurt Gödel, inevitable interpretive disputes over the language of set theory meant that Cantor's continuum hypothesis, unsolved in his lifetime, was in all probability undecidable.[25] For Gödel the idea of an infinite set – for the sake of maintaining the integrity of Cantor's original hypothesis – had to be intuitively constructed. Finally, there is the research of Paul J. Cohen which *proves* according to the axioms of set theory that Cantor's continuum hypothesis is not provable.[26] As strange as it may seem, for Cohen it is consistent with the axioms of set theory to regard an infinite set as indiscernible, or 'generic', in the precise sense of wholly lacking definable qualities.[27]

These are the three orientations of set theory which Badiou evaluates in *Being and the Event*: cardinal sets (Cantor *et al.*); constructible sets (Gödel); generic sets (Cohen). In the main I have tried to present literal explanations of the most important axioms of set theory, while at the same time restricting more detailed explanations to endnotes where appropriate. This has been done purely in order to aid understanding. In mathematics an axiom forms part of a chain of reasoning and is abstracted from the system only at the risk of collapsing it. It should be borne in mind that I have not made explicit reference to certain axioms in the main text, although most are covered implicitly in my exposition. Nevertheless I have supplied a brief appendix which provides a very basic shorthand[28] – as opposed to strictly axiomatic – description of the nine axioms of set theory which together comprise ZFC (Zermelo-Fraenkel set theory including the axiom of choice (AC)) in its entirety. The reader should treat the appendix as an optional point of reference only, and rest assured that most of the book will remain perfectly accessible without it. As a final defence I would argue that, although a mathematical philosopher, it is in philosophy rather than mathematics that Badiou's most important contribution and our main interest in him lies. Set theory clearly provides the supporting proofs of his philosophical system, not the reverse.

The reader will note the frequent references throughout the book to the 'State'. As a militant Marxist activist whose main objective during the Maoist 1970s was to affirm the 'withering away of the State' (I, 71), the political meaning of Badiou's 'anti-statism' is unambiguous. As happens occasionally with the English translation of the French État, I have rendered the latter as 'State', i.e. with a capital letter. However, in Being and the Event the State takes on a new significance, and is no longer used simply to refer to political representation. Here Badiou begins to distinguish between 'State' and 'state of the situation', in the latter case to refer to the ontological categorisation of particular elements. For example, in any social situation we can imagine the existence of different classes (e.g. bourgeoisie and proletariat) (EE, 121–8), or relations between different family members (husband, wife, son, daughter, etc.). While the political State is clearly involved when it comes to such arrangements, the important thing to remember is that Badiou does not limit the state of a situation to social relations alone. In the set theoretical sense, any collection of 'things' may be counted as a set (although Badiou recognises three further categories in addition to the political: the artistic, the amorous and the mathematical). For this reason, in Chapters 2, 3 and 4, I have followed Badiou's convention of employing 'State' where a political category is involved, and, for the most part, 'state' or 'state of the situation' in order to refer to ontology in general. Elsewhere I have used 'State' in its purely political sense.

All translations of Badiou's works are my own. At present, and in growing anticipation of its eventual appearance in English, there appears to be no overall agreement on the translation of Badiou's terminology from Being and the Event. For this reason my translations have occasionally been influenced by stylistic concerns rather than purely technical ones. *Le compte-pour-un*, which refers to the fundamental structuring principle of ontology, I have rendered as 'counting-as-one', although occasionally I have used 'counting-for-one' in the broader sense conveyed by the French verb *compter* meaning 'to calculate' as well as 'to account for something'. *L'événementialité* I have rendered as 'eventness', and *événementiel* as both 'eventmental' and 'event' (as in 'event site' (*site événementiel*)). Where other potential ambiguities have arisen I have placed the original French in brackets in the text.

1
Maoist Beginnings

The appearance of Alain Badiou on the intellectual scene does not immediately stand out for us amidst the philosophy of the late 1960s. His profile was first raised in 1967 with his recruitment to Althusser's 'Philosophy Course for Scientists', where he briefly joined the likes of Pierre Macherey, Étienne Balibar, François Regnault and Michel Pêcheux. The next couple of years were to see a temporary meeting of minds, and Badiou's assignment in developing a Marxist theory of mathematics, *The Concept of Model*, finally appeared in 1969. What was to mark Badiou's most decisive contribution of the period, however, arguably came with his article of 1967, published in the French journal *Critique*, 'Le (Re)Commencement du Matérialisme Dialectique'. Ostensibly a review of Althusser's founding studies in Marxism (*For Marx*, *Reading Capital* volumes I and II, and 'Matérialisme historique et matérialisme dialectique'[1]) this article threw down the philosophical gauntlet to Althusser and his most committed followers, and also set the parameters for Badiou's own style of Marxist-Leninist interventions which would soon follow. There is also a strong indication here of the mathematical themes which would eventually crystallise some twenty years later in Badiou's major work, *Being and the Event*.

Hegel or Sartre?

In 1967 Althusser was leading a struggle against 'theoretical sterility' in the French Communist Party. It was a struggle made all the more urgent and yet immensely difficult due to the French Party's inheritance of 'official [Soviet] platitudes'[2] after the Second World War. Then, following the death of Stalin, a challenge beckoned Marxists of a new generation to think through 'the end of philosophy' that Marx had proclaimed famously in the *1844 Manuscripts*. For Althusser the task was twofold: to recover Marxist *philosophy* as an authentic discipline worthy of renewed investigation, while simulta-

13

neously combating the theoretical misunderstandings which had grown up around Marx's writings. Thanks to Althusser, Marxism had finally entered its field of struggle and place of recovery.

In his article Badiou agrees that the years of Soviet revisionism had helped bring about three variants of Marxist philosophy. The 'analogical Marxism' that Althusser presides over views 'the relationship between the structures of the base and the "superstructures", not on the model of linear causality (totalitarian Marxism), nor on that of expressive mediation (fundamental Marxism), but as pure isomorphism' ('Le (Re)commencement', 441). The advance of Althusser, in other words, is to conceive the social totality in terms of different structural arrangements, or combinations, of the same complex whole. This, then, is a 'Marxism of identity' (by no means the first in history) and, we might add, a Marxism of *identification*, which seeks an alternative explanation for causality (what is it?) quite apart from the 'vulgar Marxism' which accepts that the economy is the driving force of every society.

Althusser famously downplays the idea of a linear or teleological causality when it comes to the determination of economic phenomena. According to Althusser, the originality of Marx's scientific revolution lies in the hidden unity which Marx ascribes to such phenomena, a set of hidden relations which are destined to remain unknowable to empirical science. Similarly there is, in the history of Marxist philosophy and particularly in the 'variants of vulgar Marxism', a profound silence on the 'ancient question of the "relations" between Marx and Hegel'. However, to reclaim the proper identity of Marx, the one so often suppressed by Marxist intellectuals (especially the French existentialists led by Sartre after the war), is to recognise first and foremost that 'the problem of the "relations" between the theoretical enterprise of Marx and the Hegelian or post-Hegelian ideology is in all rigour insoluble, that is to say it cannot be formulated' (442). The difference Althusser aims to establish for Marxist science is the pure difference of a 'space', a difference which forms itself, quite paradoxically, from the 'radical *lack*' of the Hegelian dialectic. This making-of-difference in the history of science is not so paradoxical, however, if one considers that every scientific revolution does indeed evolve from the lack of what previous theories could not detect. The history of science throws up numerous 'epistemological breaks' which, although they initially defy all common sense, in time revise the very idea of what constitutes causal relations between objects (consider, for instance,

Einstein's special theory of relativity which is born from the positive deficiencies of Newtonian physics). Crucially, for Althusser, the identity or specific difference of Marx's philosophy (dialectical materialism) is not limited to the latter's discovery of a new science (historical materialism), but extends to the meta-theoretical reading strategies which are employed in order to prove whether a science can truly be regarded as scientific or not.

The potential problems start here. For to claim, as Althusser does, that the science of history depends for its existence on a philosophy which Marx never managed to formulate in person – and could not have done so himself – is to admit that the identity of historical materialism is essentially 'impure' (447). With Marx we must therefore assume that identity is an altogether 'different' phenomenon, not limited to the object of historical materialism (which in *Capital* is political economy), but which includes the *concept* of that object. The impurity of historical materialism is especially worthy of attention. Althusser's eclectic borrowing from philosophical traditions which clearly have nothing whatsoever to do with the Marxist heritage (Spinoza, Lacan, Bachelard) claims to present us with a science of ideology – or the 'complexity of the relations between science and ideology, their organic mobility' (452) – if not science itself. We might say that what Althusser aims to reveal is the 'measure' of Marx's scientific discovery in terms which Marx himself would have been unfamiliar with, yet nonetheless still manage to convey something (an ideology) of the revolutionary significance of Marx's epistemological break as a pure 'knowledge effect'. (This is arguably the most original aspect of Althusser's return to Marx, a return not to Marx's actual world-view, but to the epistemological conditions that enabled a discovery as groundbreaking as Marx's to occur.) As such, the concept of political economy, and of *understanding* how such an object functions in the real world, requires us first of all to keep pace with the 'time-lag' (*décalage*) which necessarily separates every truly scientific system from its 'order of presentation-connection' (452–3). This is a question of how to maintain the *consistency* of a scientific system, a question which, as Badiou notes, has no straightforward solution for Marxism since 'the theoretical presentation of the *system* of a science does not belong to this science' (453). In the case of Marxism, we must assume that historical materialism can only gain its consistency by importing its theory of knowledge from outside it, and in Althusser's case from conventionally non-Marxist discourses at that (e.g. Spinozism, Lacanianism ...). This is the only way that Marxism could ever hope to produce adequate *knowledge* of its conjuncture.

What Althusser means, then, by 'dialectical materialism' is a mechanism for the production of conjunctures. There is an infinity of phases ('attributes' for Spinoza) of the conjuncture, but in general each conjuncture (is there more than one?) is made up of a set of 'relatively autonomous' instances. One of these instances will be 'dominant', as in the case of the ideology of the Church during the Middle Ages. However, such an instance or 'structure in dominance' cannot *determine* the social reality which it otherwise appears to govern. Like every great event of historical importance, the conjuncture always runs ahead of itself in the sense that its practices (scientific, political, ideological, etc.) always fall short of their combined efficacy. This shortfall might equal the 'overdetermination' of a political situation (e.g. the Weimar Republic) where the conditions for its transformation (e.g. Nazism) remain unseen and can only be re-presented once the transformation has actually occurred. The determinant practice of every conjuncture is therefore the absent cause of an 'already structured whole' (457).

What Althusser envisages with his theory of determinant practice ('economism') is Spinoza's theory of substance. The social totality is completely invested by the economy, although the latter shows up only in its 'effects' (specific practices). In other words we might say that the economy is the very substance of eternity. (As Althusser often remarks, following Engels, the economy is always determinant 'in the last instance', but a last instance whose 'lonely hour' 'never comes'.[3]) The task facing Althusser is therefore to come up with an 'adequate idea' of this structural arrangement, an idea which, as Badiou says, would *actually be* a conjuncture (458). However, before such a task can even begin there is a more pressing problem to contend with. For if determination is an absent cause, a cause gauged only in its effects, then how is it really possible to think it adequately? In Spinoza, determination is the thing already determined, or rather the process of determination remains invisible. And so any claim to be able to distinguish accurately between different aspects of a whole, or modes of a conjuncture, would appear to depend on an adequate idea of what *distinction* actually is. As Badiou says:

> The distinction of the levels of a social formation (political, aesthetic, economic, etc.) is presupposed in the construction itself

of the concept of determination, since determination is *nothing other* than the structure in dominance defined *by* the set of instances. (461)

Unless Althusser is claiming to be able to produce a conjuncture practically out of thin air – in the act of thinking or writing perhaps – it would appear that (the absent cause of) the conjuncture depends for its existence on some kind of '*preliminary* formal discipline' where the concept of determination could be worked out. To this end Badiou proposes a '*theory of historical sets*', which – as we shall see in the following chapters – would amount to a kind of formal logic enabling us to construct the conjuncture theoretically, axiom by axiom. 'This discipline,' Badiou asserts, is 'strictly dependent in its complete development on the mathematics of sets.'

Of course, at this stage Badiou's critique becomes more than just a critique. For in proposing a set of mathematical operators which regulate the sets of relations between dominant and determinant practices, etc., Badiou is anticipating a separate theoretical project. Can we not say therefore – despite the benefit of hindsight which affords us a sense of perspective here – that the 'problems' Badiou identifies on Althusser's behalf belong to an altogether different problematic from the one in which Althusser's work is actually situated? This is hardly a straightforward question, since it presumes an adequate conception of the 'object of knowledge' upon which Althusser's philosophical system depends. We might as well ask, *What constitutes an identity? By what set of determinate criteria is a conjuncture one? What would constitute the effective limits of a problematic?* In fact, Badiou's criticisms are far more modest as far as the sweeping ambition of Althusser's return to Marx is concerned. In a long footnote, however, it becomes clear that Badiou's support is qualified when it comes to the detail, and namely the general question of science. Badiou highlights at this point Althusser's tendency in *Reading Capital* to distinguish between the 'concept' (of the economy) on the one hand, and the '"mathematical" protocols of its manipulation' ('the instruments of econometrics') on the other.[4] Badiou is in no doubt that Althusser is making a grave error here. Mathematics is not employed for the purposes of defining, expressing or vouchsafing the existence of an already formed concept since, in Badiou's words, 'mathematics is ... in physics, in biology, etc., ... a productive activity' (464, 28n.; translation modified).

In Badiou's estimation, Althusser's return to Marx nevertheless marks, in and of its time, the beginning of the road to renewal in Marxist theory. Althusser enables us to see that the theoretical sterility afflicting Marxist philosophy in the post-war period is the inverse measure of its renewal. Never again after Althusser will it be possible for Marxists to pretend that work is always and in all circumstances the dominant factor under capitalism, or that work is a contest staged by the bourgeoisie.[5] It is largely down to Sartre that this crude gladiatorial portrait of man the 'species being' stifles Marxist philosophy after the war. Like Althusser, Badiou regards this image as a profound deformation requiring careful exposure. However, as far as Althusser's anti-Hegelian polemic is concerned, Badiou distances himself from any outright renunciation of Hegelian principles. Whilst acknowledging the 'major Hegelian tyranny' which has invaded Marxism down the years, Badiou is unwilling merely 'to declare oneself outside Hegel in order to exit effectively from a confounded realm' (465). The true extent of Marx's philosophical debt to Hegel may well have become confused down the years, but such confusion is the inevitable side-effect, rather than the cause, of Marxism's history of repression.[6] What the conjuncture urgently required in the meantime was a theory of politics to accompany Althusser's theory of science, a theory capable of 'reflecting the political conjuncture *in our theoretical conjuncture*, and vice versa'. It would not be too long before Badiou's demand signalled the parting of the ways between himself and Althusser.

Subjects of Contradiction

In the event the call of the conjuncture went unheeded by Althusser. The need to drive out the last vestiges of Hegel – from Lenin's *Notebooks* this time – had, by 1968, become a personal obsession. In his essay 'Lenin and Philosophy', Althusser began to redefine philosophy as the 'battle' for scientific knowledge, and as 'the class struggle in theory'.[7] For Badiou, on the other hand, everything had already changed. The events of May 68 had, in his own frank admission, 'transformed from top to bottom the content and forms of the ideological struggle and of the theoretical investigation' (TC, 8). By the following year Badiou had begun teaching courses in Marxism, Leninism and Maoism at Vincennes, and in 1970 set up a Marxist-Leninist splinter group, the UCFML (Group for the Foundation of the Union of Marxist-Leninist Communists of France). These were the years of wholesale transition – the Chinese Cultural Revolution, the Khmer Rouge in Cambodia, the NLF in Vietnam – which demanded clear, partisan commitments from French communists. The anti-revisionist and anti-imperialist struggles, both at home and abroad, could only be waged successfully with the aid of a fully integrated understanding – a combined *strategy* no less – of theory and practice. The time for science had well and truly been put on hold.

Althusser's major Maoist-inspired work is well known. 'Ideology and ideological state apparatuses' (1970) emerges as the preliminary sketch for a theory of 'ideology *in general*', ideology which 'represents the imaginary relationship of individuals to their real conditions of existence' and which 'interpellates individuals as subjects'. The essay lends itself, as countless criticisms have repeated down the years, to an 'unduly functionalist' interpretation of human agency.[8] The subject, in recognising the absolute Subject, misrecognises the objective fact of his or her personal identity (that it is structured as a fantasy) and so willingly enters into the circuits and rituals of social reproduction governed by the I.S.A.s (the Church, the school, the family, etc.). Althusser's approach to subjectivity could be stretched to parodic limits here (the Cultural Revolution as mass hysteria), and today tends to be regarded – a little unfairly perhaps – less as an accurate reflection of a political conjuncture, and more as the symptom of impending crisis in the internal politics of the French Communist Party.[9] By stark contrast, in 1970, having already split from the PSU (United Socialist Party), Badiou had freed himself from any hint of political compromise. The theoretical battle-lines were now drawn.

In the remainder of this chapter I want to consider three of Badiou's most important political essays from the 1970s: *Theory of Contradiction* (1975), *Of Ideology* (1976) and *The Rational Kernel of the Hegelian Dialectic* (1978). As well as reflecting the wider politics of the period and laying the groundwork for Badiou's subsequent writings, taken together these essays also gauge the degree and the quality of criticism which began to assail the French Left from all quarters during the 1970s. As a Maoist convert, Badiou was fair game for such 'revisionist' criticism, and by 1975 the general shift away from popular struggles of liberation was so complete that André Glucksmann, one of several Maoist agitators at Vincennes in the aftermath of May 68, was finally able to indict Marxism with the crimes of the gulag.[10]

Theory of Contradiction is part theoretical treatise and part polemic against revisionism.[11] The first important thing to bear in mind about this book is that, like all Maoist works, it is wholly enmeshed in the ideological struggles of its time. Maoism is an extreme development in the history of the class struggle in the sense that it aims to amalgamate all the elements of social practice under the strict jurisdiction of the party line. From the extension of Engels' investigations of the dialectical laws governing nature, to the principles of military strategy ('Politics is war by other means'[12]), Maoism aims its sights no lower than a *cosmology* of social practice. However, the suggestion that Maoism is a philosophical system requires a word of caution. 'Dialectical materialism,' Badiou says in the book's short preamble, 'is not a system in the sense of speculative philosophy'; 'the great philosophical interventions of proletarian leaders' are inspired by the 'concrete demands of ideological struggle' while, 'Each time, philosophy is plainly the philosophy of the *party*' (TC, 11).

The shift in emphasis from the Badiou of 1967 is tangible and is plainly conceived as part of a wider assault on the Althusserians. Class struggle is no longer ruled by an 'internal systematic necessity', but is transformed by the burgeoning, dialectical development of theory in practice. With Maoism the resolution of theoretical problems is not an abstract question. Theoretical problems instead attain their 'reason', their dynamic historic necessity, in the real-life struggles of the masses. The most decisive slogan of the Cultural Revolution in China – '"It is correct[13] to revolt against the reactionaries"' [*On a raison de se révolter contre les réactionnaires*] – is geared towards achieving this aim (TC, 15). Arguably *the* central defining axiom of Marxism as revolutionary practice ('the masses make history') recovers its full revolutionary impetus, and therefore its principle of movement, in such revolt. It is the fact that such revolt has 'reason' at its core which permits us to say that practice, although 'dialectically opposing itself to knowledge (to theory), is nevertheless an integral part of knowledge as process' (TC, 18). It therefore follows that there can be no access to knowledge not grounded, and which does not begin, in the objective reality of the class struggle.

Badiou qualifies 'reason' in three ways. Firstly, reason means a *subjective* revolt against the reactionaries – which acquires its force from within the 'unconditional and permanent character' of the class struggle – and which goes by the name of the proletariat. That society is originally divided is the first reason, and the legitimate ground, to revolt. Secondly, reason is the *objective certainty* of the proletariat's revolutionary triumph. Here reason is completely opposed to any moral interpretation in the Kantian sense. One revolts because one is compelled as a proletarian to do so, not because morally one should (the latter disposition is merely the product of a rational bourgeois norm). In this sense proletarian revolution is the most natural expression of the proletariat's 'unlimited power'. That the revolution is destined to be victorious is the second reason to revolt. Finally, reason implies the development of the circumstances that make revolution possible in the precise sense of the *direction* which Marxism brings to this development. 'Revolt arms itself with its own reason, instead of just deploying it. It *concentrates* its rational quality: it organises its reason, and disposes the instruments of its victory.' That Marxism provides the strategy for the alignment (the correct party line) of the proletariat with the objective demands of the class struggle is the ultimate reason of revolt (TC, 21–5).

Maoism, in the highly integrated nature of its dialectic of theory/practice, advances Marxist thought significantly in its approach to the key question of contradiction. Whereas Engels was held back in this respect by his adherence to the Hegelian idealist formula of the 'negation of the negation', and Stalin's dictatorship was beset by a voluntarism which subordinated a thorough understanding of the dialectic to the imperative of economic development ('dynamic materialism'), Mao, thanks to Lenin's summary remarks in the *Philosophical Notebooks*, recovers the most sophisticated axiom of dialectical thought so far: 'the primacy of contradiction over identity' (TC, 39–43). The world, and particularly the world in which Mao's anti-imperialist campaigns were once waged, is constantly being reborn from the ruins of social conflict. As such the idea of 'synthesis' only ever amounts to a superficial understanding of such conflict. It is because 'one divides itself in two' (rather than two merging together into one) that synthesis is made possible. Real synthesis is simply what Mao refers to as 'non-antagonistic contradiction': the relative 'stalemate' of antagonism.[14] Of course, in making this point Badiou is deliberately opposing Althusser, whose marginal comments in *For Marx* on Mao's theory of contradiction are woefully inadequate given the prevailing circumstances of the conjuncture.[15] 'Here,' Badiou observes, 'thought enlivens the revolt against the dismal wisdom of ecclesiastic submission. To "nothing new under the sun", [the first principle of contradiction responds with] the forever new insurgent red sun, under the emblem of the unlimited affirmative hope of rebel producers generating ruptures' (TC, 51; translation modified).

For the Maoists, metaphysics (and Spinoza is the generic target on display here) always has a conservative stake in historical analysis. It is always the metaphysical ideologues who don the cloak of objectivism in order to preserve and conceal the vested interests of the ruling class.[16] However, the first principle of contradiction, which proclaims that 'all reality is process', militates against the preservation of any particular interests. For the real Marx, the only scientific invariant is change.

It is on this point that Badiou confronts what he regards as the inherent weakness of Althusser's rival approach to the question of contradiction, which for Althusser is always an overdetermined concept. In his essay 'Lenin Before Hegel', Althusser draws our attention to the fact that, in his study of Hegel's *Logic*, Lenin equates the real historical process with the Absolute. 'Lenin takes from Hegel,' Althusser says, 'the following proposition:

> there is only one thing in the world which is absolute, and that is the method or the concept of the process, itself absolute. And as Hegel himself suggested by the beginning of Logic, being = nothingness, and by the very place of Logic, origin negated as origin, Subject negated as Subject, Lenin finds in it a confirmation of the fact that is absolutely essential ... *to suppress every origin and every subject, and to say*: what is absolute is *the process without a subject*, both in reality and in scientific knowledge.[17]

The problem with such a formulation, Badiou argues, is that the attention Lenin actually pays to the Absolute Idea in the *Notebooks* has no bearing on the question of the subject, which Lenin tackles separately. Moreover, when Lenin actually gets round to it, it is not the subject which he suppresses, but its 'idealist predicates' (Origin, God), which Althusser quite blindly chooses to regard as being synonymous with the subject itself. The historical process is a process – *qua* process – which relies on the suppression of precisely these types of dogmas, a militant process *with* a subject which moves from the in-itself of the class struggle to the for-itself of proletarian revolt (TC, 55–8).

For Badiou, not only is reality a process, but this process is itself in a state of division. This is the second principle of contradiction: 'Every process is a set of contradictions.' This second principle is no less radical in its implications for Marxism, since it completely obliterates the idea of totality. What is real is not the holistic nature of the thing (social reality viewed as a whole), but its inherent division

(TC, 61). There is a fundamental *dis*equilibrium between unity and division which sees off any unity of contraries. There is a constant struggle, a 'reciprocal exclusion', between the elements of a set; we find *'nothing in common* between bourgeoisie and proletariat, between revisionists and Marxist-Leninists, except to define … the divided unity of a historic process …'. Furthermore, 'The unity (of contraries) is a relation, not an identity. *The intersection of contraries is void'* (TC, 64). As we shall see, when it comes to the theoretical detail of Badiou's mathematical thinking the void will remain a key axiom. However, in the meantime the question arises as to precisely how, given that every process is a set of contradictions, it might be possible to pick out a single one. As Badiou notes, 'It only makes sense to speak of *one* process as far as we envisage a system of contradictions whose interdependence finds itself ruled by their qualitative subordination to *one* of the contradictions of the system.' This is the third principle of contradiction: 'in every process, there is a principal contradiction' (TC, 66).

There are numerous examples of a principal contradiction. For instance, bourgeoisie/proletariat is the principal contradiction of the global contradiction of capitalist society. At a much lower level, during a factory strike, the principal contradiction would be workers/employers. Each principal contradiction will include a number of secondary contradictions which refine the precise nature of the principal contradiction. For example, during a strike there will be disputes between workers (strikers and strike-breakers) as well as between the strikers themselves, who tend to split into opposing camps (e.g. ultra-leftists versus unionists), each one of which will also be split by its own share of internal divisions (TC, 69). Furthermore, this deepening scission requires a penultimate principle of contradiction, which states that every contradiction will have a principal aspect. For example, during the course of a strike, a decisive stage in its combat might hinge upon the dispute between rival groups of workers. In this case the principal contradiction of workers/employers would become secondary to one of its principal aspects, e.g. strikers/strike-breakers. However, there is, as Badiou admits, a problem with this rather abstract principle. For 'if principal and secondary [contradictions] convert themselves one into the other, is it not the case that the supreme law of the dialectic is a simple principle of *permutation*, a simple change of places?' (TC, 71).

In posing this question Badiou is aiming his critique at two philosophical revisionist camps: the structuralists on the one hand, and the metaphysicians on the other. Superficial disputes aside, both camps are united in their adoption of metaphysical solutions to systemic contradictions. In the case of the structuralists, the mobility or positive transformation of language (*la langue*) as a system of differences 'without positive content' is seen as being somehow internal to the system itself. While in the case of the metaphysicians the notion of 'text' obscures the disciplinary boundaries between philosophy and literature, giving rise to an infinite play of textual differences beyond the static opposition of binary pairs (nature/culture, etc.). Jacques Derrida is the philosopher who first began the deconstruction of scientific objectivism, and whose three landmark texts of 1967,[18] along with a host of other 'post-structuralists',[19] ushered in 'a new, carnivalesque order of reason'. The post-structuralist preference for 'undecidables' 'as veritable units of simulacrum'[20] would in future years barely unsettle the consistency of Badiou's scientific enterprise (indeed, for Badiou the undecidable remains an axiomatic formula). Politically, there is nothing surprising about the vacillation of avant-garde philosophers. In *The German Ideology* Marx and Engels draw our attention to the fact that for every landmark event in the history of the class struggle there will be those who attempt to hijack or subvert its revolutionary movement. For Stirner's *The Ego and His Own* read Deleuze and Guattari's latter-day *Anti-Oedipus* (TC, 72). The principle of revolutionary practice distinguishes, or separates, the Marxist-Leninists from a common enemy. But how does such practice actually manage to exit the vicious circle of movement as a *virtual* process, where 'every struggle is reciprocal benefit, every victory is defeat', and where every adversary unmasked – we assume – turns out to be really indistinguishable from a masked ally? (TC, 75)

The answer lies in the final principle of contradiction, which holds that the principal aspect of a contradiction must ultimately be divided between antagonistic and non-antagonistic tendencies. Every dialectical pair (e.g. bourgeoisie/proletariat) implies a relation between a dominant and dominated term – although such an arrangement is not in and of itself dialectical, and will remain a purely static and structural opposition in the absence of a clear understanding of the historical process. For example, consider the mutual dependence which ordinarily unites bourgeoisie and proletariat in their joint regulation of the capitalist economy. Here, any antagonism is masked due to the fact that both sides have apparently entered into a mutually binding contract based on the 'free exchange' of labour in return for wages. Here, 'dominant' and 'dominated' are purely *arbitrary* markers of the indifference of one class's relation to the other. The terms tell us nothing about the real level of domination which one class exerts *over* the other, but simply the extent to which both manage to coexist in a state of relative 'harmony', the continued existence of one being dependent on the continued existence of the other, etc. However, in the context of an event like May 68 we see that 'dominant' and 'dominated' are now *determinate* markers of the antagonism upheld by the bourgeoisie, since during the course of the national strike the latter emerges as the principal aspect of the contradiction of the striking workers, the collapse of the French economy, the injustice of bourgeois law, etc. At this point, a transformation begins whereby one of the terms of the contradiction (in this case the proletariat) makes a bid to seize hold of the dominant place occupied by the bourgeoisie (TC, 85–6). This moment of ascendancy of one class/corresponding defeat of the other is the real movement of history; it is the antagonism of a contradiction finally unmasked.

Needless to say, for Badiou the conjuncture of the 1970s had by no means exhausted its capacity for revolutionary change on a global scale, despite the growing objections of the *nouveaux philosophes*[21] to the Marxist project in France. The French situation is not the world. Moreover, the struggle between exploiters and exploited is forever being modified, as bourgeoisie and proletariat split into a myriad of upwardly and downwardly mobile class fractions. What does not change, despite these superficial and *weak* manifestations of difference, is the structural arrangement of exploitation in capitalist society and its future, historical tendency towards extinction (TC, 80). Here, then, we reach the strategic resolution of contradiction: that eventually one of the terms of the contradiction is jettisoned into the dustbin of history. There is, according to the Maoist exercise in revolutionary practice, no toleration of the halfway house offered by syndicalism.[22] Instead, the revolution lasts until the very end, until even the ashes of the bourgeoisie, its economy, laws and culture, are swept away without a trace (TC, 87).

Red Targets

Theory of Contradiction was conceived as a Marxist-Leninist intervention in a specific conjuncture, and is undoubtedly the victim of its own radical theory of supersession. Today, the legacy of Maoism has all but disappeared. However, in redirecting our focus to the surrounding context of Badiou's work, the book arguably makes a much more lasting impression. That philosophy is a *practical* activity, something which people actually *do* and therefore produce themselves – although invariably without knowing it – remains to this day a highly contemporary, and no less contentious, issue. The manifold political assemblages of May 68 – of which the long since defunct La Gauche Prolétarienne (GP) is the most famous example – epitomise this ideal with their modish 'politics of the act'. However, the fact that by the mid-1970s the founder members of the GP had traded in their activism for autobiographical reflections on their past experiences as militants would appear to confirm one thing at least: namely, that 'the bourgeoisie is the blind subject of its politics' (I, 18). For Badiou, the arrogant reflections of ex-GP militants like André Glucksmann cannot exit so easily from the ongoing reality of the class struggle, much as they would like to draw a line under their former adventures as Maoists and advocate instead that the question of history is henceforth to be read in terms of 'intertextuality'.[23] The 1970s would also witness the rightward drift of the *Tel Quel* scholars, whose editor Philippe Sollers became one of the chief targets for Badiou's Le Groupe Foudre.[24] As the leaflets of this wayward band of cultural assassins would fatefully announce, May 68 could not be spirited away like some old-fangled liberal experiment in social reform. On the contrary, the May events were part of an ongoing revolutionary movement whose momentum would be forever actively restored with the deviation of each and every leftist acolyte.

In *Of Ideology* (1976), Badiou, in collaboration with François Balmès, sets out to draw up an 'assessment' of the latter-day ideo-logues in an attempt to rid the conjuncture of the last vestiges of '"ultra-left" ideologism: Deleuze and his desire, Glucksmann and his gulag' (I, 8). Ideology is not a representation of the imaginary rela-tions of individuals to their social practice – nor is it attributable to a group fantasy of the masses. Ideology, in its classic Marxist sense, is a partisan activity, inseparable from the philosophy of the ascen-dant class and its concrete practice. Philosophy and ideology, in this practical sense, are perfectly synonymous. As Badiou and Balmès (hereafter BB) note:

> The dominant ideology, Marx says, is the reflection of the prac-tices of domination of a class. It *expresses* the 'material relations', it is not a specific *function*, operating in the element of the uncon-scious. (I, 19)

If ideology is not a function of some primary psychic mechanism, but instead reflects, albeit in an 'approximate way', dominant ideas as the very means of domination itself, then it becomes clear that ideological struggle must involve all the elements of theory and practice. Ideas are thus the immediate 'expression' of social forces. As such, contesting the forces of domination in theory becomes a practical undertaking. In the context in which BB are writing, any attempt to deny the immanence of class analysis would be, at best, to underestimate the extent to which social forces penetrate all levels of society – while, at worst, it would be to deny the role which said forces play in a particular author's practice. 'There is always an essential bond,' BB note, 'between the deliberate obscuring of the question of ideology and the refusal to take part in the most obvious class divisions' (I, 20). The intellectual performs a class-based activity. As such the suggestion that ideology is an imaginary or unconscious relation is to dissolve the antagonism that exists, necessarily and immediately, in the context of the class struggle where the intellectual consciously adopts a position. Furthermore, the accompanying suggestion that ideology is a representation of imaginary relationships is a typically dominant conception of ideology that the exploited classes have had to endure down the centuries. Take, for instance, the religious ideology of the feudal aristocracy which held that all men were equal in the eyes of God; and 'everyone knows that bourgeois juridical ideology rounds off its doctrine of social arbitration between different "partners", of an absolute equality (all theoretical) before the law as before power (universality of suffrage)' (I, 40). Ideology *is* the spontaneous struggle of the exploited against the exploiters. However, its revolt against oppression will be 'in effect *unrepresentable*, since it affirms antagonism practically, and demands concrete equality even within social relations'.

Ideology and Power

In the second part of their book BB consider the relationship between ideology and power, and how the '*unrepresentable* practice in the dominant ideology (revolutionary class revolt)' might be able to rise up in real, concrete terms. Michel Foucault's *Discipline and Punish* (1975), at that time having been published the previous year in France, had already put forward a radically new way of thinking power relations in society. According to Foucault, power in the era of modernity was no longer centralised in the person of the State as it had been in the *ancien régime*, but instead had become domesticated in the everyday workings of the social body, which Foucault defined using the figure of Jeremy Bentham's panopticon. Bentham's utilitarian doctrine enabled Foucault to propose that power was no longer a matter of punishment, but had become an essential *discipline* of social relations; that power *was* socialisation itself.

Foucault's book provides us with a materialist account, and therefore a significant advance, in our understanding of power as an endemic social practice. Rather than being vested in the people's representatives who hold power over or on behalf of the people, power exists as a largely self-regulating economy of individuation.[25] Henceforth there is no power in itself, no necessity for power to exist. Power is instead the *product* of a concrete network of social relations. In Foucault's work, however, such blanket panopticism remains ambivalent as regarrds the possibility of resistance, and particularly the organised resistance of a class subject. Foucault's view that the individual is a product of power enables him to extend his analysis of the self-disciplinary 'agencies' of power (the prison, factory, asylum, school) to include what he calls 'bio-power', i.e. a social anatomy of the human species being and the politicisation of its sexuality.[26] For BB, in the context of the ongoing class struggle, this interpretation would clearly amount to a one-sided, 'fascist' conception of politics.[27] Power as domination is dialectical, a product not of an unconscious or undifferentiated socius, but of a struggle between dominant and dominated forces.

> Certainly, the dominant ideology, representation of practices of class domination, penetrate the whole field of social practices, understood as those of the exploited. But this penetration must be understood as a contradictory process ... There is a dominant ideology only because there exists a permanent resistance to this domination. And it is from the point of view of this resistance that the domination appears as such, that's to say as representation of concrete domination, the domination of class. (I, 46)

As BB proceed to argue, only a blind ignorance of the history of the class struggle, or else an abandonment of class-based analysis, can lead ultra-leftists like Deleuze and Guattari to proclaim that: '"no, the masses were not innocent dupes; at a certain point, under a certain set of conditions, they wanted fascism, and it is this perversion of the desire of the masses which needs to be accounted for"'

(I, 48, citing Deleuze and Guattari, *Anti-Oedipus*). On the contrary in fact, the chain of events which lead, in any historical conjuncture, to the onset of fascism can be adequately explained, albeit in retrospect: 'the Spartacist insurrection in Germany, the strikes of 1920 and the movement of the councils in Italy' were all clearly integral to the rise of fascism in Germany. However, to propose that these proletarian defeats led inexorably to the point where the masses desired fascism is to underestimate grossly the sizeable body of the masses who, both prior to and during the war, *resisted* fascism. The only 'desire' of the masses is their deviation from a revolutionary path. Moreover, '"Fascist" discourse, in truth, does not exist. All that exists are the concrete (varied) forms of a violent victory of the counter-revolution' (I, 48–50).

For BB the location of resistance is where the study of power and domination must commence. The struggle against oppression and exploitation is always resisted by the affirmative revolt of the masses. Here the masses will, in true Maoist fashion, be doubly split – firstly, between dominant and dominated (the State and the mass of the exploited classes); and, secondly, between the dominated fraction of the dominated group on the one hand (the English factory workers), and those who effectively manage to carry their resistance through to the end of a popular struggle on the other (those English workers in their struggle for the Ten Hours' Bill of 1848) (I, 55–8). As BB point out, such victories in the history of the working class movement amount to more than minor concessions prized from the capitalists. Such victories have a much more affirmative character in marking a decisive blow for a rival political economy, an 'other' world-view in the ascendant: the political economy of the proletariat (I, 58)!

In every mass revolt there exists the germ of emancipation struggling for ideological expression. Furthermore, 'all the great revolts of the mass of successively exploited classes (slaves, peasants, proletarians) find their ideological expression in the egalitarian formulations, anti-property and anti-statist, which constitute the lineaments of a communist programme' (I, 66). BB rely on the historical figure of Thomas Münzer, the leader of the peasants in Germany in the sixteenth century, in order to illustrate this point.[28] Although he was a Christian reformist, BB argue that Münzer's programme held together all the demands of a communism of the masses *in embryonic form*. For example, Münzer's leadership of the peasants, although chastised by the Church for heresy before being violently suppressed, exposed the fragile unity of Christianity at a time of mounting crisis in the Church (the Reformation) (I, 69–70). BB name these rational kernels of mass uprisings 'communist invariants', which, given the fact that they express a spontaneous demand ('end exploitation now!'), remain politically unrepresentable *as such* by the dominant class. The communist invariants nevertheless always manage to anticipate – if not actually succeed in stabilising – the eventual resolution of a revolutionary process. After all, was it not that great ideologue of the burghers, the ascendant class of the sixteenth century, Martin Luther, for whom Thomas Münzer's peasant uprising of 1524 first cleared the way? The communist invariants are the avant-garde of mass political movements. Moreover, the proletariat is the first class in history able to break the disconnected cycle of historical revolts and provide these move-ments with real consistency and objective development: from the 'spontaneous justice' of the masses to the proletarian theory of revo-lution itself (I, 100).

But isn't there a familiar problem with this idea of transition? For how can one hope to maintain the real integrity of a *proletarian* science when communism as a mass movement is, according to its invariants (anti-property, anti-statism), unrepresentable? Is it not the destiny of proletarian 'logic' – '"the algebra of the revolution"' (I, 108) – and as a matter of strategic necessity, to be directed, or re-presented in its revolutionary struggle, by the bourgeoisie? As familiar as this question sounds in the history of Marxist-Leninism it nevertheless results from some basic yet highly crucial misunder-standings of Marx's central ideas. Let us pause at this stage of our exposition in order to clarify the line being followed by BB.

1. *The class struggle.* Although evidently composed of dominant and dominated forces, it is *not* the case that domination exists in any pure state, or is somehow 'caused' by the class 'in power', e.g. the bourgeoisie. The key distinction here is between domination/resistance – or dominant/dominated forces – which is an entirely natural feature of every society, and the predomi-nance of the ruling class in securing for itself certain material advantages, which is not.

2. *Proletarian organisation.* Given the essentially divided nature of class struggle, there is no reason why the genuine integrity of proletarian science should be diluted by bourgeois directives since there are no longer purely bourgeois directives. Furthermore, as the *Communist Manifesto* spells out in no uncertain terms, the

proletariat's success in furthering its class aims lies in its ability to tie its fortunes to those of an ascendant class *when and only when* the demands of the latter happen to coincide with its own (and of course the *Manifesto* notes how the identity of the ascendant class will vary over time and between places).[29] Consider, by way of illustration, the sudden conversion of Proudhon to the French Revolution of 1848, when on 24 February the timid pacifist uprooted trees in the Place de la Bourse in order to reinforce the barricades and accepted the task of printing pamphlets urging the overthrow of Louis Philippe.[30] The recruitment of the bourgeoisie to the cause of the people in times of national crisis – what Marx viewed as the capacity to convert spontaneously from a programme of reform to one of direct action – epitomises the communist mode of organisation.

'The organisation of class,' remark BB, 'is the decisive contribution of the proletariat to thought itself'; 'Proletarian organisation is the body of new logic.' Moreover:

> From this point of view, that which is in play today in the debates for or against the necessity of a centralised party rightly mobilises philosophers of all sides. The question is in no way tactical, but engages a general struggle over thought itself: what is logic today? (I, 107)

Thought exists on exactly the same plane as the class struggle, and so must be approached, not as the restricted concern of bourgeois intellectuals, but as being synonymous with the material conditions of that struggle. It would be wrong to imagine, as the utopians have, that the weight of ideology under capitalism collapses the proletariat's ability to comprehend the true measure of its exploitation by the bourgeoisie (invariably to the extent that it becomes the task of bourgeois intellectuals to 'educate' the proletariat in this regard). It is the nature of ideology to be divided, and so too of the class struggle to remain an open conflict. The historical contradiction of proletariat/bourgeoisie depends upon the structural contradiction of productive forces/social relations of production under capitalism. As such the proletariat's development as a class (both intellectual and material) runs in tandem with the bourgeoisie's continuing socialisation of the productive forces of society. To summarise in a sentence: the proletariat's revolutionary potential resides in the organic bond which it manages to forge with the bourgeois intellectuals – and, to an even greater extent, which it succeeds in *breaking* at key historical moments.

As BB admit, one might be forgiven for believing that the Maoist theory of knowledge itself marks a break – or at least anticipates one – with the founding formulations of Marxist-Leninism. Could it be that Maoism, conceived at the height of its world-historical power, brings about the conditions for a break with Marxism? The risk could hardly fail to escape the authors' attention. The Maoist theory of knowledge which hinges on the intellectuals taking their lead from the masses, rather than providing the latter with direction, certainly brings with it the possibility of a split with Lenin, if not a complete reversal of his basic formulas in *What Is To Be Done?* (I, 122). For Mao it is the masses, rather than the intellectuals, who spontaneously generate revolutionary ideas. Instead of the fusion of Marxism with the working class movement, in Mao the party becomes the principle of the division of true and false ideas. Here, the party is the eternal return, rather than the synthesis, of the revolutionary cycle of knowledge (I, 121). Every revolutionary movement is therefore 'traversed [as in the case of the Paris Commune] by a profound division between ancient ideas of the Proudhonian type and new ideas' (I, 122).

Although this appears to signal a transgression of the role which Lenin assigns to the party vanguard, for BB the dialectic of mass/class does in fact satisfy the conditions for a revolutionary movement with direction. For whether one adheres to the view that the party vanguard moulds the proletariat's revolutionary experience 'from within' (Mao), or whether it infuses the proletariat with revolutionary consciousness from outside (Lenin), still one concedes that the organic bond between Marxism and the proletariat is the logical mechanism of the 'real living history of the revolution' (I, 127). Moreover, whereas Lenin assumes an eventual synthesis between Marxism and the working class, on closer inspection such an apparent merger only ever marks the *crossroads* of a revolutionary situation, which is always subject to further assessment and rectification by the party (I, 127–8). The living reality of Marxism is the never-ending struggle between true and false ideas in the corresponding material forms of proletariat and bourgeoisie; 'it is the struggle, which is the very life of the organisation, between two lines, two voices and two classes' (I, 127).

BB's analysis is intended to contest the appropriation of the so-called politics of the masses as upheld by Deleuze and Guattari on the one hand, and André Glucksmann on the other. For BB, the splits in the French Left which continued to occur throughout the 1970s only added discipline to the struggle of the revolutionary working class movement, thereby advancing its cycle of knowledge. In the context in which BB are writing such splits do not mark that movement's subjective defeat. On the contrary, they measure the depth of its historical progress and the underlying vitality of its revolutionary substance. However, one might be inclined to question the 'Marxist' character, and therefore the historical consistency, of BB's Maoist approach to the question of resistance. For if we accept, as BB contend, that there is no power without the corresponding resistance of the masses, then couldn't it equally be claimed that there is no such thing as power in itself? This is precisely the position of Foucault, for whom power is not repressive, but instead applies on each occasion to a productive *agency* of subjectivity: political militancy, citizenship, sexuality, or whatever. In Foucault's work the egalitarian ideal which heralds the dissolution of the sovereign power is rejected in favour of an ethics – or, better still, an existential interpretation – of power. According to this model, the resistance of the class subject in overthrowing the old regime becomes part of the essential discipline of establishing new forms of domination. One doesn't simply throw off one's chains in fighting against repression: *one produces the spectacle of the subject who attains freedom.*[31] With Foucault we are seemingly back on the terrain of Jean-Paul Sartre.

The influence of Sartre goes unacknowledged by BB, although is fairly implacable in much of Badiou's work, especially his Maoist writings, even if Sartre is rarely mentioned by name.[32] That social conflict remains internal to its intelligibility as the 'social ensemble' of singular events is the thesis put forward by Sartre in *Critique of Dialectical Reason*. It remains to be seen how this influence evolves in Badiou's more recent works.

Hegel and/or Marx?

Badiou's next important collaboration of the 1970s, *The Rational Kernel of the Hegelian Dialectic* (1978), is the final instalment in his series of Maoist essays. In this work – largely a translation of one of the chapters from an essay written by the Chinese philosopher Zhang Shiying during the Cultural Revolution – Badiou, along with Joël Bellassen and Louis Mossot, aim to prove, with the aid of their own supporting commentary, that the break with Hegel heralded by

French philosophers over the previous ten years is somewhat premature. It is always a misguided and disingenuous attack which aims to rid the philosophical battleground of Hegel's influence, not least because in so doing one also attacks Marx under the cover of political expediency. This is not the type of reading of Hegel which Badiou can accept, and it remains the case that in Badiou's work there is no significant break with the philosophy of Hegel. The imagined break with Hegel is always political, always politicised, and fused with all the trauma of Marxists' attempts to force Hegel's 'idealist system' to conform to the instrumental requirements of a materialist dialectic. There is no passage beyond this essential dualism of Marx/Hegel, which, as Badiou *et al.* conclude, is a question of the 'dialecticity' of the dialectic itself (NR, 91n.).

The tradition of Hegel in France originates almost entirely in *The Phenomenology of Spirit*. The readings of Hegel which Kojève inspired and which were adopted after the war by Malraux and the surrealists (Bataille and Breton) on the one hand, and the existentialists (led by Sartre) on the other, paved the way for an idealist Marxism where the Hegel of the *Logic* was completely ignored. Even when Althusser unintentionally restores this Hegelian bond in his discovery of a materialist Marxism he stubbornly refuses to acknowledge the debt to the 'materialist Hegel of the *Greater Logic*', instead conceiving Marx as the 'anti-Hegel of metaphysical materialism' (NR, 15). For Badiou *et al.*, the time had come to confront these philosophical exercises in ignorance in order to expose the conflict which lies at their heart: 'the maintenance and the scission of the dialectic between Hegel and Marx' (NR, 17).

By contrast the reception of Hegel in China since 1949 amplifies all the contradictions between conservative and revolutionary readings of his work. In the Chinese context following the revolution, something of the mortal Hegel appears, the Hegel whose idealist system is vulnerable to interventions (bearing in mind also that the actual terrain of *The Phenomenology* had been shaken by Napoleon's triumphant arrival in Jena in 1806). In China the critique of Hegel defines two key phases in the history of the Republic. Firstly, from 1956 to 1959, during the time of the Great Leap Forward, Mao Tse-tung commends a study of Hegel's 'unity of contraries', and later the 'identity of thought and being', both of which appear in works by Zhang Shiying (*On the Philosophy of Hegel* (1956) and *On the Logic of Hegel* (1959)). The second period, from 1972 to 1975, begins with Lin Biao (the former head of the Red Army University and vice-chairman of the Chinese Communist Party) and the long-running controversy sparked by his plenum on Mao's 'genius' at the CCP's Ninth Congress in 1970.[33] Intent on suppressing the ominous rise of the cult of personality, Mao responded by calling for 'the study of the history of Chinese and Western philosophy and on the critique of the *a priori* theory of genius' (NR, 21). Among the 'several histories of Western philosophy' which were published, Zhang Shiying's *The Philosophy of Hegel* emerged in 1972.

Badiou *et al.*'s translation of Zhang Shiying's book provides the platform for an engagement with the official current in Maoist thought. However, it seems equally fair to say that this work also stands as a valuable, although somewhat overlooked, contribution to French Hegelian scholarship of the period. In terms of the future direction of Badiou's work, *The Rational Kernel* is a preliminary indication of the mathematical turn which his thought would take in the next decade.

In his text Zhang highlights the main principles of transformation which govern the dialectic (movement and the interdependence of phenomena, contradiction, the passage from quantity to quality, etc.) and prevent it from collapsing into purely abstract, metaphysical accounts of difference. For every set of phenomena there is a 'necessary connection' between the elements of the set on the one hand (smell, colour, form, etc. in the case of Hegel's bouquet of flowers[34]) and an 'immanent genesis of differences' within the set which governs its overall evolution on the other (NR, 26–7). Hegel's presentation of this logic begins with his analysis of the concepts of being and nothingness and the presumed conversion of one into the other. However, as Badiou *et al.* note, idealism typically surrounds this passage when it comes to the question of beginning. As they observe:

> Taken in the beginning, the Hegelian dialectic will not develop itself under the form of work of contradiction. It will function otherwise: one will set out from a unique term, being, and it will rather have the appearance of a form of repetition, a logic of difference in which that which is the driving force is not the process of division of identity, nor a process of merging contraries (being and nothingness absorbed in becoming ...), but the double inscription of identity under the form of two marks whose referent is absolutely undifferentiated: being and nothing are two marks for the void. (NR, 29n.)

The fundamental difficulty which confronts the Hegelian dialectic, and the question for science as a whole, is 'iteration'. Here, rather than the disjunction between being and nothingness which implies a genuine, dialectical transformation of one into the other, we encounter only the repetition of the first term. Difference obeying the principle of repetition, then, and not difference as dialectical movement. How does one resolve this internal contradiction? Hegel, rather idealistically as it turns out, regards the concept of becoming as the effective mediation of being and nothingness, and idealistically in the following sense. For becoming is not purely the means of bringing about the passage from being to nothingness ('becoming-identity'), since it also falls prey to the problem of iteration, i.e. the 'becoming-contradiction' of being and nothingness as absolutely different, inseparable terms (NR, 32n.). Here, then, contradiction becomes *immediate* and therefore demands no resolution since it involves no effective movement (this is the metaphysical approach of Spinoza – although not his only one – where nature is thought 'under the aspect of eternity': *sub specie aeternitatis*). Recognising the problem, Hegel proposes that becoming must be doubly determined: on the one hand, from nothingness commencing its passage into being, and on the other, from being commencing its passage into nothingness. However, as Badiou *et al.* remark critically, instead of resolving the problem of *a* beginning, here Hegel merely confronts us with the problem of two (NR, 34n.). The relation of one to the other is more complex than Hegel would have us believe, since every presumed disjunction between a pair of dialectical terms (being/nothingness) would in fact appear to depend on their prior conjunction and vice versa – although in both cases this is precisely what the becoming-contradiction rules out. The Hegelian question of beginning is therefore, at the 'start' of the logic, a '"*closed* circuit where that which is first becomes last and vice versa"' (NR, 37n., citing Hegel). This is a form of Hegelian idealism which Badiou strongly opposes.

Virtually the same tension informs the Hegelian critique of representation. For the metaphysicians, the relation of essence/phenomenon is seen as being mutually exclusive, where we might imagine an object to exist at two levels – the object's 'real interiority' versus its 'exteriority for us' – with no determinate relation between them (NR, 38n.). In fact, the relation between essence and phenomenon, inside and outside, exists, although is subsumed by the whole. We might understand Hegel's critique better by recalling the spatial metaphor of the 'Möbius strip' as employed by the psychoanalyst Jacques Lacan. The fact that the strip, a long rectangular piece of ribbon, has been twisted through 180 degrees and joined at both ends means that, taken as a whole, the inside versus outside distinction cannot be maintained. The relation between the two is revealed *only when the strip is cut* – which of course results in its negation. However, as Badiou *et al.* maintain, it is important to view 'the split correlation of exterior/interior ... as a process' rather than the static deficiency of a negation (or what Lacan calls 'lack') (NR, 39–40n.).

This raises once more the question of movement, and how we might aim to expose a contradiction which *is* the very fabric of being. As Zhang argues in his essay, the philosophy of Hegel is split *internally* between an idealist system and a materialist dialectic. It follows that the 'idealist' dialectic of Hegel is not opposed to the 'materialist' dialectic of Marx; instead *both* are opposed to metaphysics (NR, 88n.). (In this sense we might call 'history' the universal tension between Hegel and Marx.) The end or the apparent inertia of a given contradiction in reality therefore belies its internal dialectic, where lies the secret – the 'rational kernel' – of its movement.

Of course, we could not end an exposition like this without a final word on another philosophical influence which Badiou and his fellow Maoist collaborators blatantly avoid the merest mention of. The absence is understandable. Deleuze's *Difference and Repetition*, published in France ten years before *The Rational Kernel*, introduces us to a world of difference and repetition set adrift completely from the Hegelian concepts of identity and contradiction. For Deleuze, difference is not the medium of identity, nor does repetition somehow frustrate the becoming of a contradiction. Such conceptions merely encourage us to interpret movement as a means to an end – an 'abstract logical movement' which passes through the negative – when in reality movement involves 'inventing vibrations, rotations, whirlings, gravitations, dances or leaps which directly touch the mind'. Movement can quite positively go nowhere – or 'now-here' as Deleuze has it in his sideswipe at Hegel's faith in abstract universals. We might say that for Deleuze history is stuck in a rut while simultaneously travelling at the speed of light. For in spite of the apparent inertia of a becoming we still experience movement immediately in the *singularity* of a repetition, or what Nietzsche calls 'eternal return'.[35]

The possibility of false movement simply does not arise in Deleuze's work. The dominant speculative tradition of philosophy from Plato to Hegel which opposes logic to metaphysics in order to penetrate its supernatural realm of simulacra – the realm of play and deceit – is one which Deleuze famously rejects, or at least would claim to subvert beyond all rational sense. Indeed, such has been the impact of Deleuze's efforts to upset the dominant metaphysical tradition, infiltrating it with a band of 'unknowns' (Lucretius, Hume, Spinoza, Nietzsche), that to approach philosophy in future with the same degree of faith in its rationalist heritage would appear to depend on a supreme talent for bringing about nothing short of a classical renaissance. In this respect Badiou will remain undaunted by the anti-philosophers and postmodernists in aiming to achieve precisely this end.

2
The Science of Being

The 1980s would become the 'winter years'[1] for those philosophers who, like Badiou, continued to work relentlessly on revolutionary agendas. With the decline of Maoism as a credible political force, the 1980s were to mark a period of theoretical recovery and *regroupement* for a dwindling band of Marxist thinkers.[2] However, for Badiou the labour of thought would lose none of its militant vitality in the interim. Amid philosophy's retreat from the sciences and the accompanying multiplication of its schools, Badiou's attachment to the idea of a subject-oriented, universalist approach to the study of history deepened. The paradigmatic shifts in French academia and the vicissitudes of global 'culture' which heralded, in the mind of Jean-François Lyotard, a postmodern condition of incommensurable interests were, for Badiou, little more than an illusion: 'From the practical renunciation of egalitarian universalism one strictly infers that the specialist knowledges where one confines thought, outside the walls of journalistic cretinism at least, assure only the revenues of the civil functionary' (TS, 11).

In this chapter it will be my aim to argue that Badiou's methodology, and his approach to philosophical questions following his political writings of the 1970s, represent a robust challenge to current postmodern trends in philosophy. Here (and in the following two chapters) I will focus on Badiou's most important work to date, *Being and the Event* (1988), and in this chapter concentrate on the mathematical ontology which underpins the book. Rest assured that this will not involve a detailed treatment of formal logic, of which I assume no prior knowledge on the reader's part. Badiou's aim as a pure scientist is to force the separation between mathematics (in its Platonist mode) and philosophy. Furthermore, the ambitious range of Badiou's work on logic, mathematics, politics and literature is enough to convince us that his is a universal philosophy.

The Mathematical Turn

As was noted briefly in the previous chapter, Badiou's *formation* in philosophy was a mathematical one. The 'overtaken conjuncture' of *The Concept of Model* (1969) – 'happily interrupted' by the events of May 68 (CM, 7) – put to one side his experiments in scientific practice and ushered in a series of Maoist collaborations in the face of mounting political revisionism. However, the 1970s, which witnessed the defeat of Leftism in France and the retrenchment of structuralism's new wave around more traditional European democratic ideals, was not a time to be theoretically isolated. Between 1975 and 1979 Badiou juxtaposed his Maoist collaborations with a 'thematic repertoire' of seminars on 'Political theory, Logic and mathematics, Circumstances of history, Psychoanalysis *stricto sensu*, Literature and theatre, God, [and] Classical philosophy' (TS, 12). *Theory of the Subject* (1982) was the result of this repertoire which brought together two 'great German dialecticians' (Hegel and the poet Hölderlin), the two modern French ones (Mallarmé and Lacan), along with 'four of the five great Marxists' (Marx, Engels, Lenin, Mao) – Stalin being confined to the index. This figure of four (the 'double scission') is what Badiou regards as the *strong* version of the Hegelian dialectic; for Badiou, there is no need to think beyond what is, for the postmodernists, the deficiency of the Hegelian syllogism. Logic – including any presumed anti-logic – is always already present in Hegel: 'That the dialectical scansion supposes the four terms of the double scission (place, force, subjective, objective), and not the three of alienation (position, negation, negation of the negation), [Hegel] establishes in a famous passage from the chapter on the Absolute Idea.' In Hegel's *Logic* the mediated term of a syllogism, rather than being excluded from the subject of a conclusion, is in fact only *formally* excluded, while being *universally included*. For Hegel it follows that '"the negative or difference is thus counted as a duality"' (TS, 66, citing Hegel).

The fact that postmodernism attempts to undermine Hegel on the ground of the negative (as a synthetic or unifying logic which ignores difference) is ironic, although perhaps hardly surprising. This is, after all, the preferred image of vulgar Marxism, and hence the soft target for philosophical revisionists. To read Hegel's *Logic* strictly to the letter, however, is to encounter an altogether stronger adversary, and to enter a problematic which dispenses with Hegelian logic only at the peril of dispensing with philosophy itself. Badiou's response to this kind of slack approach in *Theory of the Subject* is twofold: to affirm the circularity of the dialectic (the tendency of history to repeat itself *ad infinitum*), while at the same time retaining a sense of periodisation (how can one introduce scission into the infinite?). For Badiou, the dialectic must be understood in its authentic *dialecticity*, in the dual permutations of *both* its structural *and* historical sides, not as a means towards the resolution of a historic problem somehow exterior to itself (the class struggle which is, in essence, unresolvable anyway), but towards the *being* of the dialectic itself. 'It is the dialectic itself which we must divide, at the very edge of its dialecticity: structural side, historic side. Logic of places, logic of forces' (TS, 71).

A science of logic, then, is what is called for here in order to recover the subject (that discredited scrap of the historical process) on the verge of its being/non-being; what Badiou, reading Lacan, calls 'the too-early/too-late of its fortune' (TS, 153). It is crucial not to confuse science in this Hegelian and Lacanian sense with the empirical science which, as Badiou notes, continues to misconstrue Freudian psychoanalysis as a means of authentic self-reflection. The unconscious, it is quite true, has never been 'proved' – no more, Badiou adds, than one officially announces the event of a revolution. The (subject of the) unconscious is instead the 'thing' of controversy which its disputed existence inspires. Furthermore:

> The unconscious is this being which subverts the metaphysical opposition of being and of non-being. For it is the effect of lack-of-being [*manque à être*] (effect which has the name: transference). (TS, 152)

The subject stands on the threshold of the impossible – what Lacan calls the Real[3] – both psychoanalytically and politically a rare occurrence. In psychoanalytic terms, the cure is not the end of the symptom, nor therefore does it mark the termination of analysis, but the point at which the subject becomes readjusted to its 'own repetition'. While politically, 're-education' provokes 'A radical toppling of the subjective position, that is to say the interruption of repetitions induced by the anterior (class) position' (TS, 160). In either case the subject is the anchorage of subversion.

In terms of the overall development of Badiou's thought, *Theory of the Subject* is quite evidently an abstract fragment of a far greater work to come, even if its loyal attachment to materialist categories seems less inspired by the question of pure logic, and more the result of a lingering political antagonism towards the 'undertaker's assistant Mitterrand' and the other traitors of the French Left during the 1970s (TS, 60). Badiou's valiant effort to retain the global efficacy of the dialectic as the disguised substance/subject of imperialist society presumes, far too prematurely, that one already has the answer to the inaugural question of ontology. However, such a question does not immediately concern the subject.

The inaugural question of ontology as the science of being which propels the work of the ancient Greek atomists is broadly comparable to the question posed by modern nuclear physicists – namely, *Why is there something rather than nothing?*[4] For Badiou this question is not a conventionally scientific one and is largely genealogical in its adherence to the historicity of the perplexingly entangled relationship between philosophy and (mathematical) science. It also would appear to be inescapably metaphysical in orientation. From Anaxagoras' introduction of Mind into early Greek cosmology in an attempt to explain the 'presence of order in Nature'[5] to Heidegger's meditations on the enigmatic 'coming to presence' of theory (*theōria*),[6] the history of science is tormented by the possibility that the 'objective wonders' of the universe are in fact attributable to the humanistic power of scientific interventions. Nietzsche, in the celebrated Book Three of *The Gay Science*, puts the case as strongly as any cosmologist when he writes:

> Let us beware of presupposing that something so orderly as the cyclical motions of our planetary neighbours are the general and universal case; even a glance at the Milky Way gives rise to doubt whether there may not there exist far more crude and contradictory motions, likewise stars with eternally straight trajectories, and the like. The astral order in which we live is an exception; this order and the apparent permanence which is conditional upon it is in its turn made possible by the exception of exceptions: the formation of the organic. The total nature of the world is, on the other hand, to all eternity chaos, not in the sense that necessity is lacking but in that order, structure, form, beauty, wisdom, and whatever other human aesthetic notions we may have are lacking ...[7]

Like Lacan's incorporeal unconscious, the primordial site of Badiou's ontology is discordant, a random flux of atoms and void.[8]

Considered as the basis for a scientific world-view,[9] we might regard it as an anti-evolutionary schema. Universal being is the Absolute, unconditioned in nature, which postulates a species resistant to all further genetic mutation. While the temptation among metaphysicians (i.e. those for whom science and philosophy have today become indistinguishable) has traditionally been to lament poetically the dispersed presence of being, Badiou's ontology attends to the 'harshness' of being of the void 'foreclosed not only from representation, but from all presentation'. Unlike Heidegger for whom being is always being-there (*Dasein*), Badiou's being is stripped of its 'aura' to the point of (its own) 'deductive consistency' (EE, 16). Badiou's task is therefore to rewrite the 'genealogy of discourse on being' in terms more akin to being's 'radically subtractive dimension' by dispensing with the poetic ontology of Hölderlin, Trakl and Celan in favour of the mathematical ontology of Cantor, Gödel and P. J. Cohen.

The 'Presentation of Presentation'

Badiou's ontology is not the formal object of philosophy. The proto-scientific enterprise of *Being and the Event* rules out any epistemological theory of knowledge. The book's central thesis – 'ontology = mathematics' – is metaontological (EE, 20), although it remains for philosophy, rather than mathematics, to verify the truth of such a thesis. Mathematical knowledge is guaranteed by its own existence in thought. Its deductive proofs, *qua* deductive proofs, are immanent to the totality of the mathematical universe, and as such require no further demonstration. Truth, on the other hand, arrives from another dimension, proceeding from a sudden *intervention* in thought which disturbs the mundane pattern of deductive logic. Badiou's stated aim as a philosopher, militant above all, is to force this intervention in thought by 'assign[ing] philosophy to the thinkable articulation of two discourses (and practices) ...: mathematics, science of being, and the intervening doctrines of the event, which, precisely, designate [non-being]' (EE, 20). The immediate problem however, which is the objective of philosophy, is how to ensure a degree of discursive consistency to this thesis given the fact that *'philosophy is originally separated from ontology'*.

Badiou's dilemma recalls the famous question of Heidegger's *Dasein*. In *Being and Time* being is impeded by the temporality of its being-in-the-world, and withdrawn from its authentic 'ontical' – as opposed to ontological – presence. In direct contrast to Heidegger's poetic ontology of deferred presence, Badiou opposes a mathematical ontology of presentation. For Badiou ontology need not mourn the passing of its 'original disposition', since that which presents being *is* the reflection of its own essence, or the in-consistency of its own discourse on being, which he terms the 'presentation of presentation'. Moreover:

> If such is the case in effect, it remains possible that it is being-as-being which is at stake in this [ontological] situation, since no access to being offers itself to us apart from presentations. At the very least, all possible access to being is gained by way of a situation whose presentative multiple is that of presentation itself. (EE, 36)

Whereas with Heidegger we assume that being is separated from its 'original disposition' as a result of its forgotten philosophical heritage (for Heidegger this heritage is the philosophy of the Greeks), Badiou wants to say that being is both a-temporal and anterior to language. For Badiou the separation of philosophy from ontology is philosophy's universal condition, not evidence of its fall from an original state of grace. Consider the analogy of the psychoanalytic symptom. Is it not the famous Freudian slip, in disrupting the articulation of speech, which attests to the essential being of the unconscious, and hence the invariance of a principle which resists the development of language over time? In Lacan's labyrinthine ontology being is the exact point where the subject is born in the symbolic sense, the 'quilting point' (*point de capiton*) at which the amorphous mass of pre-libidinal experience crosses over into language (*langue*). It is *this* contradictory moment where the subject becomes split – and contradictory inasmuch as this splitting (*Spaltung*) is the only means of becoming *a*, i.e. one, subject – which Badiou wants to gain access to. In order to be one, one has to be separated from something else, and so on, *ad infinitum*. For Badiou, following Lacan, if anything is ontologically irreducible it is precisely such a moment of separation/attachment, the infinite being wrested from itself, which marks the subject's coming into – and going out of – existence.[10]

As well as atemporal and anterior to language, Badiou's being is also intransitive. Presentation is purely tautological in that it presents the in-consistency of being as such, rather than in the form of a verb which takes a direct object. For example, whereas the subject can ordinarily be defined by its transitive relation to a certain class of objects ('one is *x*'), for Badiou being will be strictly self-predicating and present nothing other than the being of its own presentation. Badiou names this unequivocal predicate 'multiple', and its means of articulation 'counting as one'. Let us consider a fairly straightforward example.

The 'Eiffel Tower' is a multiple which can be counted as one. It is made up of a multiplicity of component parts, each one of which bears a unique relation to all the others. Of course, we must be careful here to clarify precisely what we mean by 'unique', for this term can either refer to a multiple which is unprecedented and without equal, or else a multiple which is defined by a specific set of relations. (Badiou names these conceptual variations 'event' and 'situation' respectively.) Clearly the Eiffel Tower satisfies both conditions. On the one hand what we have before us is *the* Eiffel Tower, which is in every conceivable way beyond comparison, while on the other we have *a* giant piece of modernist architecture which was constructed for the Paris Exposition of 1889. In the first sense its uniqueness is unparalleled, the remnant of a historic occasion which defies adequate presentation. In the second its uniqueness is wholly exclusive in relation to other national monuments and their intrinsic properties.

Every multiple is 'split' as a multiple of *presentation* and a multiple of *composition*. Leaving aside the concept of event, each situation involves presentation as 'inconsistent multiplicity' and composition as 'consistent multiplicity' (EE, 33). For example, in the first instance the Eiffel Tower commands widespread recognition as a national monument without being universally appreciated as such, while in the second its unique association with the Paris Exposition is indisputable despite being incongruous due to several subsequent modifications to its design, such as the raising of its height in 1959 by 21 metres. The multiple is composed of multiple properties, and yet presented as one multiple; and presented as a multiplicity of relations yet nonetheless composed of multiple ones. However, there is no signification to speak of here, since no one multiple, in being predicated on its own multiplicity, ultimately refers to any unitary concept – even of itself. The multiple is a multiple *of* multiples, and is therefore absolutely self-sufficient as a 'pure multiplicity', or 'multiple without one'.

Badiou is at pains to alert us to the fact that the multiple's presumed oneness is only the *result* of it having been counted (EE, 32–3). Being as one is always a retroactive fiction, it haunts the situation in arrears, and is only a *function* (not the *concept*) of presentation. For example, on closer inspection the Eiffel Tower's presumed identity as one belies a situation which presents a multitude of supplementary variables: tourists, Gustave Eiffel,[11] the pathological site of dramatic suicides, Nazi newsreel propaganda, surrealist literature (Raymond Queneau's 1959 novel *Zazie dans le métro*) ... each one a world or situation unto itself as far as its own internal relations are concerned. The 'Eiffel Tower' is a term of absolute difference. As such it remains indifferent to anything – including any presumed manifestation of itself – beyond the bounds of its own unique situation.

The Being of Number

Our example may be misleading. To begin with, the counting as one does not involve the ordering, or the calculation, of an 'integral', i.e. the sum total of infinitesimally small quantities which comprise a whole. There is no 'parts versus whole' distinction in Badiou's ontology. Neither does the counting as one aim to assign 'value'[12] to mathematical objects. The counting as one is an operation of consistency, which is to say that it seeks to establish the philosophical conditions where measure and calculation can take place. Although such a task would appear to have little relevance for non-mathematicians, Badiou's aims are ultimately far more comprehensive than they first appear.

The starting point of Badiou's mathematical philosophy is his critique of Platonism. The latter is defined by Benacerraf and Putnam in the introduction to their seminal collection *Philosophy of Mathematics* as a belief in 'the *discovery* of truths about [mathematical] structures which exist independently of the activity or thought of mathematicians'.[13] Despite being a self-proclaimed Platonist himself this is not a definition which Badiou chooses to accept, since he argues instead that according to Plato the independent existence of mathematical structures is 'entirely relative' (CT, 95). But what does Badiou mean by this? For even a rudimentary grasp of Platonism will confirm that, for Plato at least, mathematical structures are ideal, mind-independent forms or essences.

In the *Meno*, when Socrates confronts the slave-boy with the diagram of a square and elicits the requisite logical insight from him, we take this as an illustration of how mathematical ideas can be learnt by anyone rather than being generated in the mind of the mathematician.[14] Badiou would certainly agree that mathematical structures are not innate.[15] However, by 'entirely relative' Badiou doesn't mean that mathematical ideas are simply a matter of contingent, situation-specific identities and beliefs. What he does mean is that an idea, in order to be true, will depend on the universal conditions of its presentation ('reminiscence' for Plato) in thought. What Socrates proves during the course of his interview with the slave-boy is the extent to which a complex mathematical idea can be found to inhabit the 'blank mind' of a slave. 'More particularly in terms of mathematical ideas, the entire concrete demonstration of the *Meno* is to establish the least educated, the most anonymous presence in thought: the thought of a slave' (CT, 96). On this evidence it follows that the only transcendent condition of truth for the human being will be his or her reduction to a state of ignorance (in matters of geometry, virtue, or whatever).[16]

For Badiou 'thought is not, is never confronted by "objectivities" from which it will be separated. The Idea is always already there. If it was not "activatable" in thought, it will remain unthinkable' (CT, 96). The Pythagorean gesture whereby numbers are thought of as being immaterial, and mathematics is viewed analogously as providing divine access to the mysteries of the cosmos, is the *sine qua non* of modern scientific enquiry. At least one eminent physicist, Stephen Hawking, has referred to his work as an attempt to comprehend 'the mind of God'.[17] However, attempts by mathematicians to co-opt Platonism into this holy alliance by identifying the latter with the discovery of transcendent mathematical structures is 'certainly inaccurate' on Badiou's terms. On the contrary:

> The fundamental concern of Plato is to declare the immanent identity, the co-belonging, of the known and the knowing spirit, their essential ontological commensurability. (CT, 96)

In support of this rather unconventional brand of Platonism, Badiou appeals to the intuitionist branch of mathematics. Intuitionism is an extreme methodological position, contrary to standard Platonism, which rests on the assumption that mathematical ideas are immediately knowable without being universally true. For Badiou, however, as is the case for the mathematician Paul Bernays, there is no necessary contradiction between Platonism *stricto sensu* and intuitionism;

on the contrary, the two 'complement each other'.[18] The detachment of mathematical objects from the thinking subject is itself intuitive and *internal* – rather than external – to the processes of thought.

As a proponent of this radical, somewhat unyielding critique of mathematics which he terms a 'Platonism of the multiple' (MP, 85), Badiou's task is to explore the ways in which this pure elementary intuition can operate, let alone be understood, in more customary philosophical terms. This exercise involves a critique which can account for 'the modes according to which mathematics is, since its Greek origins, a *condition* of philosophy' (C, 157). In Badiou's estimation the relation between philosophy and mathematics is today defined by three tendencies: the grammatical/logical analysis represented by Frege and the early Wittgenstein; the epistemology of concepts; and the 'matrix for structural generalisations'. Badiou's contention is certainly not that his philosophy – which he ranks alongside that of Cavaillès, Lautman and Desanti respectively – can somehow escape the conditioning tendencies of mathematics. What he sets out to do instead is to retrace 'mathematical eventness' (*l'événementialité mathématique*) in the 'singular thought of the philosophical act' (C, 158n.). Essentially, this translates as a philosophical and historical liberation of mathematics from its central myths. For example, in the case of German romanticism Badiou describes how the concept of infinity undergoes a secularising process of temporalisation. Here, infinity becomes a limit or 'horizon' in need of repeated negation. Despite ridding itself of its divine being, mathematics in the age of romanticism is subsumed by the concept of time – 'the historicity of finitude' – thereby effectively replacing one type of religiosity with another (C, 162–78). In distinguishing himself from postmodernism – what he defines disdainfully as 'classico-romantic eclecticism' (C, 163) – Badiou challenges philosophers of mathematics to resist practically the temptations of romanticism and embrace mathematics in its bare ontological truth: namely, 'there is only the infinite multiple, which presents the infinite multiple, and the unique stopping point of this presentation presents nothing' (C, 177).

Badiou is under no illusions that the classical fortunes of mathematics as ontology can be revived. Contemporary philosophy is dominated by the so-called 'linguistic turn', attributable in Badiou's estimation to the mathematisation of logic as formerly practised by Frege, Russell, Whitehead *et al.* Badiou strongly opposes the latter tendency, rejecting its central thesis that logic is 'mathematicised under the form of a syntax, or a formal theory' (CT, 127). Although Badiou does not deny that language has displaced mathematics from the centre stage of philosophical enquiry, he does deny that there is anything intrinsically logical about the connection between philosophy and language. Furthermore, given the crisis of metaphysics and the reign of multiplicity which have infected philosophy since the (nominal) end of romanticism, the challenge today is to establish a distance between mathematics, as such and in itself, and its numerous syntactic applications. In other words, a question not of signification, language or meaning, but of determining the limits of thought itself. This question is both difficult and precarious, for the 'being of number', i.e. the status of mathematics as pure thought, is not a question of objectivity:

> The Number is not an object, or an objectivity. It is a gesture in being. Before all objectivity, before all united presentation, and in the untied eternity of its being, the Number opens itself to thought as formal carving in the maximal stability of the multiple. (CT, 149)

In *Being and the Event* Badiou appears, at certain points, to embrace the metaphysical crisis in thought that brings about the complex splitting of philosophy into a host of specialisms and sub-disciplines. His rejection of 'being as one' in favour of a 'complete theory of the multiple', and his elevation of 'pure difference' over and above 'simple repetitive diversity' (EE, 43), exhibit all the signs of the absolute difference and multiplicity most often associated with postmodernism. However, what sets Badiou apart from the postmodernists is his strong resistance to the Nietzsche and Heidegger-inspired 'overturning' of Western philosophy from Plato to Hegel. Badiou sees little merit in this nihilistic exercise. The problems of classical thought are both self-sufficient and ongoing, and therefore any attempt to overturn them must assume, quite prematurely, that they are outdated.

The (Re)turn to Platonism

Badiou's aim in Book I of *Being and the Event* is to return the dialectic of one/multiple to the stage where it first emerges in ancient, pre-Socratic philosophy, and is recounted in Plato's *Parmenides*. The *Parmenides* is the most elusive of all the dialogues, steeped in dramatic irony and role reversal: Socrates, the overzealous and inexperienced pupil, meets the sage Parmenides and is duly taught a lesson in philosophy. The symbolism of Plato's text can hardly be lost on Badiou, although this in no way leads him into exploring the frames of the dialogue or unearthing its rhetorical structure. Nor is he remotely interested, unlike the textual scholars, in reading the *Parmenides* as an allegory of Plato's relation to Socrates. Instead, Badiou views the *Parmenides* as the original site where the essential formulas of dialectical logic are unleashed for the first time. The stakes in retrieving the terms of the encounter are sufficiently high, for this 'exercise in pure thought' bears on 'all the formulaic hypotheses as to the being of the one' (EE, 41).

The dialogue itself begins with Socrates' opening remarks on the theory of forms. There must be universal essences or forms, declares Socrates, which enable a unique thing to possess opposed properties. For example, Socrates is both 'one', because he is one among several spectators, and 'many', because his right is different from his left side, his front from his back, his upper from his lower halves, and so on.[19] It is at this stage that Parmenides mounts his challenge to Socrates. If every unique thing partakes of a universal form then it follows that there are as many forms as there are unique things.[20] This revelation leads to the deductions which comprise the remainder of the dialogue.

In his meditation on Plato (EE, 41–7) Badiou restricts himself to the dialogue's final four hypotheses which concern the positive and negative qualifications of the one and the others in respect of the thesis 'the one is not' (EE, 41). Badiou's decision to begin his analysis here, midway through the dialogue, is based on strictly methodological grounds. There is no possibility of 'resolving' the antinomies of being and oneness which proliferate in Plato's text. Nevertheless, classical scholars have tended to frame the problems of the final hypotheses in ways that would seek to demonstrate the consistency of the *Parmenides as a whole*. Badiou's method is radically opposed to any such approach. Rather than working through the antinomies in an attempt to explain the text's (in)coherence, Badiou isolates a 'coherent' element in the text in an attempt to account for the antinomies. The element in question, the thesis 'the one is not', is according to Badiou the founding axiom of ontology, the logical impasse which blocks the path of thought. At the same time, however, the implications of this impasse are inconsistent, 'dissymmetrical', specifically in relation to the one itself:

The spring of this dissymmetry is that the non-being of the one is analysed only as non-being, and tells us nothing of the concept of the one ... (EE, 42)

At the close of the first hypothesis, Parmenides excludes the one from all participation in being to the point where the one is divested of its own character.[21] The problem again surfaces in the fifth deduction where Parmenides declares that even the one which 'is not' must still partake of certain relational properties[22] including, *ipso facto*, being. Given the seemingly indispensable relation of non-being to the one, Badiou aims to advance the analysis a decisive stage further by seeking the being of determination itself; a determination wholly divorced from the one and vice versa (EE, 42).[23]

For Badiou, as for Deleuze, oneness can only be presented adequately in terms of multiplicity. However, given that 'the one is not', it must follow that multiplicity as 'pure presentation' is 'anterior to all effect-of-one, to all structure' – a fact which renders it 'as such, unthinkable' (EE, 43–4). Multiplicity rules out all relations between concepts and categories, including their non-relations. Deprived of all determination to the point where even its non-being is excluded from being, there is only one other 'thing' that the concept of the one can possibly be: *nothing*. At this point Badiou arrives at the final, negative qualification of Plato's text: 'If the one is not, nothing is' (EE, 44).

Badiou is well aware of the nihilistic implications of accepting the final thesis of the *Parmenides* as sufficient, and proceeds to highlight the ambiguity of the French word *ne* in an attempt to distinguish between two sides of the expression 'nothing is': *rien n'est* and *rien est*. Rather than nothing being a negation of all that is, this further qualification enables Badiou to put forward the thesis that nothing is the essential ontological principle, and the structure of 'being as being'. For Badiou, there is, strictly speaking, only multiplicity, or the 'multiple without-one'. In analytical terms this multiplicity concerns the gap between 'the inconsistent multiple, the being-without-one, the pure presentation' and 'the consistent multiple, the composition of ones' (EE, 45).

Uniqueness, or the state of being a singular one, is the aporia which haunts the *Parmenides*, leading countless studies headlong into an infinite regress. What Badiou intends with his analysis is not to identify the aporia as the undermining weakness of Plato's text, but instead to accept it as the essential nodal point, the dialectical site as it were, of the presentation/composition of multiplicity itself. What we might otherwise call *oneness in the making*. The one is not the Idea. Nor does it even feature as one of the five fundamental Ideas of 'being, movement, rest, the same and the other' which appear in Plato's *Sophist* (EE, 47). The situation of the one is *necessarily* aporetic:

> No being separated from the one is conceivable, and that is in fact what the *Parmenides* establishes. The one is only the principle of every Idea, grasped from the side of its *operation* – of participation – and not from the side of its *being*. (EE, 47; my emphasis)

Badiou's method in his meditation on Plato is perhaps vaguely reminiscent of Althusser's in *Reading Capital* where Althusser argues that the apparent dissymmetry of Marx's scientific project is, in fact, perfectly consistent with a set of symptomatic absences or oversights which he discovers in Marx's mature works. In both cases the methodology is reductionist in establishing the scientific protocols for unearthing the text's bare theoretical framework. However, the real forerunner of Badiou's ontology, as we have already noted in passing, is Jacques Lacan.

The Science of the Real

Lacan doesn't stop at the reformulation of the Freudian Oedipus complex. For Lacan, the universal origin of prohibition is never questioned, and so this non-questioning becomes a postulate, is prescriptive, and hence neither purely descriptive nor purely normative. The law of being is dependent upon (the being of) a negative ontology. As Mikkel Borch-Jacobsen puts it on behalf of Lacan himself:

> The whole Lacanian system encloses and barricades itself in the a priori of the 'no,' interpreted as the universal law of humanity: 'Do not identify'; 'Do not be what you are'; 'Desire yourself beyond every object'; 'Be nothing'.[24]

Lacan's famous formula 'the unconscious is structured like a language' does not therefore mean what we might otherwise think it does. The unconscious is not a discourse on truth, a metalanguage, which the analyst interprets in order to relieve the subject of its traumatic symptoms. The subject is a myth, essentially *nothing real*, while language is manifestly *un*equal to the task of speaking the truth. What language provides instead is a social contract[25] in the form of a linguistic convention which allows the subject to manifest itself, *to come into being* as it were, in the fullness/emptiness of its own speech. The question of the subject quite literally cannot be stressed enough: its essential non-being is either recognised or it is not. But there is no question of the subject being cured in any objective or definitive sense since the cure always comes and goes by courtesy of another subject.

In his later seminars Lacan began to take more seriously the problematic status of language in psychoanalytic discourse in an attempt to regain a degree of authority over what was, for him, a scientific discipline after all. If language is unequal to the task of speaking the truth, then its inequality threatens the integrity of clinical practice by undermining the presentation (as the scientific proof by replication) of approved psychoanalytic procedures. Lacan's systematic reformulations of Lacanian doctrine can therefore be viewed at once as the defence of both a discourse and an institution.

Lacan confronts the scientific equivocations of 'Lacanianism' by drawing attention to the discourse of mathematics. His use of mathematical algorithms drawn from set theory is not some playful exercise in poetic invention, or a 'language game' where everything is assumed to be made out of signs. It is an attempt to symbolise the various stages of psychosis in a way that avoids the arbitrary pitfalls that one associates with language as a referential system of words and their meanings. For Lacan the disruptive influence of language is seemingly there from the beginning, retroactively furnishing the subject's void identity with its 'I'. Language, as well as existing prior to the point of individual subjectification, is also immanent to it, since there is no guarantee that subjectification will occur (for the subject) at all, even and especially if the subject's coming to consciousness is a myth. If language always shoots excessively wide of the mark of meaning, then in order to (re)present this paradox to the subject, faithful analysis needs to reveal to it the myth that regulates its condition. For Lacan mathematics unlocks the door to this negative dimension, leading the truth of speech (*parole*) where language ultimately cannot follow.

The Science of Being

In *Being and the Event*, Badiou aims to surpass Lacan's science of the Real with his own science of being. It is an ambitious goal. Henceforth there is no longer any Real impasse to existence. Rather it is *on this side of* (rather than beyond) the Real that we must establish the idea of scientific process. 'Consistency' is the key dynamic informing Badiou's ontology, comparable to Deleuze and Guattari's use of the term *puissance* to describe both a capacity for existence and the power of a number to be raised exponentially. The being that Badiou identifies with mathematics entails the bracketing off of every realist reference point, of every reference to an outside world which is not governed by a space of variables – an 'axiomatic'. Badiou is under no illusion that mathematics can present reality as it really is or was. If mathematics operates as a method of *unveiling* then it does so only in the sense of *a-lētheia*, i.e. truth as unveiling *itself* (of no being).[26] With this aim in mind Badiou's algebraic formulas refer to nothing beyond their own adequate expression. The system of alphabetic numeration which Badiou chooses to employ in *Being and the Event* (Badiou uses the Greek letters α, β, γ, etc. in order to represent discrete elements) is an arbitrary, as opposed to digital, form of notation. However, this does not mean that Badiou's scientific objectives are merely restricted to the level of developing a new form of mathematical notation.

According to Badiou mathematical ontology is 'subtractive'. By subtractive he means that ontology subtracts itself from the established significations of a given language (in this case we take 'language' to mean any formal system of rules with its own symbols and syntax). For instance, consider a situation in which two variables, x and y, are said to have two values, -2 and $+2$. Since the difference between the two values cannot be expressed – or else is expressed only at the expense of cancelling it out – we say that the difference is 'indiscernible', or else subtracts itself from all attempts at 'differential evaluation' (C, 182). When all permutations equal 0 we say that the 'difference' is the same in all cases. For Badiou, there are four subtractive dimensions of ontology including the indiscernible, the undecidable, the generic and the unnameable. What they broadly share is their ability to suspend any evaluative norm. In the case of the indiscernible, for instance:

> If no formula can discern two terms of the situation, it is affirmed that the choice of making verification pass by one rather than by the other has no support in the objectivity of their difference. It is then a matter of an absolutely pure choice, separated from all presupposition other than of having to choose ... If no value discriminates what you have to choose, it is your liberty as such

which is the norm, to the point where in fact it confounds itself with chance. (C, 190)

This confounding of liberty and chance is what Badiou calls truth. Truth is the free independent variable in a situation, although statistically speaking it is not within the power of the mathematician to control it. Truth is what seizes the scientist on the brink of discovery. In Lacanian terms truth is the 'bar' of being which the subject cannot overcome. Crucially, however – and this is where Badiou's break with Lacan occurs[27]– although barred from the being of truth the subject can at least rally selflessly to its cause. The subject is always an active part of a procedure into truth, and the fact that truth exists beyond the realm of complete understanding does not mean that the subject's presumed lack of knowledge is not positively invested in the future event of truth.[28]

Cantor and the Theory of Sets

I wish to conclude this chapter by offering a short introduction to the work of the nineteenth- and early twentieth-century German mathematician Georg Cantor. Arguably no other thought – mathematical *or* philosophical – manages to encapsulate the modernist scientific paradigm – its stakes and objectives – quite so well as Cantor's theory of sets. As we have seen, *Being and the Event* exhibits a dual form of expression, and apart from philosophy can equally be treated as a series of meditations on the historicity of mathematical science. As such, no presentation of Badiou's major work would be complete without a rudimentary introduction to set theory. In what follows I have restricted the use of mathematical proofs, and have chosen instead to rely on a literal explanation of Cantor's inaugural axioms.

Cantor's set theory begins from the received wisdom regarding number which dominated mathematical thought up until the end of the nineteenth century: namely, the concept of infinity is unattainable, i.e. infinity is not a number which can be arrived at by counting. Although, as Badiou remarks, the idea of infinity as a virtual limit or horizon establishes itself in the era of romanticism, marking the separation of philosophy from Christianity, it originates in Aristotle's *Physics*, where nature is held to be the non-accidental cause of an evolutionary cosmos. For Aristotle, nature is the principle of motion and rest, or, as Badiou puts it in characteristically ontological fashion,

'Nature is the being-as-being whose presentation implies movement, it *is* movement, and not its law.' However, this definition leaves Aristotle facing a dilemma, since if movement is an infinitely all-embracing power then what sense is there in saying that '*there is* movement'? Or in other words, 'why is there movement rather than absolute immobility?' (EE, 86–7). Aristotle's pre-Galilean, speculative brand of physics assumes that the only way of settling the problem is to establish ontologically a place which *excludes* movement, thereby relieving nature of its infinite – and infinite in the sense of wholly indifferent – power (EE, 88). Aristotle calls such a place 'void', which he defines as a '"place in which nothing is"'. The void amounts to an 'excess' on every situation and acts as 'the cause of transport' for material processes. Moreover, if the void is inconceivable, unpresentable as such, it can at least be 'another *name* for matter' (EE, 92).

In Badiou's meditation on Aristotle (EE, 85–92) the latter emerges as the first in a long line of thinkers who propose a nominal solution to the material problem of the presentation of being-as-being. The void is the 'proper name of being' and the 'subset' which is 'universally included in every situation' (EE, 100). However, there is one, fundamental formula which distances Badiou from Aristotle and irreversibly ushers in the modernist paradigm of mathematical thinking. Although quite prepared to treat the void as an (infinite) space, Aristotle refuses to accept that such a space 'has to be thought as a pure *point*' (EE, 92), and indeed, one might add that Aristotle's rejection of the idea that a point in space can be infinitely divided is highly prudent.

Highly prudent, that is, until the arrival of Cantor.

Cantor stands the Aristotelian idea, dominant in philosophy down the centuries, that the relationship between the finite and the infinite is analogous to the one between the parts and the whole, completely on its head. According to basic Aristotelian reasoning the part will always be smaller than the whole to which it belongs, or else it loses its status as a part and becomes a new whole in its own right. Cantor asserts on the other hand, quite improbably, that the part is *equal* to the whole, or that the set of things which is equivalent to one of its parts is *infinite*. But what is Cantor's definition of infinity, and is it likely that we could hope to gain an adequate idea of infinite number beyond what we simply imagine to be its uncountable size?

What leads Cantor to make his assertion is the notion of an 'infinite set'. Consider two sets of elements, *A* and *B*. Let *A* be the set of positive integers (1, 2, 3, ...), and B the set of even numbers (2, 4, 6, ...). B is a part, or 'subset', of A. For every element of A let us subtract its double from B. Similarly for every element of B let us subtract its half from A. Since this operation establishes, in theory at least, a one-to-one correspondence between the elements of A and the elements of B, we can assert that the subset B is equal to its set A, or *the part is equal to the whole*. Furthermore, assuming that this operation can be counted to infinity, we can say that the relations between the subset and its set are infinite. However, Cantor is unable to let things rest here, for if it follows that there are as many even numbers as there are positive integers – or, by a comparable mode of reasoning, as many positive integers as there are fractions – then we are confronted by a seemingly insurmountable paradox. For how can we even entertain the idea of a one-to-one correspondence between sets whose subsets are as numerous as the sets themselves?

The problem of establishing a one-to-one correspondence between sets leads to Cantor's continuum question, which is: how many points are there on a straight line in Euclidean space? This is not a question of calculating magnitudes in the usual way, for if the number of points on a straight line between 0 and 1 are equal to the number of points between 0 and n then the question of how to establish any type of interval between points would appear to be insoluble. Given the infinity of infinite sets how can counting even begin? Cantor's answer to this question is the theorem of cardinal number, which asserts that 'for each cardinal number and each set of cardinal numbers there exists exactly one cardinal number immediately succeeding in magnitude and that the cardinal number of every set occurs in the series thus obtained'.[29] Leaving aside the proof of this theorem[30] we are able to accept that there are, indeed, an infinite number of infinite sets and that counting between them is possible. With the creation of 'transfinite' number – which Cantor symbolises using the Hebrew letter aleph: ℵ – the infinite is raised miraculously from a mere potential to an actually existing number open to intuition.

In their attempts to grasp a mathematical infinity the work of Cantor and his followers has not drawn universal acknowledgement from mathematicians, although as Gödel would remark, the refutations of the foundations of set theory derive as much from philosophical disagreements as to the nature of mathematical objects as they do from strictly mathematical falsifications of the axioms themselves.[31] The question of the underlying consistency of set theory would in this case be no less a *wager* on truth than a matter of presenting a 'conventional' lesson in axiomatic verification. But how, one may ask, can mathematics live up to its scientific status if set theory is partly regulated by what will remain uncertain and, ultimately, unknowable to it?[32] What possible meaning could truth have in such a self-defeating system?

Without being able to provide here a detailed account of the paradigmatic significance of this question for set theory or Badiou's response to it,[33] we can summarise things in more general terms by saying that truth – and the truth of the infinite as represented by Cantor's continuum hypothesis is the ultimate truth for Badiou – is 'intrinsically undecidable'. The consistency of set theory does not depend entirely on its own axioms, but instead must be supplemented with the appeal to intuition as and when required.[34] Clearly there are countless examples from the history of science which remind us that a principle of undecidability will often function as a heuristic device which may lead to accommodations between competing scientific theories, or, in very rare instances, complete 'breaks' with the epistemological foundations of science.[35] Put simply in other words, truth does not emerge as a result of any prior anticipation of a scientific breakthrough, but will invariably subtract itself from the received wisdom of a problematic, thereby confronting us intuitively, and so pushing back the limits of a present state of knowledge.

This hypothesis evidently requires some further unpacking, although, paraphrasing somewhat, it is essentially what enables Badiou to surmount at least some of the central paradoxes of set theory. For him, truth is unknowable from within the immanent confines of any situation. Truth is the void object = x of philosophy which follows in the wake of what is profoundly indiscernible for the subject and goes by the name of the event.

3
The Event of Non-Being

Having examined the scientific method of *Being and the Event* it would seem appropriate to consider whether such a method provides adequate foundation for a political science. Is it not, after all, the aim of classical thought – a tradition within which Badiou installs himself – to contribute towards the coming about of a truly 'democratic' society? As we shall see in the next chapter, Badiou regards politics as one of four philosophical conditions of truth whose universal precursor is the event. Although ontologically unthinkable, the event induces a set of political (or artistic, or scientific, or amorous) consequences to be drawn from the site of its aftermath. However, nothing is certain as far as the event itself is concerned, and before moving on to consider the political implications which may (or may not) follow in its wake, let us first examine the logical twists and turns which lead us towards its actual occurrence.

In Book I of *Being and the Event* Badiou introduces an exacting vision of ontology which we can now summarise in the following four stages.

Firstly, we have seen how Badiou regards the reciprocity of being and the one as a retroactive fiction. The multiple is 'without one', even to the extreme extent of being *barred* from itself (to adopt the Lacanian neologism). Secondly, if being as one 'is not', then we have seen how, in Badiou's reading of Plato, 'nothing is' (*rien est*). Rather than regarding nothing as an outright negation, Badiou names nothing 'the structure of the void' or otherwise 'the phantom of inconsistency' (EE, 68) which recalls the determinate negation of Hegel's '*Aufhebung*'. Finally, the void itself is 'the proper name of being', the element which is 'universally included' in every situation (EE, 100ff). This final definition both affirms and seeks to go beyond Aristotle's *Physics* – where the void is conceived as 'the cause of transport' for material processes (EE, 91) – and is arguably the most radical in ushering in the modernist paradigm of Cantor's theory of sets, which for Badiou marks the onto-logical extension of Platonism.

What follows in Book II of *Being and the Event* can be described as a topology of multiplicity. In a broadly similar vein to Deleuze, Badiou regards the dogmatic image of one world as the illusion which keeps the subversive power of multiplicity at bay. However, while alert to the illusion Badiou's scientific method is intent on defeating it. For Badiou the one is not, and so only presumes a *counting as* one where multiples in an infinite process of presentation/composition structure a situation. For Deleuze, on the other hand, any possible splitting of multiplicity is immanent to the one, and as such requires no logical mediation.[1] In *Difference and Repetition* Deleuze rejects science in favour of a Platonic philosophy of difference,[2] whereas in *Being and the Event* Badiou for his part holds that philosophy maintains a (conditional) dialogue with mathematics. It is on this point that Badiou supports the classical Hegelian architecture of the *Logic*[3] without reverting to a theory of substance in the Spinozist mould. Despite the reversal in fortunes which took place in the respective philosophical legacies of Hegel and Spinoza in France during the 1970s,[4] we repeat that there is no corresponding 'break' anywhere in Badiou's work with the philosophy of Hegel. For Badiou, the 'genius' of Hegel lies in splitting infinity – the Substance which the Spinozists regard as the Absolute of materialist analysis – in two.

There are *two* infinites in Hegel, the good and the bad, where 'that which constitutes the good infinite is the *presence* of the bad' (EE, 185). However, in accepting that Hegel's is a generative ontology where 'the pure multiple detains *in-itself* the counting-as-one', and where 'every point of being is "between" itself and its mark', we encounter the classic Hegelian problem of transgression: how can one cross a limit without *already* having overcome a prior limitation? 'In effect, the limitation [*la borne*] is the non-being by which the limit happens' (EE, 183). In other words, in Hegel's logic, there is nothing which is yet to happen which has not – in the global sense – happened already (EE, 182). The question we must pose therefore, in seeking to prove the idea of *progress* to the infinite, is can we conceive a degree of symmetry between same and other, pure presentation and structure, situation and counting as one?

The Multiplicity of Nature

This kind of question implies a somewhat unreconstructed return to the philosophy of Marx as well as Hegel, although Badiou's topology of multiplicity has nothing to do with the famous 'inversion of Hegel' which is often rather simplistically attributed to Marx and also to Engels. For the latter, Hegel's idealist 'error' lay in asserting the primacy of mind over matter whereby 'what we cognise in the real world is precisely its thought content – that which makes the world a gradual realisation of the absolute idea ...'.[5] According to Engels, Marx's materialism sets out to turn the dialectic of mind and matter 'right side up' by grounding the idea in the historical forces of production, thereby positing mind as the highest embodiment of matter or nature. It is indicative of the material conditions in which Marx and Engels were themselves writing – and perhaps the unaccounted for genius of both – that the 'driving causes of history' were revealed in the specific class antagonism of the time – bourgeois and proletarians – as well as in the historical form of such antagonism – 'The history of all hitherto existing society is the history of class struggles.' It is also indicative of the maturity and objective 'simplicity' of the aforementioned 'driving causes of history' – the 'interconnections with their effects'[6] – that the scientific investigation undertaken by Marx and Engels could pose 'the question of the relation of thinking to being' as a pivotal one for the philosophy of the nineteenth century.[7] However, any analysis which involves a materialist 'inversion' of the terms 'mind and matter' would certainly fall short of an adequate understanding of the present historico-social situation. As Louis Althusser has argued with considerable power in this respect, 'A man on his head is the same man when he is finally walking on his feet', meaning quite simply that the inversion of the *terms* of Hegel's philosophy makes no objective difference to its *content* or – employing Althusser's preferred terminology – its 'problematic'. Instead, for Althusser philosophy becomes a question of a '*new relationship* between *new terms*' whose structure-superstructure is conceptually 'overdetermined' in the present conjuncture.[8]

Althusser's theoreticism, along with the multiple variants of neo-Marxist scholarship which comprise its legacy,[9] aim to mark a controversial and unfinished 'break' with the humanism of Marx's early works and the accompanying concept of alienation. With Althusser the anthropology which makes man the rational, thought-bearing citizen of the State, spontaneously transforming thought into action, is nothing but a vulgar simplification of concrete reality. It is enough to recall that Althusser's key methodological definition in *For Marx* rejects the idea of a dialectic of theory and practice, distinguishing instead *theoretical* practice (science) from the theory of theoretical practice (philosophy).[10] There is, we must therefore assume after Althusser, no straightforward, determinate relation between theory and practice, mind and matter, thought and being, which govern the multiplicities of determinations in social formations.

Nor for that matter, it must be said, is such a straightforward, determinate relation evident in Hegel, a fact which Althusser conveniently glosses over throughout his writings, arguably to the detriment of his Marxist scholarship.[11] As indispensable as his contribution to Western Marxism remains, one may also recall that Althusser's preface to the English edition of *For Marx* is at pains to alert the reader to the status of philosophical essays which are '*simultaneously*, interventions in a definite conjuncture' and 'which obviously demand correction'.[12] The question of the currency of Althusser's work and its situation in relation to Marxism need not detain us here. However, the *singularity* of Althusser's intervention in post-war French philosophy and the unrivalled theoretical militancy – 'fidelity' in Badiou's language – which his name has signalled for both French Communism and its opponents are two key lessons of which the Badiou of *Being and the Event* evidently approves. We will return to the question of singularity later on in this chapter.

Like Althusser, Badiou's scientific enterprise distances itself from Hegelian phenomenology. For Althusser all consciousness is ideological, although ideology is not a reflection of the real world, 'but an image of the ideological consciousness'.[13] Althusser defines ideology as one of four determinate practices (the others being science, politics and the economic) which, taken together, register the overdetermined complexity of a social formation (its problematic). Moreover, 'the *problematic* of a thought is not limited to the domain of the objects considered by its author, because it is not an abstraction for the thought as a totality, but the concrete determinate structure of a thought and of all the thoughts possible within this thought'.[14]

Badiou acknowledges the contribution of Althusser's theoretical anti-humanism for philosophy, although, for Badiou, Althusser's legacy nowadays remains of largely political rather than scientific interest.[15] Ideology/consciousness exists for both outside the realm of pure science. In Althusser's case ideology can comprise the raw material which theoretical practice transforms into knowledge, although the production of knowledge is beyond the realm of 'practical recognition' and hence what Althusser terms a 'process without a subject'.[16] For Badiou knowledge is also a subjectless procedure.

However, on this precise point there is a definite parting of the ways, since in Badiou's case the subject is by no means absent from the historical process, and is quite capable of appropriating knowledge retrospectively (Badiou names the subject's encounter with knowledge, 'approximate truth') (EE, 435). The concept of truth aside, however, the influence of Althusser's *Reading Capital* is insurmountable for Badiou when it comes to what he regards as the identity of thought and being,[17] or what Althusser for his part terms the 'thought-totality':

> Far from being an essence opposed to the material world, the faculty of a 'pure' transcendental subject or 'absolute consciousness', ... 'thought' is a peculiar real system, established on and articulated to the real world of a given historical society which maintains determinate relations with nature, a *specific* system, defined by the conditions of its existence and practice, i.e., by a *peculiar structure*, a determinate type of 'combination' ... [18]

Can we therefore say that both Althusser and Badiou advance philosophical systems based on what each defines respectively as four practices (science, politics, ideology and the economic in Althusser's case), and four 'generic procedures' (science, politics, art and love in Badiou's)? The temptation at this superficial level of agreement is to answer yes, although the difference between their respective positions is marked in key ways, mainly because Badiou provides a far more systematic treatment of science than Althusser was ever capable of providing.[19] Like Deleuze and Guattari in *What Is Philosophy?*, Althusser adopts the Spinozist model of thought where the *concept* reigns supreme.[20] Here, Althusser requires that 'the production of knowledge ... takes place *entirely in thought*, just as we can say, *mutatits mutandis*, that the process of economic production takes place entirely in the economy ...'.[21] Accepting that each of Spinoza's attributes of thought and extension is infinite enables Althusser to infer that 'the *relation* between the order of real historical genesis and the order of development of the concepts in scientific discourse ... is an *imaginary* one'. Furthermore, on this basis, 'we can admit no *one-to-one correspondence* between the different moments of these two distinct orders'.[22] For Althusser, Spinozist, the relation between thought and being can be defined in this respect as one of *singularity*. The problematic of nature is such, so extreme, that the progress from one historical conjuncture to the next is absolutely infinite in kind, i.e. it excludes all the others. In nature, the one is all. It cannot therefore be *counted* as one. Or at least it can only be counted as one on condition that what is counted – individuals in a situation – and what is counting – the State – are identical: *Deus, sive Natura* (EE, 137).

Unlike Althusser's brand of Spinozism Badiou's axiomatic conditions of thought are somewhat different. As we have already seen in the previous chapter, the idea that there exists a one-to-one correspondence between elements deemed to be infinitely multiple is the central tenet of Cantor's continuum hypothesis. But can we say that set theory yields a mathematical approach broadly compatible with Badiou's earlier Marxist – or, strictly speaking, Maoist – principle of contradiction?[23] Badiou regards set theory as that which brings about a fundamental break with the language of speculative ontology and its dialectical pairs of 'one/multiple' and 'whole/parts'. 'The multiple consists of being without-one, or multiple of multiples, and the categories of Aristotle (or of Kant), Unity and Totality, cannot serve to apprehend it.' (EE, 95) Badiou's avowed aim in *Being and the Event* is to leave behind the 'still-born' legacy of dialectical materialism (EE, 10). However, the traces of Marxism – and Maoism – arguably persist, here and there, despite the introduction of this radical, 'post-Cantorian' variety of what Badiou names 'subtractive ontology'.

Multiplicity is always split between the multiple of presentation and the multiple of composition, inconsistent and consistent multiplicity, 'established in the division of the counting-as-one, the inconsistency upstream, the consistency downstream' (EE, 33). This universal ebb and flow of matter in motion appears on the face of it to resemble the dialectical philosophy which, in Engels' essay on Feuerbach, 'reveals the transitory character of everything and in everything; nothing can endure against it except the uninterrupted process of becoming and passing away, of ascending without end from the lower to the higher'.[24] Badiou's mathematical ontology does, however, make some important qualifications regarding multiplicity.

Firstly, the presentation of multiplicity/composition of multiplicity is a mutually exclusive process 'without one'. Here multiplicity recalls the universality of contradiction as elaborated by Mao in the tradition of Lenin and also of Engels. 'The interdependence of the contradictory aspects of a thing,' Mao writes, 'and the struggle between them determine the life and impel the development of that thing. There is nothing that does not contain contradiction; without contradiction there would be no world.'[25] For Mao – quoting Engels in *Anti-Dühring* – the process of contradiction is '"a practically endless succession of generations, in infinite progress"'. Unlike structuralism where the concept of structure (*la langue*) is reproductive in order to accommodate structural transformations which simultaneously comprise the whole, contradiction extends so far as to fracture every particular stage of the system's genesis into an infinity of sub-systems. 'Processes change, old processes and old contradictions disappear, new processes and new contradictions emerge, and the methods of solving contradictions differ accordingly.'[26] The unity of a thing is only notional, temporal and temporary. As such the only 'thing' that is certain is that *there are* elements in relative states of presentation and composition, of coming into being and passing away.

Secondly, in recalling what was said in the previous chapter with regard to number, multiplicity does not exist within the confines of a neatly sealed composite totality. Drawing a further analogy with Badiou's *bête noire* structuralism will prove illuminating here. *La langue*, according to Saussure, is a system of differences 'without positive terms' where the meaning of any one unit of language depends on its relationship to other similar units within the system as a whole. However, as Bennett observes, to be able to ascribe meaning or value to *individual* units of language assumes that the system is 'granted all the attributes of a person or philosophical subject in being endowed with the capability to undertake operations in relation to itself'.[27] Multiplicity maintains no such illusion of a universal or particular one. Instead, all is open to change in the sense that Marx, writing in *The Poverty of Philosophy*, proclaims that capitalism, in the fullness of time, annihilates everything, including all the abstract concepts hitherto employed in its understanding. Multiplicity follows no 'royal road to science', but neither should we be persuaded by the positivist illusion that its scientific status can be reliably vouchsafed by Marxist philosophy. Nowhere in Marx and Engels' writings is it argued that 'Marxism' (a void term for Marx if ever there was one[28]) should be blindly called upon as a theoretical tool regardless of the historical circumstances in which we find ourselves. Marxism is, no less than any other, a philosophy of its time, while the objective 'matter' of multiplicity is eternal.

So, yes, quite evidently the 'Marxist' inspiration is there in his work despite Badiou's strict insistence that his is a mathematical discourse. However, for Badiou there would be a profound dissymmetry to any 'dialectic' of multiplicity, since multiplicity marks a rupture with rational thought, while the dialectic is always a higher project of mind. Unlike the 'science' of historical materialism, the science of the pure multiple has no interest in and makes no claims to be able to clarify historical problems or concepts. There is also a further consideration. What Engels describes in a famous essay as the 'essential difference' between the 'brilliant intuition' of the Greeks and 'strictly scientific research in accordance with experience'[29] is evidently not a distinction upheld by Badiou, for whom both intuitionism and Platonism are scientific categories of research. Unlike the dialecticians of the nineteenth century Badiou starts out from a quite different set of premises about the natural world and man's place in it. Man does not wield the mystical power of science over nature. Instead, science investigates whether 'man' amounts to an object of science; whether there really is anything in man worthy of being.[30]

In Book II of *Being and the Event*, Badiou introduces the founding relations of the multiple, derived from set theory, of which there are two: 'the original relation of *belonging*' and 'the relation of *inclusion*'. Belonging, which employs the term $\in$, 'indicates that a multiple is counted as element in the presentation of another', while inclusion, which employs the term $\subset$, 'indicates that a multiple is subset of another' (EE, 95). Badiou is alert to the mistaken prejudice which views these relations as two ways of *thinking* the multiple: 'the same' multiple cannot be 'thought differently', for to do so would be to relegate it to the categories of Unity and Totality. 'It is entirely irrelevant,' Badiou asserts, 'to believe that α is at first thought as One (or set of elements), then as Whole (or set of parts)' (EE, 96). The *variety* of α occurs simply by virtue of its relation to other multiples – but this relation alters nothing of the essential being of α itself. And yet, given the 'ontological neutrality' of any one element, how can *any* definite relation hold between multiples, and specifically the two relations, belonging and inclusion, under consideration here? Put simply, how can any one multiple, in being indifferent, imply the existence of another?

The first stage of Badiou's response relies on what he calls 'the axiom of the set of subsets' which states that 'if a set α exists (is presented), then the set of all its subsets also exists'. This axiom permits us to overcome the problem of relations between multiples in the following manner: assuming we have the set α then we also have whatever elements it includes, even if such elements merely amount to the iteration of the set itself, or its re-presentation: $\alpha \subset \alpha$. The notation for this set of subsets is $p(\alpha)$, which 'is *a multiple essentially distinct from α itself*' (EE, 97). The problem of relationality is overcome, in other words, when a given multiple is defined by the existence of another multiple which the initial multiple is not. This axiom enables us to arrive at 'the theorem of the point of excess', which states that 'the multiple of subsets of a set consists inevitably of at least one multiple which doesn't belong to the initial set' (EE, 98). However, the proof of such a theorem is conditional, for as we shall see in due course, in set theory 'measure' is 'strictly unassignable' (EE, 98).

Even a cursory reflection on number is enough to make us realise that counting (as measure, calculation or consistency) is very often less about the categorisation of elements than it is about *establishing* their categories of existence. Counting is never an operation entirely distinct from its terms. Instead, each time one counts one is counting not exclusively for independently existing things but also for the existence of the counting apparatus, i.e. the structure which allows counting to get going in the first place. The counting as one always presumes a counting of counting. In order to present one multiple there must already have been, paradoxically, a means of re-presenting it.

The theorem of the point of excess dispenses two types of multiplicities: '*ordinary* multiplicities', 'which have the property of not belonging to themselves', and '*eventmental* multiplicities' (*multiplicités événementielles*) 'which have the property of belonging to themselves'. The event is the forbidden multiple, prohibited from being. It is being's gap or interval. Here we recall the 'empty intentionality, never filled' that Lacan calls 'metonymy'. What attains being (its 'elusive signified') only actually does so '"at infinity"'.[31] In the Lacanian sense, the event would be the actual *bar* of subjectivity: /, which is invested in Lacan's formula: S/s. For Badiou, this prohibition, although unpresentable, at least has a name: 'void',[32] or what is indicated by the mark ϕ. The event cannot be, its non-being is unthinkable.[33] However, before arriving at its own presentative formula we shall need to gauge its prohibitions, or the rules that prevent it – ordinarily – from happening.

As was noted in the previous chapter, the void marks the absolute 'point' of being. The void is 'universally included in every situation'. Given the void's 'unicity of inexistence', no element is able to resist its disjunction. Like the mathematical zero, we say that the void is infinitely multiple. However, the consequences of such indiscriminate behaviour would appear to be absurd, for an element of the void is an element of anything and therefore, what amounts to exactly the same thing: an element of nothing. For Badiou, however, this 'absurd chimera' is precisely what vouchsafes the proof of the distinction between belonging and inclusion, for although it is the case that the null set, in being unique, possesses no element or multiple, it does possess a subset: *itself*. In other words, while belonging to itself – written thus: $\phi \in \phi$ – is, for the void, forbidden, the void is nonetheless included in itself: $\phi \subset \phi$. Between the void and its mark, ϕ, there is nothing, not even the void. But this 'nothing' is still part of the void. The following example should help to clarify the issue.

We have known since Marx that social relations are intimately tied up with the productive forces of the economy. 'The windmill,' writes Marx, 'gives you society with the feudal lord; the steam mill, society with the industrial capitalist.' A multiple is ordinarily presented as subset of another; it is included in the situation of which it is a component part, or 'sub-multiple'. However, bearing in mind that capitalism also brings about the conditions of its own eventual collapse, we say that no thing belongs to it (neither nothing nor the void), not even itself. To the question *what is eternal?* Marx responds: 'There is nothing immutable but the abstraction of the movement – *mors immortalis.*'[34] In the fullness of time capitalism annihilates everything, every last vestige of social stability, including its own productive efficiency. The void – death – is the only objective certainty in the universe, a certainty which there is no possibility of transcending.

But can we say that what is unpresentable in this sense – what is void or never belongs – is naturally antagonistic, as in the case of an unlawful mode of production? For Badiou the solution rests with the state of the situation.

What is unpresentable is by no means unrepresentable. For Badiou 'all presentation is two times structured' which means that 'presentation is never chaotic. I say,' says Badiou, 'only this:

> inasmuch as chaos is not the form of the donation of being, the obligation arises to think that there is a reduplication of counting-as-one. The prohibition of all presentation of the void is immediate and constant only if this point of flight of the consistent multiple, which is precisely its consistency as operative

result, is in its turn plugged, or buckled, by a counting-as-one of the operation itself, a counting of counting, a meta-structure. (EE, 110)

The necessity of the consistent multiple, of its consistency as one ('as operative result'), is to block the 'point of flight' which makes it multiple. Put differently, in order to police the border of any territory effectively, (the law of) counting must first prove its capacity to arrest its terms. Badiou calls this secondary counting framework, with explicit political overtones, 'state of the situation', whereby 'the structure of a situation – of any structured presentation – is counted as one'. It is the State which bears ultimate responsibility for counting its population, and this concept clearly owes its inspiration to Althusser's famous prototype. In 'Ideology and ideological state apparatuses' we recall how the State's task is to guarantee the obedience of subjects who must recognise the State 'in the name of a unique and absolute Subject'. Of course, although 'in the majority of cases' the subjects obey the law, there are always those '"bad subjects" who on occasion provoke the intervention of one of the detachments of the (repressive) State apparatus'.[35] For Badiou, as we shall soon discover, this 'intervention' marks the beginning of the process of subjectification, or what he also calls 'fidelity'. Moreover, since an intervention will involve subjects who manage to escape the system, the process is activated by what Althusser calls 'misrecognition'. The act of *not* being counted by the State is the main condition for the subject to come into being.

The State is a counting apparatus, but the subjects it counts are not numerical. In the work of Deleuze and Guattari we recall how the State is the ultimate counting machine, 'a phenomenon of *intraconsistency*' which 'makes points resonate together, ... very diverse points of order, geographic, ethnic, linguistic, moral, economic, technological particularities'. But the populations in question are not numerical. For Deleuze and Guattari the State, or *States*, must be thought in the qualitative rather than quantitative sense as 'collective mechanisms that simultaneously ward off and anticipate the formation of a central power [the 'State-form']'. Moreover, the ultimate form of consistency is a 'threshold of consistency, or of constraint' which 'co-exists with what has yet to cross it'.[36] One might say that the State is constituted in the shadow of its own dissolution.

Similarly, for Badiou, what haunts the state of the situation is the void, whose errant structure paradoxically guarantees the relative stability of counting. It is 'formally impossible', as we have already seen according to the theorem of the point of excess, 'that *everything* which is included (every subset) belongs to the situation' (EE, 113). The State is therefore the transparent constitution of what is not, populated with outsiders and nomads in addition to a qualified citizenry. Furthermore, if counting is doubled then so too is each of its terms (situation and state of the situation; or, analogously, presentation and representation; or again, belonging and inclusion). This deduction permits Badiou to establish four 'decisive concepts of a typology of donations of being' which are: *normal*, 'a term which is at the same time presented and represented'; *outgrowth*, 'a term which is represented, but not presented'; and *singular*, 'a term which is presented, but not represented' (EE, 115). Finally, *void* is a term which is neither presented nor represented.

State, Class and Part

'It was certainly a grand acquisition of Marxism,' Badiou says, 'to understand that the State had no relation, in its essence, to individuals, that the dialectic of its existence was not that of the one of authority to the multiple of subjects' (EE, 121).

Badiou's axiom of the state of the situation applies equally to nature – an application largely ignored by Marxists – a nature which he defines as being merely 'stable'. It is certainly not the case that the state of nature harbours the anarchy famously invoked by Hobbes. Indeed, in response to Galileo's famous pronouncement that the book of nature is written in the language of mathematics Badiou follows an altogether more rigorous formula. In accepting that 'Nature' is composed entirely of natural elements it could easily be deduced that 'all (that is natural) is (belongs) in all, except that there is not all'. As we have already demonstrated, auto-belonging ($O \in O$) is forbidden. Put simply in other words: *Nature doesn't exist* (EE, 159–60).

No doubt there will be a strong temptation to dismiss this formula as a *reductio ad absurdum*, the inevitable consequence of attempting to cast the net of mathematical thinking far too randomly. However, this would be to confuse Badiou's aims with those of the scientific realists for whom the idea of a proposition is that it must necessarily correspond to some feature of objective reality. When Badiou employs an empirical example, as in his meditation on Marxism (EE, 121–8), it is for completely different reasons. For Badiou, science must expose what it, science, *is not*, or cannot reveal. Can we there-fore assume that Badiou's selection of the Marxist paradigm in exemplifying the state of the situation is based on the assertion that Marxism's historical defeats – and its resulting 'dogmatism' – stand as the most 'advanced' lessons (axioms) in the development of a science of the State? It would certainly appear that way, a fact that equates with Badiou's attachment in *Being and the Event* to a Marxist prob-lematic more or less consistent with his own 'history' as a Marxist. It seems fair to say that Badiou's faith in Marxism's involvement in the historical contradictions that it, Marxism, continues to be sympto-matic of – and 'the Cold War' is only a nominal indication here[37] – is a Marxist-Leninist position, recalling as it does Lenin's saying that Marxism's truth, in theory and in practice, is generated from within its own historical weakness.[38] Moreover, taking this to be Badiou's position leads us to acknowledge the reliance of mathematical ontology on empiricism, where the latter provides the 'raw material' which science then uses to vouchsafe the integrity of its own system.

Badiou illustrates his theory of the State by invoking the 'great masses – these parts, which are often parties – at the same time empirical and moving, that constitute the rich and the poor' (EE, 122). The State has no interest in individuals, since counting always concerns the structure and its parts rather than the terms of the situation. 'Even the coercion ... that the State exercises on such and such an individual, in no way signifies that the State is *defined* by the coercive "interest" that it will feel for this individual, or for individuals in general' (EE, 122). Nevertheless we can accept the principle that 'the State is the State of the dominant class' – the guar-antee of representation – even if things are slightly more complex in practice. For a start the bourgeoisie is only traditionally the class *in* power, corresponding to a particular phase of the development of the productive forces of society, etc., rather than the class *of* power in the absolute or universal sense. The bourgeoisie possesses 'the means of production, property, the concentration of capital, etc.' although such possessions evidently help to further its own interests as a class, and furthermore have 'nothing to do with the constitu-tionally representative character of government'. The State is 'always defined by representation', it re-presents a thing (property) which is 'already historically and socially presented' by one of its constituent parts (bourgeoisie). Recalling our typology the bourgeoisie is *normal* ('economically and socially presented, and re-presented by the State'). It is the social democratic variety of the State.

The State does however confront a key historical antagonism. On the one hand the State must remain historically *'tied'* to the society that it represents, e.g. in its maintenance of some form of consistency in ensuring relative degrees of social stability ('peace', 'justice', 'prosperity', etc.). On the other hand, in only being able to represent situations which have already been historically presented and which it can therefore scarcely claim credit for bringing about, 'the State – conceived as operator of counting and guarantee of the universal reassurance of one – is necessarily a separated device' (EE, 123–4). It is unquestionably the case that the Marxist idea of the State – the question of its 'constitution' – is separated from any suggestion of particular interests (an equally Rousseauian theme to which we will return in the following chapter). Communism also dictates that the free expression of one is conditional upon the free expression of all.

But surely this poses a very real difficulty for the State as the supposed guarantor of counting, for if an individual 'is not counted as one as "itself"' then how could the State ever represent him effectively as one of its parts?

The problem might be resolved if we were to shift attention away from the State as a disciplinary apparatus, and concentrate instead on the role of civil society as the container of a dynamic equilibrium of individual wills (Gramsci). However, Badiou is hostile to any idea of politics as a form of either domination or consensus (EE, 384). Instead, the true individual is a militant, being presented but not represented, and only ever appears as a *singular* term, thereby evading representation by the State. 'Proletariat' is the historical name for that term. Or, adopting the mathematical writing: {Proletariat} (EE, 124).

As Étienne Balibar's earlier formulation of the proletarian situation has it – drawing similar parallels despite having been written in a different conjuncture[39] – '*The concept of the dictatorship of the proletariat* [if we accept this to be the real object of Marxist-Leninism] *has nothing essentially to do with the conditions and forms of the "seizure of power".*' Moreover, for his part Badiou highlights a 'mortal ambiguity' in the works of Lenin and also of Engels on precisely this point, which might be expressed as follows. If the State, or the power of dictatorship, is essentially ambivalent to the class holding it at any one time, then what function does the State provide *for* the proletariat? Lenin's response to this frequently posed question was pragmatic enough:

Dictatorship is rule based directly upon force and unrestricted by any laws. The revolutionary dictatorship of the proletariat is rule won and maintained by the use of violence by the proletariat against the bourgeoisie, rule that is unrestricted by any laws.[40]

It is because coercion is reciprocal to the separation of the State that *'the State does not found itself on the social bond that it will express, but on its dis-connection that it forbids'* (EE, 125). It is always the 'peril of inconsistency' which throws the masses together, not through freedom but through necessity (the threat of 'permanent civil war'). Indeed, one might add that it is not the illusion of democracy that holds the State together, since the people are quite capable of recognising that their political representatives lie and are corrupt, but the mortality of their life, their 'being-together', that rules out any revolutionary organisation of the State. The State is a term of *outgrowth*, being represented but not presented, and 'as such ... leaves itself so easily neither destroyed nor even attacked' (EE, 127). This is a fairly blunt report for political militants, although it does at least draw out an inversion in the question of absolute State power. Namely, that if the State, conceived as the power of dictatorship, is essentially ambivalent to the class holding it at any one time, then what use is it for the proletariat? Or again, bearing in mind the instrumental nature of the question: *why should* the proletariat aim to seize State power at all since clearly, framed in this manner, *not* holding it no less precludes the proletariat's rule of dictatorship than holding it would otherwise do? This is not a rhetorical question. On the contrary, its purpose is to harness the multiple formulas for the realisation of proletarian dictatorship, the 'unlimited regime of the individual', which might be written summarily thus: $P \subset P$, where P = 'proletariat'.

According to this logical application of the term, 'proletariat' does not refer to a 'class in-itself'.[41] Those terms counted as proletarian are included in the proletarian situation without necessarily belonging there, i.e. without necessarily *being* proletarian.[42] Furthermore, in accepting this we are obliged to admit that for every proletarian term there must also be another element which will be, generically speaking, 'bourgeois'. For as we have seen already, the axiom of the set of subsets states that the multiples included in a set α form another set to which they belong, $p(\alpha)$, which is written thus: $\alpha \in \beta$. It became the cause of notable regret for Lenin that the communist principle of individuality continued to be conditioned long after the Russian Revolution by its class character. The wholly inclusive nature of the administration of a given society in a state of genuine, socialist transition cannot ultimately do away with its representatives. Instead, it relies on such participation in order to function as 'a more democratic, but still *State* machinery'.[43] On this basis 'the Marxist description of the State is formally correct, but not its general dialectic', which Badiou refers to as 'the dialectic of the void and excess' (EE, 126). What we have here is a daunting paradox for Marxists, since on the one hand the singularity of the void can only be (mis)taken for the non-representation of the proletariat as the subject of experience, while on the other hand the 'excess' of bourgeois democracy remains the universal condition of revolutionary change. We can see that the 'contradiction' of the dialectic of the void and excess is, in the final analysis, a thoroughly non-antagonistic one.

Of course, there is a missing dimension at work in Badiou's meditation on the State. For although we might agree that communism is conceivable in terms of a typology of being (a type of social equation as Lenin believed) we must be wary of attributing the power of actual decision-making to any scientific apparatus. For all the supposed logic and universality of the state of nature, mathematical ontology arguably falls some way short of grasping the strategic demands of communism (or any form of political organisation for that matter) *as practice*. As we shall see later on and in the following chapter, the State's function is always a political problem forged from the point of the undecidable. It remains to be seen whether Badiou's idea of politics can provide any reason for political optimism in this regard, and indeed whether it presents anything *radically new*. In the meantime, however, it is towards Badiou's concept of the event that we will need to turn our attention next.

The Event and History

So far we have only been dealing with nature, which is merely 'natural', 'stable', 'consistent', 'normal', 'ordinary' – definitions which apply equally to the universal condition of States and, in Aristotle's judgement, 'the universality ... of the middle class' (EE, 121). In this sense multiplicity is 'axiomatically homogenous' (CT, 57). These are the conclusions which Badiou reaches in respect of mathematical ontology as the science of being as being, and which he sets out in Books I–III of *Being and the Event*.

Badiou's objective in Books IV and V is to introduce us to the concept of the event which, in direct contrast to the status of mathematical ontology, is 'that which is *not* being as being'. As was pointed out in the previous chapter, the gap which Badiou seeks to open up between philosophy and mathematics is a militant aim, and a question of intervening in the history of mathematics in order to guarantee its true philosophical status. Such an event is irreducible to any kind of logic or intuition, although having said that the axiomatic system we have been considering up until now will prove indispensable to our understanding of philosophy's occurrence. The event of philosophy always registers an impact, disturbing an equilibrium of whatever kind, or in other words and invoking Badiou's generic categories, *ruptures* the prevailing scientific, political, amorous or artistic norms of a situation.

Badiou's concept of the event gathers its inspiration from Heidegger's lectures on art, where we learn that '"all which appears other" – other than the very appearance, which is nature – is confirmed and accessible only "as not counting, as a nothing" ... I will retain from Heidegger,' Badiou adds, 'the root of his proposition:

> that the *place* of thought of that-which-is-not-being is non-nature, that which presents itself *other* than natural, or stable, or normal multiplicities. The place of the other-than-being is the a-normal, the unstable, the anti-nature. I will call *historic* that which is thus determined as the opposite of nature. (EE, 193–4)

What Badiou is also drawing on, besides art, is Heidegger's concept of time. Ordinarily people inhabit a homogeneous time where their daily routines are punctuated by the law of the clock. Ordinary time is clearly imperative, since it enables a society to date key events and co-ordinate its public life collectively. However, such a concept of time is phenomenologically inauthentic since it presents time as a sequence of successive moments or 'nows'. For Heidegger, this is not time in the truly historic sense of the word. Instead, time occurs in the fleeting disquietude which makes us wonder how a particular event can be properly accounted for. All of us will have experienced situations which appear to exceed the bounds of ordinary time, moments when a minute lasts a lifetime, or when a week seems to fly by in next to no time. This is what Heidegger calls 'ecstatic temporality', or time taking place in its authentic moment of ek-sistence. For Heidegger this is the time which the temporal regimes of past, present and future *naturalise*, the time which *makes history*, and which reveals itself against a backdrop of abject normality.

Badiou's interest in history as 'eventness' (*événementialité*) clearly falls into this latter category. If nature is stable, 'the omnipresence of normality', then history as anti-nature is 'the omnipresence of singularity' (EE, 194). History in this sense lies dormant, bordering on a happening, which Badiou refers to as an 'event site'. The site is an 'undecomposable' term or multiple 'on the edge of the void' which 'blocks the regression of combinations of multiples to the infinite' (EE, 195).

It is important to note that the relation of history to nature is profoundly dissymmetrical. Unlike natural multiplicity which 'conserves' elements once they appear, the event site differs in not presenting its elements, apart from the element from which it is, itself, composed. The site is quite content to be naturalised – 'to undergo a statist normalisation' – although, crucially, the same cannot be said in reverse, i.e. *nature cannot be singularised*. History is relative to the circumstances of its appearance, to the particularity of its *local* situation, while nature is absolute – a place where nothing is the same – admitting a *global* coexistence of terms. For Badiou, the result of this dissymmetry allows us to dispense with the 'vulgar Marxist conception of the sense of History'. 'We can think the *historicity* of certain multiples, but we cannot think *one* History' (EE, 196–7).

Arguably this is a hierarchical conception of history. Badiou invokes a 'typology of situations' for the purpose of distinguishing between 'those in which there are event sites and those in which there are not'. Natural situations will not have a site, since nature merely re-presents multiples which have already been presented in a situation. The historic situation on the other hand will possess at least one multiple which manages to a-void the global law of re-presentation. The site of the historic situation therefore occupies the extreme margins of action. Nothing 'below' the site is part of it (EE, 195). Moreover, 'All action of radical transformation originates *in a point*, which is, from within a situation, an event site' (EE, 197).

This is certainly not the type of history which people encounter in the course of their everyday lives. For Badiou, history is never the subject of ordinary experience. Instead, history on his reading amounts to the monumental variety which replicates the glories of past events and ushers in some form of heroic action. Badiou's approach follows closely on the heels of Heidegger for whom history is always a question of the 'being-there' which chooses the authentic path towards its own destiny. Politically speaking history is certainly not neutral. However, we must be careful not to mistake the historic situation or event site for Heidegger's *Dasein*. The event itself is certainly not buried somewhere 'within-the-world'.[44] There is something altogether more miraculous and other-worldly about the eventness of being. 'The confusion of the existence of the site,' Badiou explains '(for example: the working class, or a given state of artistic tendencies, or an impasse of science ...) and the necessity of the event is the cross of determinist or globalising thoughts' (EE, 200). The uncertainty of the event is its very condition of being. There is never an adequate occasion to decide whether what appears to be happening *is* in actual fact. Indeed, such is the level of profound scepticism which naturally tends to greet any act of true originality (political, artistic, scientific ...) that the mere rumour of the event is enough to ward off its possibility. The event site is always on the brink of the void, of being dismissed before 'it' even has a chance to come into being.

Badiou's mathematical formula, or 'matheme', of the event is as follows:

$$e_X = \{x \in X, e_X\}$$

where e_X signifies the event and X signifies its site. In Badiou's words, 'the event makes one-multiple on the one hand from all the multiples which belong to its site, on the other from the event itself' (EE, 200). Badiou draws here on the 'syntagm' of the French Revolution in an attempt to illustrate the event's dual character. Given the history of France between 1789 and 1794 we are, in theory at least, able to count for practically all of the terms which belong to this historic situation where we discover, among others, 'the electors of the general States, the peasants of the Great Fear, the *sans-culottes* of the towns ...' as well as 'the guillotine, the massacres, the English spies ...'. However, during the course of this presentation, and at a certain point, something (else) happens: the event assumes an identity. With regard to the French Revolution, Badiou proposes, a *declaration* is made (by the French revolutionary leader Saint-Just that 'the Revolution is frozen'), which halts the dissemination of multiples in its tracks. Needless to say the content of such a declaration is not in itself enough to bring about this punctuation (syntax being void for Badiou), as indeed any declaration may be little more than a question of timing. What is decisive, however, is that by virtue of this act of intervention what is mobilised is not just a set of random encounters bordering on the indiscriminate (the pointless disorder of French republicanism), but the 'French Revolution' as '*an axial term of the Revolution itself*'; and, furthermore, one invested with the power of qualification, i.e. of *deciding* what does and what does not belong to the site; of what attests to the revolutionary singularity of the Revolution and what doesn't.

Of course, we must accept that the event is, in terms of our interpretation of it, a purely retroactive phenomenon. Only when it – the 'it' being the composition of terms which may in certain situations turn out to be void, i.e. have nothing to do with the Revolution – is count-*ed* can the event *then* be said to exist. Whether in reality the intervention marks the beginning or the end of the event – whether or not the situation has in actual fact exhausted itself – is insignificant. What signifies the event as such is the abstraction in a singular point – a declaration or some other act – of that which turns out to be a pivotal moment in history. The point where history stands 'irreversibly' poised on the brink of change.

Unlike nature, the event (of history) is not a fact. In the midst of the complexity of a given situation and lacking any unified plan for action – or objective criteria for defining 'revolutionary situation' in advance – 'revolutionary activity' would appear to be an intuitive affair. However, Badiou's axiomatic method is reluctant to leave the situation open to chance. The event is not a question of simply trusting in the vain hope that, given the 'right' set of circumstances, something might just happen. Is there, then, any way of verifying the event's non-being or perhaps even gauging the likelihood of a given set of circumstances arising – or not as the case may be – from the site? Badiou's answer to this question is simplistically frank: we just can't tell. 'If an event exists,' he explains, '*its belonging to the situation of its site is undecidable from the point of the situation itself*. In effect, the signifier of the event (our e_X) is necessarily supernumerary to the site' (EE, 202). The upshot of this undecidability is therefore formulated via the following hypothesis. Either the event belongs to the situation by virtue of its own self-reflexive separation from the void (what Badiou calls the 'ultra-one'), or the event does not belong to the situation and is therefore subsumed by the void (where '*nothing* of the kind ever took place') (EE, 203). Clearly the latter qualification would only seem to confirm what is *already* established i.e. that the event, *qua* the event of non-being, is undecidable. The qualification of the event is indeed a circular operation (EE, 202). However, this is not by any means a barrier to the event's existence for us. On the contrary, undecidability, rather than deferring the proximity of what is, is precisely what is at stake when coming to grips with the event as the 'rational attribute' of what is not (EE, 220).

Badiou's Wager: Pascal

What defeats uncertainty in circumstances that would appear to present equally uncertain propositions is not the conviction that one of them is objectively true. Settling on the truth of either is instead a question of making a decision as to which one must, in a given set of circumstances, be chosen. Such a procedure is what Badiou names 'intervention', and draws its inspiration from the (anti-)philosophy of the seventeenth-century French philosopher and scientist Pascal. What attracts Badiou to the work of Pascal is the range of interests held by the latter, both in the arts and sciences, and which culminated in the work which is most often associated with his name: the *Pensées*. In this work – unfinished in Pascal's lifetime and published posthumously from notes and essay fragments – the question of presentation abounds.

The *Pensées* offers a strong repudiation of the scepticism handed down from Descartes, which in Pascal's day had become the staple of philosophical enquiry. For Pascal truth is grounded, not by way of this 'doubting' reason, but by means of knowledge which is purely intuitive. 'It is through the [heart] that we know first principles,' Pascal writes, 'and reason, which has nothing to do with it, tries in vain to refute them.'[45] The *de facto* separation of reason from the senses thereafter confronts human beings with a stark challenge. Set adrift from reason, all that remains is for human beings to bear witness to the wretchedness of their own existence, and of the infinite gulf which separates reason from instinct. When all paths appear to be equally futile the suggestion of there being a more rational choice tends to be eclipsed by the strength of an individual's faith in his present circumstances, even if such faith tends to imply (for non-believers) the apparent absence of absolute truth. Here Pascal's thought provides us with an effective way out of the difficulties that frustrate the very idea of the event; granted that the event, as that which *is not*, is undecidable. *If* it exists *then* it either belongs to the situation of the site or it does not. However, since the event's occurrence is not something which can be established beyond reasonable doubt, it makes little odds to the question of the event's belonging whether it, the event, actually occurs or not. What matters instead is that the subject 'goes through the motions', resolutely acting *as if* the aim of his energies was accurately trained on the object of his desires. Whether or not we later find out that our faith in the event was misguided is of secondary importance, since 'nothing' has been lost in the process, while equally everything stood to be gained. This highly original although no less controversial mode of thinking, commonly referred to as the 'wager', is Pascal's most celebrated contribution to modern philosophy and forms the basis for his theory of mathematical probability. But how exactly does the idea of the wager help to inform Badiou's approach to the event?

Firstly, the intervention guarantees, not the event's actual occurrence, but that the uncertainty surrounding it *was* interrupted. From the point of view of any presumed participants the event is not 'under way' in the sense of individuals being contemporaneously recruited to its cause. The event has no cause, and so 'There are no heroes of the event' (EE, 229). The intervention marks an interval of the event – or an interval separating one event from another – not a term of the situation, since the intervention cannot safely harness the event's singularity. All it can do instead is, by means of what is simultaneously an act of recovery, rescue the remnants of a situation which, to all intents and purposes, happened. But no event need 'genuinely' have taken place for an intervention to be made. As the countless religious inquisitions and political show trials which populate our social history ably demonstrate, there is always sufficient scepticism surrounding the alleged act of heresy or treason to divide the State *de jure*, its prosecutors and defendants, in two.

This is essentially what happens. The intervention is 'unlawful', suspending the law of order we ordinarily attribute to the State. Given the fact that the State is unable to account for the event, the intervention performs the task of nominating it, or giving the event a name. Every crisis of the State can usually be found in a declaration that 'In the name of ...' ('justice', 'peace', 'the Republic', etc.) the law is being challenged. Needless to say, the crisis following in the wake of the event always exceeds the accountability of the State (hence the 'state of emergency' and 'special powers' which it uses to restore order). There is a duty, which is the 'affair of State', which demands that every situation marked by an intervention is divided between a crime and a culprit, or an event and a site.

Here the question of the 'Two' enters into the equation. In order to fulfil its proper representative function the state must be able to guarantee a form of correspondence between the event and the site where – we can only presume at this stage – the event belongs. However, as a term of outgrowth the state harbours no relation to the event as singularity and cannot represent it. Indeed, as we have seen, it is this necessary shortfall between the adequate counting of the state and the presentation of a genuinely revolutionary term that conditions the state's very existence (as well as its apparent precariousness). To summarise:

> Each time a site emerges as the theatre of a real event, the state – in the political sense, for example – sees all too well that it is necessary to mark out the pair of the site (factory, road, university) and of the singleton of the event (strike, riots, disorder), but cannot manage to fix the rationality of the bond. In the same way a law of the state sees in the anomie of this Two – and it is the admission of a dysfunction of counting – the *unknown hand* (the outside agitator, the terrorist, the perverse professor). It is unimportant whether or not the agents of the state believe what they say. What counts is the necessity of the statement. For this metaphor is in reality that of the void itself: of the unpresented *operating*, and of what the state comes to say about it, by designating a cause exterior to the situation. The state seals off the appearance of the immanence of the void by the transcendence of the guilty. (EE, 230–1)

The intervention does not found the event. Instead, it merely intervenes in a situation whose consequences are always already decided in the act of being seized by the State. The intervention, which brings into circulation the name of the event, will always ultimately (re)compose the State's interests, its arbitrary powers, and its wider constitutional aspirations. But what chance is there that the intervention might otherwise serve a truly militant aim, i.e. one whose consequences *remain* unified, holding themselves together as it were, in spite of the rule of law? This paradoxical mode of intervention is what Badiou calls 'Time' which, 'if it is not co-extensive to the structure, if it is not the *sensible form of the Law*, is the intervention itself, thought as interval of two events'. Time enables the intervention to actually *occur* rather than simply following mechanically and aimlessly in the wake of what has already gone before it. Although incapable of presenting the exact moment of the event, time at least draws out the event's presumed consequences – to the point of the occurrence of another event. Badiou ridicules 'speculative leftism' for adhering to the misguided belief that the intervention somehow 'authorises itself only by itself, and breaks with the situation with no other support than its own negative will'. To intervene is always, formal constraints aside, to enter into a new situation or, more exactly, to enter a situation *anew* (EE, 232). The intervention always enacts the transformation of an existing set of circumstances that cannot be anticipated from where one originally started out. Such is the unbridgeable gulf of being.

Badiou's idea of the intervention reinforces for us the true significance of Pascal's wager. For one never wagers on the possibility of the event itself, since one cannot anticipate what cannot happen. The intervention is the possibility of accepting or rejecting the event's consequences, and it is on *this* that we wager while all the time recognising that, once the event has actually occurred, we are now entering into an entirely different world.

4
The Politics of Truth

Politics must be subtracted from the State. In the remaining Books (VI–VIII) of *Being and the Event*, Badiou sets out to meet the final challenge of his system. For Badiou, truth is the ultimate aim of philosophy whose conditions (art, politics, science and love), once met, liberate philosophy for itself. Badiou's pair in support of this project, truth and subject, is one which has long since fallen into disrepute in the eyes of the postmodernists, obtaining scant references in the writings of Derrida, Deleuze and Guattari, and Lyotard. However, as we shall see, there arguably remains far more in the way of political mileage to be had from Badiou's theory of the subject than the postmodernists are willing to concede. Badiou's subject is not, as Deleuze and Guattari would have it, a 'poor approximation of thought',[1] neither does it serve the interests of any dominant reality. Instead, the subject is born from the chance-ridden circumstances of historical events and their 'being-true'. The question of true *perception*, of the subject being able to discern the event's truth for itself in the absence of any State involvement, is the higher ambition of Badiou's philosophical enterprise.

The Mark of Fidelity

We have already considered in the previous chapter how the intervention manages to put into circulation the name, if not the actual being, of the event. Intuitively we can see that the event must be arrested, punctuated at some point, even if only in the form of a nominal definition which adds nothing to our overall understanding of it. The 'French Revolution' might *appear* to refer to the set of all revolutionary phenomena to have occurred in France between 1789 and 1794. However, whether the intervening historical period has succeeded in faithfully transforming the fledging ideals of the French Revolution in line with the changing aspirations of the French Republic is not an objective issue, and today still remains largely open to question. The event, strictly speaking, is always foreclosed from ontology. Therefore ontology must take on the role of gauging the degree of correspondence between the terms of the *post*-eventmental situation (in this case those of French republicanism) and the supernumerary name of the event ('French Revolution'). This procedure is what Badiou calls 'fidelity', and is driven along by an intense faith on the part of the subject. At first sight, 'French Revolution', as the name of universal egalitarian democracy, may appear to have passed over into the corporate annals of Western capitalism. Yet this is not to say that the infinite multiplicity of the Revolution – which today lies politically dormant – cannot be revitalised, if not with the aid of Saint-Just, then at least with the arrival of a new proper name in the history of French republicanism.

Fidelity is 'the set of procedures by which one discerns, in a situation, the multiples whose existence depends on the putting-in-circulation – under the supernumerary name that conferred an intervention – of an event multiple' (EE, 257). The fidelity procedure retroactively regroups connections and disconnections to the event. Consider the dialectical plight of the faithful and the heretics whose mutual antagonism comprises the very substance of every institutional setting. The Christian Church following the founding intervention of St Paul or the Russian Revolution following Lenin's transfer of power to the Soviets do not simply go uncontested. The intervention causes splits, forcing the event to depend for its very survival (as 'what happened') on the counting as one which evaluates each of the resulting situation's respective sets of parts. The fidelity procedure, we might say, is an institution of parts. In the case of the Russian Revolution one cites the factionalism of the Bolsheviks versus the Mensheviks, and later on the Trotskyites versus the Stalinists, along with the corresponding sets of parts which allegedly testify to this historic event. The fidelity procedure's task is to decide, in each case, whether and to what extent the presented multiple is faithful to the event or not. Following on from an intervention the fidelity procedure invokes truth and draws up a kind of attendance list for the main protagonists, reporting on who is to be marked present and who absent, which terms are to be included in the situation and which ones excluded.

The fidelity procedure, employing this form of judgement, is a subjective operation, although Badiou refuses to allow it the status of 'a capacity, a subjective trait, [or] a virtue'. Instead, he explains, 'Fidelity is a functional relation to the event' which succeeds the intervention and is marked *only in its effects*; it performs a structural operation, and 'is not a multiple-term of the situation' (EE, 258). Badiou draws here on what mathematicians call the 'axiom of choice' in order to establish that a function can exist without being manifestly proven.[2] Similarly the objective existence of a fidelity operator (a noun or proper name linked to the preceding intervention) is quite different from the way in which this operator actually functions during the course of an evaluation. Can we therefore say that fidelity, as a body or institution, enjoys relative autonomy from the state? 'A fidelity is strongly distinct from the state,' Badiou explains, 'if it is in some way *unassignable* to a defined function of the state, if its result is a part which, from the point of view of the state, is particularly lacking in sense' (EE, 263). One need merely recall the 'slippage' (*glissement*)[3] of the Cultural Revolution in China, that mass signifying chain which in due course went off the rails, as the most striking example of the unassignable in question. Of course, in general, in the wider (objective) scheme of things, the fidelity procedure changes nothing, and exposes no part of the state apparatus, since the state simply counts as one multiples which are '*already* discerned'. The fidelity procedure in the end always has the 'backing' of the state apparatus. 'Certainly,' Badiou acknowledges 'fidelity, as procedure, is not.'

> At each instant however, an eventmental fidelity is seizable in a provisional result, which consists in effective inquests where it is registered that multiples are, or are not, related [*connexes*] to the event. (EE, 259–60)

There will always be those who question the integrity of mass political movements, whether for alleged stage management or ultimately for selling out to a higher power. Yet this is *precisely* what the fidelity procedure understands and, furthermore, founds itself on this deconstructive 'principle'. The state is 'only a crude approximation, in actual fact nil, of what fidelity is capable of'. Fidelity stands for degrees of relative autonomy – synonymous with the flourishing of the many student movements of 1968 – which are merely akin to *finite* exercises in a kind of hyper-self-criticism. Rather than providing reasons for being/non-being we might say that the fidelity procedure dispenses alibis for past behaviour. Either the multiple was (reportedly) there at the site of the event or was not, and can therefore be connected, as a fidelity operator ('counter-revolutionary', 'revisionist', 'fascist'), to the supernumerary name of the event ('Imperialism', 'the Twentieth Congress', 'the Third Reich') or it cannot. There is no equivocation and no right of appeal. Fidelity is surrounded with all the *accoutrements* of the state; it presents itself as a 'counter-state' or 'sub-state' (EE, 258). What ultimately makes the difference is the *measure* of distinction between sub-state and the state itself, as well as the *hazardous trajectory* which leads out of order to chaos.

The relentless circularity of the dialectic (from order to apparent chaos and back again) provides good reason to highlight the political significance of fidelity and its deductive procedures. Politics is not, after all, undermined by the truism that its current agenda is bound, sooner or later, to become outdated. On the contrary, the strength of the political intervention instead rests in *defying the law of nature (and interrogating truth)*, thereby putting off the possibility of defeat until another time. (This is what art also aspires to in its 'suspension of disbelief'.) For Badiou, politics – which (dis)appears as an ungraspable ontological agency – 'puts the State at a distance' (AM, 160). In this sense we might say that fidelity is a part of the body politic itself.

Cantor Revisited

'A thought,' Badiou declares, 'is nothing other than the desire to finish with the exorbitant excess of the state' (EE, 312). There is something – everything! – excessive about state power, and in Book VI of *Being and the Event*, Badiou devises, by way of a series of mathematical exercises, a framework for the 'expansion' of the separation of politics from the State.

The State corresponds, in the popular imagination, to the very notion of ultra-power. More precisely, we assume the State to be quantitatively *larger* than any individual or one of its parts. However, the ancient Euclidean axiom, 'the whole is greater than the part', is abolished by Cantor's theory of sets. After Cantor it can be established, in strict accordance with the axioms of set theory, that there are as many fractions as there are whole numbers, or as many whole numbers as there are squares. As long as one can go on counting *ad infinitum* the idea of infinite number encounters no contradiction. However, Cantor's theory of infinite number also poses, or rather *collapses*, a fundamental paradox, namely: is it really sensible to assume the one-to-one correspondence of elements that are as numerous as the relations between them? What sense is there in designating a 'multiple' of relations which are *already* multiple or infinite (Badiou's 'multiple of multiples')? After all, Pascal's wager is enough to alert us to the fact that 'Unity added to infinity does not increase it at all, any more than a foot added to an infinite measurement.'[4]

In order to clarify the problem we need to return to what was said in the previous chapter on nature and infinity. Nature, we will recall, is absolute. In an open universe like ours, there are no 'boundary conditions'[5] (to borrow a key term from Stephen Hawking's research in gravitational physics) which limit its potential inflation. This rule can also be applied to the idea of natural numbers. Consider the sequence of natural numbers: 1, 2, 3, ..., etc. Since we could imagine counting this sequence indefinitely there is little sense in believing that such an operation would somehow 'lead' to the infinite, arriving there at some point in the future, since for every point reached there is always an infinite distance between where one is and the 'ultimate' point of infinity. Natural numbers are *ordinal*, i.e. they denote rank only. Instead of 1, 2, 3, ... we might just as well write 1, 1, 1, ... bearing in mind that such sequences of numbers tell us nothing about the relative value of any one term. This kind of infinity is a question of pure repetition and void succession. Nature, as infinity, far from being the height of disorder here exhibits the utmost stability.

Cantor's solution to the problem of the natural infinite is to denote an immediate and positive successor to the finite ordinals using the Greek letter ω (omega). As Badiou observes, this 'number' destroys the 'ancient speculative opposition between the finite, quantitatively varied and numerable, and the infinite, unquantifiable and unique', and unleashes 'the infinite proliferation of *different* infinite quantities' (EE, 301). The so-called 'limit cardinal', or first infinite number, ω_0, no longer founders on the conundrum of how to surpass the limit of the finite numbers. It is due to a scientific prejudice attributable to Kant, Badiou points out, which would seek to ascribe to the infinite the routine dimensions of time and space (EE, 293–5). Regardless of the place where we choose to bound the set of finite numbers, all that matters is that the number *immediately succeeding* this set is superior in quantity. From here on in the concept of finite number comes in 'second place', i.e. is derived from that of the infinite (EE, 179).

Cantor's theory of *cardinal* number, which concerns those numbers equal to or superior to ω_0, states quite simply that the number of subsets of a given set is always greater than the number of its elements. For where we have a cardinal ω_0 we can conceive at least *one* cardinal, the set of its parts $p(\omega_0)$, which is quantitatively greater in size (EE, 304). Moreover – and this is an absolutely crucial and decisive feature of Cantor's discovery – *there is no set of all cardinal numbers.*[6]

The theory of cardinal number *quantifies* Badiou's earlier theorem of the point of excess, which is worth recalling here.

> The theorem of the point of excess gave a local response to the question of the relation between a situation and its state: the state counts at least one multiple which does not belong to the situation. And consequently, the state is *different* from the situation of which it is the state. The theorem of Cantor, for its part, gives a global response: the power [*puissance*] of the state is – in terms of pure quantity – superior to that of the situation. (EE, 303)

That there can be a scale of measure which enables us to count as one a multiple as being quantitatively superior to an initial multiple (that 'the state counts at least one multiple which does not belong to the situation') advances things significantly. For if the state of the situation counts at least *one* multiple, which then, on further inspection, turns out to be 'greater' or 'smaller' or 'equal to' another, then it follows that this state is constructible in accordance with a strict hierarchy of differences. Furthermore, translating the theorem into the language of politics loses nothing of its axiomatic import. The State ordinarily exhibits supreme indifference towards individuals. However, what if, following the theory of cardinality, it was no longer indiscriminately excessive in its means of representation, but instead became associated with the power of *distinction*? Such power at least heralds the idea of equality. For is it not the most politically advanced axiom of equality which declares that the State is able to assume the figure of '1' (AM, 155–67), that it manifests itself in the shape of a person (if not an adversary) before the people, and that human beings are capable of acting each in accordance with his or her distinctly human capacity? As the communist declaration of the radical English Puritan Gerard Winstanley has it, '"From each according to his powers, to each according to his needs."'[7]

However, there is a persistent paradox at work here. For if the state is capable, in a given situation, of counting different terms as one, then its *power* of distinction is completely hazardous and arbitrary.

Representations are, for Badiou, 'situated' but not '*situatable*' (EE, 307). Politically speaking, the figure of democracy cannot be objectively measured. In Pascal's sense, politics would be the supreme wager on a set of circumstances whose 'democratic' consequences cannot be known in advance. The State, as a means of representation, is an errant structure. Similarly for mathematical ontology: on a cardinal scale of measure 'it is *impossible* to determine where the set of parts of an infinite set situates itself on the scale ...' (EE, 306). Any attempt to determine the set is made only at the risk of either over- or underestimating the magnitude of the terms in question.

Leibniz, Language and the Indiscernible

There is a diplomatic solution to the problem of the state whose power of representation is disproportionate in relation to its terms. Language, as a means of conciliation, is the 'filter', or 'the medium of this commensurability' between presentation and representation, situation and its state (EE, 319). As Wittgenstein argues, it is language which sets limits on (our understanding of) the world, and as such it is only prudent, politically speaking, that we remain silent on those subjects which we cannot talk about (EE, 322).

In response to the problem of commensurability, or what we might regard as the defiant, global contradiction of state power,[8] Badiou embarks upon four 'endeavours', two of which I will consider in the remainder of this chapter. The first involves the philosophical enterprise of Leibniz, which inspires the work of philosophical grammarians like Wittgenstein. The second will involve the 'generic procedure' and a more detailed treatment of the question of truth.

Leibniz's philosophy inhabits several fields of investigation, and it is easy to get carried away with the idea of a 'possible world' which has also provided, down the centuries, plenty of ammunition for the satirists.[9] The idea of 'worlds infinite in number' certainly encourages imaginative speculations on the possibility of differentiating science fact from science fiction. Badiou, however, is not interested in such possibilities. For Badiou, the only possibility at stake is the possibility of science itself, not its global environment. Badiou's interest in Leibniz is therefore not a sociological one. Instead, it is much more in keeping with the aims of a pure scientist seeking to gauge the disposition of a rival's work.

Badiou begins his meditation on Leibniz by locating the latter's philosophy in the scientific paradigm of 'constructivism' which, simply defined, holds that mathematical objects, rather than existing in themselves, have to be constructed. Leibniz proposes that this construction should (ideally) rely on a universal language, and although not the first philosopher to pursue its creation, Leibniz's writings are regarded as more or less foundational for the branch of Anglo-Saxon philosophy which formerly went by the name of 'logical atomism'.[10] We have already seen a brief example of constructivism at work in the guise of nominalism, or the naming which succeeds the intervention. However, unlike Badiou for whom the name is supernumerary, Leibniz's attachment to nominalism is ontologically formative.

There are two principles involved in Leibniz's formal logic: 'being-possible' 'which governs essences', and 'being-existent', the principle of 'sufficient reason'. In the first case the principle of non-contradiction, or the formal principle of identity, states that two things are 'formally identical' if there is no difference between them. This principle does not guarantee actual existence, since 'two things' whose abstract properties are found to be identical would be parts of one and the same concept. Here Badiou observes Leibniz's distinction between 'essence' – sometimes also called 'entity'[11] – and 'existent'. Badiou equates essence with the multiple which '*tends* towards existence': 'every non-contradictory multiple desires to exist' (EE, 350).

In the case of being-existent or 'world' we encounter 'different possible multiple-combinations' which sufficient reason counts as one. For Leibniz, nothing in the world is left to chance. There is no decision to make – no axiom of choice – or wager as to why we inhabit this world rather than any other. The sense of a multiple-essence is perfectly rational and determined, even to the extent that the reason employed in its proof must also be proved to be rational, if necessary by resorting to pure tautologies. The resulting 'primitives' are as much evidence as we need for existence (EE, 351). If an entity is *possible* then we ultimately take it to mean that the entity itself *exists*. Yet isn't there an emergent difficulty with this tendency towards non-contradiction given that – once more – what we are tending towards can always be infinitely divided?

For Leibniz the relief from the infinite is 'God', who is 'the constructibility of the constructible, the programme of World', and the 'supposed complete language'. Badiou invokes the famous Leibnizian question at this point – 'Why is there something rather than nothing?' – in order to confirm the decisive role that language plays in Leibniz's system. 'The question,' Badiou observes, 'functions as a crossroads for all the constructible significations of the Leibnizian universe.' Furthermore:

> The axioms [essences] impose the question, and reciprocally the response completes the question – which supposes the axioms – validating that it was posed, confirming the axioms that it utilises. (EE, 352)

Put simply, there is no place for individuals to doubt that there is 'something', in which case we are able to presume that the multiple *is* therefore presented. And there is no place to doubt it because it is *God's own language* which we employ for any such doubting. We might add that, unlike Descartes, Leibniz refused to regard 'clear and distinct ideas' as immediately knowable or resulting from our deductive powers of cognitive reasoning. As Hidé Ishiguro puts the case so well on his behalf, 'not only are we unable, according to Leibniz, to talk about concepts or ideas without words, we cannot even *think* in concepts or ideas without words or "characters" (symbols)'.[12] 'Of this power from which nothing thinkable can subtract itself,' Badiou explains, 'for us the most striking example is the principle of indiscernibles.' Leibniz's principle of indiscernibles states that if what is true of *A* is also true of *B* then *A* is identical to *B*. 'If two beings are indiscernible, language cannot separate them' (EE, 352). After all, why would God – the 'complete language' – wish to treat two beings, which really were identical, any differently? There is the flicker of equality in Leibniz's principle of indiscernibles which enables us to reflect on 'differences' between individuals in terms of our uses and abuses of language, although such a proposition is not without its fair share of problems. For if language rather than being is the reason for difference then how could equality, as pure indifference, truly exist? 'If all difference is attributable to language and not being, *presented* in-difference is impossible' (EE, 353).

For Leibniz there is no event. The present perpetuates itself under the aegis of sufficient reason, and there is no interruption or 'intervention' which could naturally explain this manifest or 'local' continuity. Only globally is it reasonable to assume that we will be able to evaluate how 'successive states' come into being and time. Furthermore, these two registers – global and local – are not mutually exclusive, and there is no ultimate point of separation (void) between them. The celebrated differential calculus informs us that *x* is a variable, *dx*, which although converging towards the 0 axis on the plane of an abscissa, never actually meets it. What is more, as far as language is concerned, the symbol or name, although 'ultimately' indifferent with respect to its referent, remains intrinsic to it. This is precisely Badiou's characterisation of constructivism. As we have seen already in the previous chapter, there is never a pure 'Two' in nature, i.e. a perfect coincidence of one and the other.[13] The idea of a complete language is therefore one which requires continuous construction (EE, 354).

In Leibniz's philosophy 'the continuous is closed on the one, and far from being errant and undetermined, its quantitative expansion assures the glory of well-made language according to which God constructs the maximal universe' (EE, 355). Moreover, although there is a *general* principle underlying this 'quantitative expansion', individuals are only at liberty to understand and apply it approximately. However, for Badiou there is still the lingering suspicion that this type of 'difference' is regressive, indifferent, and rests ultimately on an 'unfounded universe'. What is Leibniz's response to this not uncommon criticism? We find the answer in his theory of the monads.

In order to ward off absolute inconsistency or the void from his system, Leibniz constructs the monads – '"metaphysical points"' – which he regards as 'substantial unities absolutely undecomposable'. However, if we assume – as it appears we must – that these monads, in being 'absolutely undecomposable', are unaffected by one another, then it can also be assumed that they are 'quantitatively void' and distinguished only by their internal qualities (EE, 357). The monads are the nearest we have come yet to a theory of the subject, if we understand by 'subject' a being of 'pure interiority', essentially uncaused by events in the outside world. However, politically speaking, Leibniz's theory of the monads might well give us cause to be sceptical. For what real point is there – save a politically conservative one – to a subject who, for all its supposed independence, remains indifferent to anything outside it? And if the 'Law does not crack [the subject]' then what stakes could ever be involved in its deployment? For all the 'audacity and anticipation' of Leibniz's principle of indiscernibles – which Badiou will himself modify somewhat – in Leibniz's hands the principle cannot escape the 'moral and political conclusions' of a 'conciliator', for whom Leibniz the Philosopher-Statesman was himself so well renowned (EE, 357). Moreover, we might add, this monad-subject – 'required by the absence of the event, the impossibility of the intervention, and qualitative atomism' – would appear to obey the central tenets of post-modernism, for it is the latter which best exemplifies how difference is ruled, not by antagonism, but by the peaceful coexistence of different linguistic communities. The postmodern or neo-conservative age is one where, despite the attention to difference on the surface of things, hierarchically nothing really changes. It is difficult to see truth ever fulfilling a decisive political role in the Leibnizian universe, and in recognition of this apparent shortfall the question of truth is where Badiou sets his sights next.

It might appear to be an idealist philosophy which, in Badiou's case, attempts to return truth to its age-old pedestal of *alētheia* (revelation). After all, throughout the latter half of the twentieth century French philosophy experienced the earth-shattering archaeology of Michel Foucault,[14] whose work aimed to penetrate the institutional practices and power relations which go towards the production of regimes of truth. Badiou's decision to uphold truth as a positive philosophical category with its own set of scientific validity criteria would appear to be out of step by comparison. Take Badiou's critique of Leibniz for instance. Leibniz arguably does fail in his attempts to come up with a consistent existential foundation for the principle of indiscernibles. However, the concept of limit in Leibniz is arguably far less distinctive in its own right – and therefore more problematic as an object of criticism – than Badiou is prepared to accept,[15] not least because Leibniz had his own peculiar way of formulating the problem which failed to acknowledge the subtractive dimension of ontology, i.e. the idea that truth, in the classical sense, subtracts itself from language. Surely one of the supreme insights of Leibniz is the idea that truth is able to function in ways which tend to restrict any form of unanimity among its subjects. Reflecting on this fact might give us cause to view Badiou's critique of the limitations of Leibniz's philosophy in terms of the latter's moral and political conservatism as misguided. For given the widespread political degradation that Badiou quite evidently abhors, why aim truth any higher than the facile tautologies that comprise the politics of the present? What have the people done to deserve the intervention of any would-be philosopher king? We might further point out that Leibniz's philosophy is hardly an apology for conservatism. For instead of perpetuating a politics of slack conciliation to the detriment of a politics of truth the strength of Leibniz's enterprise surely lies elsewhere in *exposing* – inadvertently, although no less effectively

– politics as a baroque spectacle, a dazzling pageant in a hall of mirrors where the existing State constitution turns out to be nothing more than a simulacrum.[16] These are, I believe, strong criticisms which we will need to explore further in the following chapter. For the moment, however, let us move on to consider Badiou's concept of truth on its own terms.

Truth's History

Badiou's concept of truth is derived from Lacan. Truth is always post-eventmental and retroactive. It illuminates what was, or would have been, resulting from an intervention, so bearing witness to what happened. Badiou also acknowledges a further distinction, strongly Hegelian in principle, between truth and knowledge. For Badiou 'a truth is always that which makes a hole in a knowledge'. The task is therefore 'to think the relation – which is rather an un-relation – between, on the one hand a post-eventmental fidelity, and on the other hand a fixed state of knowledge ...' (EE, 361).

> The key to the problem is the mode by which a fidelity procedure *traverses* the existing knowledge, starting from this supernumerary point that is the name of the event. (EE, 361)

There is a complete end in itself to wisdom that Hegel named the 'End of History'. Man's assumption of knowledge marks the supreme dilemma for philosophy since, in *attaining* it, man, as historical individual, risks being annihilated (along with philosophy). Both Lacan and, following him, Badiou, recognise the dilemma. The fulfilment of knowledge is, in the words of Maurice Blanchot, a 'strange surplus'. For Lacan, the 'subject supposed to know' is not the end of history but the beginning – of *desire*.[17] There is, historically speaking, always a gap in knowledge which demands to be filled. This desire for what ultimately cannot be known is what Lacan calls truth, and is accomplished in the act of true or 'full' speech. The aim of true speech is to *expose* (the illusion of) the limits of language, to break through the 'language barrier'.[18] Completeness is always the illusion that truth stands for.

For Badiou the fidelity procedure is the means whereby truth is 'discerned' or, more precisely, its limitations are assessed. Following in the footsteps of Lacan, Badiou recognises that truth is founded on a constitution (a social contract) of terms, which it then becomes the task of knowledge to classify. He calls this classification an 'inquest'. 'An inquest,' Badiou declares, 'is therefore a "finite state" of the process of fidelity' or a set of 'minimal reports [*constats*]' on the name's (dis)connection to the event (EE, 364). Taken together as a result, what this finite set composes is an 'encyclopaedia' that permits us to decide whether the truth of the situation is 'true' or merely 'truthful'. This is a fine distinction, although crucially for Badiou it remains central – and internal – to the dialectic 'truth/knowledge':

> Let us insist therefore that the one-multiple of a truth – the result of true judgements – is indiscernible and unclassifiable for the encyclopaedia. This condition founds *in being* the difference of the true and of the truthful. We are beginning to see that a condition of this condition is that a truth is infinite. (EE, 367)

Knowledge has a shelf life. Truth, on the other hand, does not. However, the distinction must be qualified somewhat precisely because, for example, 'the set of whole numbers' comprises an infinite set which is intuitive and hence immediately knowable. Truth can always temporarily coincide with knowledge (although this is not its true aim). Indeed, it is part of the order of knowledge to derive its determinations from the fidelity procedure or what we might otherwise call the 'historical process'. 'Vulgar Marxism' provides Badiou with a good illustration. 'The workers' is an infinite 'class' – i.e. an epistemic category – and, historically speaking, 'was not the sum of empirical workers'. However, 'This did not prevent knowledge (and, paradoxically, Marxist or Marxian knowledge itself) still being able to consider that "the workers" fell under an encyclopaedic determinant (sociological, economic, etc.).' For Badiou this 'coincidence' of 'political truth' and the 'knowledge of History' that Marxism once stood for is proof of the distinction between truth and knowledge, and that the distinction can be formulated (EE, 368). Moreover, since each inquest is comprised from a set of either positive or negative judgements it is not difficult to work out that there will be opposed categories of truth. 'Truthfulness' is *negatively* determined and falls under the aegis of the encyclopaedia. Its declarations are somewhat pragmatic and, possessing 'sufficient reason', promote what Badiou refers to as the 'community of interests'. On the other hand, truth proper is *positively* determined, and therefore resists the encyclopaedia or language of the situation. Truth, whose multiples are connected to the name of the event, remains '*indiscernible and unclassifiable* for knowledge'.

Badiou formulates '*a truth*' as '*the total positive infinite – the recollection of* x (+)*'s – of a fidelity procedure which, for every determinant of the encyclopaedia, contains at least an inquest which avoids it*'. Furthermore, 'Such a procedure will be called *generic* (for the situation)' (EE, 372). There is a familiar ring to the fidelity procedure which recalls the Lacanian 'dialectic of desire', where truth and knowledge enter into terminal conflict – a 'fight to the death for pure prestige' – for '"something other"'.[19] Badiou's 'a-truth', which is an infinite part of the *inquest* – the latter being a *finite* state of the situation – reflects what Lacan in his later seminars referred to as the '*objet petit a*'. For Lacan human desire, being finite, was a part without a whole, or a 'part-object', whose lack persisted even in its own absence. The *a* (as in the French 'other', *autre*) always belies complete mastery and is therefore, without a hint of exaggeration, what forces human history to transcend any given set of (finite) circumstances.

With Badiou the Lacanian vocabulary is dispensed with, and we have already noted the reasons why in the opening chapter of this book. In the early 1970s 'desire' was being appropriated by Deleuze and Guattari in a way which deviated sharply from the standard interpretations of the French Hegelians. In the wake of the *Anti-Oedipus* desire became associated with a brand of philosophy which was to remain an object of political antagonism for Badiou. Despite this, conceptually there are founding similarities between Lacan's concept of desire and Badiou's little complex of terms which comprise what he calls, rather prosaically, the 'generic fidelity procedure'. Not wishing to confuse or imply any significant differences between their respective positions, however, we must make some important observations about the generic procedure.

The generic procedure is what facilitates the passage from the old to the new. It is a procedure which aims to assert change. But how is change possible? For as we have seen, Badiou admits that there is a real impossibility in declaring that any one situation succeeds, and is therefore different from, another. The generic procedure maintains that what cannot be discerned in a situation *is* the situation's 'general truth', or the 'truth of its own being, considered as foundation of all knowledge to come' (EE, 361). Given a situation where at least one part is finite we say that this part is indiscernible, or is a generic part of the situation, which produces the situation's a-truth.

By way of illustration let us consider the example of 'love', as Badiou does at various stages in *Being and the Event*. It is highly instructive that Badiou regards love – Hegel's 'non-antithetical relation to the other' – and not desire as the rational kernel of individual psychology, for in making this point Badiou is clearly borrowing from Hegel's *Phenomenology*. Love is an encounter between two people where despite the mutual separation of the lovers there exists at least one part of their being-together that is, for both, indispensable for each. (This is what Hegel calls 'being-for-another', or simply 'existence'.[20] For Badiou, it is the actual infinite finally revealed in the operation of counting.) This being is not a question of knowledge since the lovers are invariably blind to what they have in common. All that matters *'for them'* is that this unknown and indiscernible element *is* what keeps them together (EE, 374). Of course, in the event of their separation this unspoken bond would no doubt prove to have been misplaced, although, crucially, any supplementary revelations about their love are only deemed truthful from the point of view of a 'new' situation. Truth is infinite and immune to exhortations voiced in the language of common sense ('she's no good for him', 'they make a lovely couple', etc.). We might say that truth is decidedly unpronounceable or *unnameable* (for the situation). Only after the event does any presumed insight put on the mantle of truth (which it ultimately *cannot be*). Wisdom is the casualty of experience. As Hegel says, the Owl of Minerva takes flight at dusk. However, without being wholly seduced by these Lacan-inspired, Hegelian platitudes we must also accept the subject's immanent capacity to be a part of truth, and indeed to *realise* what is truthful, during the course of a generic procedure. Although the subject cannot attain the whole truth it does not automatically follow that the subject will be negated or 'want-to-be' (*manque à être*) by virtue of what it does not presently have or cannot hope to achieve. Truth always suspends the normal expectations of a situation, sometimes forcing open a gap in knowledge which enables the subject to emerge in the fullness of time.[21]

To recap, there are two categories of truth. Firstly, there are those encyclopaedic truths which are subtracted from knowledge during the course of a generic procedure, and which involve questions of 'fact'. Badiou excludes 'all sorts of other practices' from truth, notably 'commerce and all forms of "good works"'. Secondly, there is the question of 'principle' (*droit*) which it falls to science alone to investigate – in this case whether there really is 'sense to talk of an indiscernible part of any multiple' (EE, 376). Strictly speaking, however, Badiou regards science not as a question of truth – which it is the task of philosophy alone to think – but as one of its four conditions. With this distinction in mind let us now turn our attention towards one of them. For although science has undoubtedly shared, in the course of its history, something of the vision of politics to change the world, it is politics as a decidedly subjective discipline which manages to invest, for better or worse, the highest degree of faith in humanity.

Rousseau: 'At the Edge of the Abyss'[22]

Politically speaking, Badiou is no Hegelian. There is no 'right' which confers the rational juridical foundation of the State. For Badiou truth, not right, is the highest aim of political philosophy.[23] Politics, in this Platonist realm, is henceforth the means of *conditioning*, and thereby restoring, the autonomous reign of the thinking subject. But there are some important qualifications here, since real politics is not a matter of governmental decrees or round table summits. Politics is a singularly inventive act, and one which relies upon the most faithful militant practice on the subject's part. In Badiou's estimation there is one philosopher whose life and work serves as an adequate model for a politics of truth, and that philosopher is Rousseau.

Unlike Hegel, Rousseau was an inhabitant of a society whose Spirit had *not* already arrived, and whose future was still being conditioned by the shock upheavals of eighteenth-century Europe's revolutionary coming of age. More than any other philosopher in history Rousseau provides, in the detail of his combined life and work, the impression of a society *animated* in change (*'le tourbillon social'* which Saint-Preux encounters in *The New Eloise*) yet wholly realisable only in the imagination. *The Social Contract* is the most complete expression of the philosophy of Rousseau, whose goal 'is to examine the conceptual functions [*réquisits*] of politics, to think *the being of politics*. The truth of this being rests in "the act by which a people is a people"' (EE, 379). Rousseau was not concerned with the politics of transition as advocated by the supporters of constitutional government, nor would he have been in favour of the respective philosophies of right and of revolution which came to dominate the political landscape of the nineteenth century. Instead, Rousseau's social contract theory is the *strong* version of contractualism which seeks immanent expression in the people itself, a people whose only form of 'legitimacy' is to *exist* as a body politic. The enterprise of Rousseau, unlike that of most contemporary scholars of political philosophy, retains for us politics as 'a *creation*, local and fragile, of collective humanity' which is 'never the treatment of a vital necessity'. For Badiou we must reject the idea of man as an instinctively political animal (one who seeks out the company of other human beings), and concentrate instead on the social pact among free agents that comes about rationally, although somewhat paradoxically at the same time, completely by chance (EE, 380).

The defining term of *The Social Contract* is the 'general will' which Badiou identifies with the ontological formula of the event. The standard criticism of Rousseau revolves around how the particular will becomes transformed into the general will on the basis of a presumed agreement between persons who, precisely because they express particular wills, would only appear to be capable of making a social pact by force. This is in fact the position of Hobbes, for whom the people alienates its sovereignty in the form of a ruler (monarch or government), who then exerts power over them as a means of avoiding further conflict. But this will not do at all, since the event (of the general will) is a 'hazardous supplement' of the situation rather than a product of force. Indeed, 'general will' is only the generic part of what happened, which must be qualified retroactively by the fidelity procedure, i.e. in the form of a calculation or inquest into truth. Otherwise put, 'the general will is the operator of fidelity that commands a generic procedure' (EE, 381).

The advantage of the concept of the general will over alternative brands of social contract theory (notably Hobbes's) lies in its avoidance of so-called 'statism', where the sovereign power *enforces* individual rights – usually by employing whatever means it deems necessary in the circumstances – thereby committing a breach of the contract. For Rousseau no such situation need arise in theory since, under the auspices of the general will, whenever an individual right is threatened this merely proves that said individual was acting in his own particular interests rather than in consort with the general will. But isn't there a rather sophistic explanation masquerading as a principle here – and, indeed, one that obtains in Badiou's idea that the general will is essentially indiscernible, i.e. (part of a) generic (procedure)? For if the general will is indiscernible, then how do we know for sure that it is ever actually being expressed? We might recall that the problem strikes Rousseau himself in Book IV of the *Contract*, where in the chapter on 'Voting' he makes the following point:

Each man, in giving his vote, states his opinion on that point; and the general will is found by counting votes. When therefore the opinion that is contrary to my own prevails, this proves neither more nor less than that I was mistaken, and that what I thought to be the general will was not so.[24]

In a situation such as this why should we be convinced that anything other than the rule of the majority is operating – a majority which, although legally right, is simply voicing its own particular will? Badiou acknowledges the problem explicitly, recalling that Rousseau's way round it lay 'in posing that the will is split by the event-contract'. Thus:

The *citizen* designates in everyone their participation in the sovereignty of the general will, the *subject* designates the submission to the laws of the State. The term [*durée*] of politics has for measure the insistence of this Two. There is politics when an internalised collective operator splits particular wills. (EE, 381)

In other words, politics is the qualitative *act* of the decision, which remains divided in each individual, rather than the decision's final, quantitative result (which inevitably is expressed in terms of the rule of the majority). Here we can gauge the literal sense in which 'The general will is a relation of co-belonging of the people to itself.' For if the general will essentially expresses a relation to self then it must follow that *each* individual, as one part of this collective will, must also express, in theory at least, the same relation. Moreover (and this is a virtually decisive point), this would appear to exclude any rule of the majority from legitimately holding power, since if every 'majority' is in principle divided within itself then it cannot effectively represent the general will of the people – or at least it would only appear to do so by default. This is the nature of Rousseau's distinction between 'decrees' and 'laws'. Laws are the foundation of any social order and, since they *enable* governments to enact decrees, governments (which are only majority assemblies) cannot pass them. In order to be legitimate, laws require the assent of the whole people. This is not to say that laws must enter into every aspect of the people's lives, or that they are oppressive of individual freedoms. On the contrary, they are the basic axioms which enable individual freedoms to exist in the first place.

What most often pass for laws in society are in actual fact only decrees according to Rousseau. A government passes decrees simply in order to satisfy the particular interests of various competing groups in society. The government's role is that of an executive, balancing interest group against interest group, delegating power to its deputies, and therefore *discriminating* on the grounds of race, class and party. Although such partiality – in its good form promoted as the 'culture of difference' – is often viewed as one of the exemplars of Western liberal democracy, this is not the true aim of a politics founded on equality – or indeed on truth. However, the fact that Rousseau famously – and in many latter-day minds notoriously – regarded equality as being indivisible among the people – i.e. realisable in each only on condition of being realisable in all – has resulted in him being regarded as the architect of totalitarianism. How well does Rousseau's theory hold up on such a charge?

'Totalitarianism' is a name which results from the collapsing together of some very diverse and dubious *non*-political 'expressions', notably Stalinism and Nazism. Therefore, to respond simply, the so-called totalitarian State would appear to be completely removed from any concrete historical reality. It is an all-too-convenient symbolic fiction. Although unquestionably an emotive expression, 'totalitarianism' is a linguistic operator which ultimately communicates nothing about 'totalitarianism' as lived experience, or what this term might actually mean for societies presently labelled 'totalitarian'. Moreover, any valid expression of the general will is not a question of power. For Rousseau power is 'transmissible' while the general will is 'unrepresentable' (EE, 383). Therefore we can assume that the mere 'empirical reality' of States in no way confirms that they possess one ounce of legitimacy between them. This illegitimacy has been the historical legacy of the revolutionary militant and the paradox of the stateless citizen, e.g. Rousseau, Marx, Trotsky.

How does this help us in understanding politics as a militant process of truth? In light of the above it seems fair to say that the State operates (illegitimately) where there are 'factions'. 'As Rousseau notes,' Badiou remarks, 'the original pact is the result of a "unanimous behaviour [*comportement*]". If there are opponents, they are purely and simply exterior to the body politic, they are "strangers among citizens"' (EE, 383–4). Every 'really political decision' is one that conforms to the 'ultra-one' of the people; it is one that actively and systemically subtracts subsets (of particular interests) from the set (of the whole people) of which they are a part.

Politics is not a question of 'right' or 'left', good or bad, or needless to say of voicing opinions in the language of the situation ('parliamentarism' for Rousseau). Such is nowadays more than ever the vocation of the career politicians and their army of public relations experts. Instead, politics as a militant activity is a hazardous and unpredictable exercise largely because, unlike the career politicians' preoccupation with consensus, the political militant's sole aim is truth. Objectively speaking, truth is a dangerous supplement for politics, and one which is just as likely to end up confounding the subject with heavy doses of scientism as in spreading enlightenment (e.g. the dogmatic exaltation of socialist planning during China's Great Leap Forward in May 1958). Truth has no particular interests. It reveals itself while remaining indifferent to any consequences. Its only condition is that the whole people faithfully and logically devote themselves to its cause, believing that there is truth, even and especially at times where truth is wholly absent – indiscernible – in the situation in which they find themselves.

Badiou identifies two related difficulties in the *Contract* which demand attention here. Firstly, the question of the intervention which in Rousseau is that of the 'legislator', and secondly the question of politics' 'survival' as a generic procedure (EE, 385). The legislator does not hold any legislative power. Laws are founded according to the will of the people. The legislator's task is merely to submit laws for public approval. The problem arises, however, that if the legislator remains indifferent to the act of popular sovereignty then his role would appear to be elevated to the level of a divine authority: one who drafts laws while remaining completely immune to them. For Badiou this does not present a logical hurdle since, as was remarked at the end of the previous chapter, the intervention (here the 'intervening legislator') always directs a 'new' set of circumstances whose connection to the original event, not being obvious, *must be made*.

A decisive example is the Russian Revolution of 1917 where, in a country generally regarded as being among the least ripe for revolutionary change, a set of circumstances arose – the 'Imperialist' 1914–18 War, the strong organisation of the Bolsheviks, the association of the peasants and the workers, the collapse of social democracy, etc. – which became united in a single slogan: 'All power to the Soviets'. The legislator, in naming a situation, is that rare being who manages to subtract an element from each part of the situation, thereby militating a political expression in the form of the general will. '[The legislator] is the one who changes the collective occurrence into a political term. He is the intervener in the vicinity of popular rallies' (EE, 386).

Of course, the lot of the legislator is also a double-edged sword, and one that today tends to tip the balance at every opportunity, although not towards politics as a generic procedure, but towards the selfish and reactionary populist agendas of the majority (cf. Gramsci's 'science of numbers'). How is politics able to survive, its true aims intact, alongside the bogus rhetoric of this majority, where 'equality' simply equates with whatever happens to be in any given phase of society? How can politics exist as *a* – i.e. one – *consistent set* of popular aims from one situation to the next (especially, we might add, since the one 'is not')? For Badiou the question presents itself as Rousseau's 'impasse'. Thus:

> Rousseau's predicament when it's a matter of passing from the principle (politics finds its truth only in a generic part of the people, every discernible part expresses a particular interest) to its execution (the absolute majority is supposed to be an adequate sign of the generic) leads him to distinguish *important* decisions and *urgent* decisions … (EE, 387)

Clearly the politics of the militant (indiscernible), having suddenly become majoritarian (discernible), risks having its original set of aims outweighed and overturned, since it is now ruled by the majority. Rousseau's answer to the dilemma is the creation of 'two tiers for certain decisions, as in the case of constitutional revisions' (the system of 'qualified majority' voting which exists today). However, the problem still remains as to who exactly decides whether a 'political' situation should be classified as either important or urgent. Isn't there a danger here of politics being relegated from concrete practice to a remote system of evaluating particular situations in advance (an 'encyclopaedic classification of political circumstances'), thereby draining them of their singularity (EE, 387)?

What this question ultimately boils down to is the universal dilemma facing legislators. Given that law is a sovereign act, one which concerns all the people (not just the majority), not only can no law ever be legitimately passed by government, but the implementation of each new law suspends the contract and, *ipso facto*, the general rule of law. The law is not democratic, and the majoritarian manner whereby laws are passed and come into effect convinces us that there is a significant – if not somewhat untimely – gap between the act of popular *sovereignty* and the onset of *democracy*. Democracy is a 'form of the executive'; it involves a 'democratic governmental decree'. But crucially it touches on no aspect of either politics or law (EE, 388).

In times where the received wisdom (the encyclopaedia) casts doubt on the survival of any generic brand of militancy we can rest assured that politics *is* at work each and every time the agenda of a 'democratic' party is seen to deviate from the constitutional rights of citizens. This acute brand of perception which operates 'at the edge of the abyss', on the brink of the void as it were, occupying the margins of action, is for Badiou the measure of Rousseau's original contribution to politics. Only by submitting our revolutionary ambitions to the most thoroughgoing form of civic duty can a just constitution of the people emerge. Thus the survival of the professional revolutionary is guaranteed, if only at the expense of a kind of transfixion of the political landscape. It is during these phases of relative calm before the storm that the need for a hardened form of political practice is ever more keenly felt. Quoting Marshall Berman – quoting Marx – confirms for us that for all the tried and tested failures of the '"so-called revolutions of 1848"' they at least '"denounced the abyss"'. For Marx the abyss would have been the abstract humanity represented by the bourgeois class. Speaking in 1850, when revolutionary optimism had once more given way to bitter disappointment, the spectre of communism continued regardless to '"[weigh] upon everyone with a 20,000-pound force"'.[25] Like his inheritor Marx, Rousseau is the harbinger of this void – the first in modern history – the one who forces us to *feel* the nagging pressure of circumstance, even when faith has vanished from the situation, but where our political conscience still compels us to be on the lookout for truth.

For Rousseau the question of how politics is able to guarantee its own consistency in spite of the impact of historical events was ultimately one for 'the dictatorship'. The latter was not to be confused with a permanent form of power, but only to be invoked in times where 'generic truth' is 'suspended by an event' (EE, 389). '[I]t is important,' in Rousseau's own words, 'that [the dictatorship's] duration should be fixed at a very brief period.'[26] However, where laws prove to be less flexible than circumstances demand – and while 'everything cannot be foreseen' – the need for a dictator then arises, not to suppress the general will, but in order to lead it decisively towards its truth. On such occasions we might therefore say that the dictator *is* the general will, since 'That which upholds the procedure is uniquely the zeal of the militant-citizens, whose fidelity engenders an infinite truth that no form, constitutional or organisational, adequately expresses' (EE, 389). For Badiou, this obstinate form of (non-)expression is what passes for the very essence of politics.

As Rousseau declares towards the beginning of Book II, 'truth is no road to fortune, and the people dispenses neither ambassadorships, nor professorships, nor pensions'. There is no appeal to a higher power where truth is concerned, no alienation in a leader, whether a dictator or some other charismatic man of destiny. Truth must ultimately be for the people, undivided by factions or parties, to appropriate for itself. Finally, in historic situations such as these, we find ourselves in a situation where *everyone* belongs.

Philosophy and the 'Finally Objectless Subject'[27]

Allow me to summarise the exposition so far of the passage from the event to truth. There are four nodal points. First of all, and as was noted in the previous chapter, the event is always undecidable. Owing to its extreme singularity we are unable to tell whether 'what appears to be happening' actually is or not. Secondly, what ensues in the time or interval which follows is the post-eventmental fidelity procedure. Following on from a militant intervention, the event is named ('Russian Revolution', 'ready-made', 'multiple'). Here the task is one of adequate connection of the fidelity operator (a noun or proper name) to the supernumerary name of the event. Can Lenin for the Bolsheviks, Marcel Duchamp for Dadaism, or Albert Lautman for mathematics, truly be tied to the event or not? (Note that the fidelity operator involves not one, but *two* terms.) This is not an objective question, but instead it relies on a subjective fidelity procedure. The question, in other words, is conditioned by the task of the day, the situation at hand. Less a question of whether Lenin 'really took part' in the Russian Revolution (we know he did), and more one of whether his reputation emerges from an inquest into its truth intact. Furthermore, the question is retroactive, since the truth about what happened becomes, for us, a matter of deciding what would have been, there and then, in the future anterior of a situation we reconstruct after the event. A problem therefore arises. Thirdly, language tends to equivocate on the truth of what actually occurred. Truth is always indiscernible in the language or encyclopaedia of the situation, since our available knowledge only ever leads us to *assume* that an event could have occurred in a given way, with a certain set of consequences, etc. Furthermore, assuming that 'Marcel Duchamp' is itself only an approximation (a (re)construction) of a hypothetical singularity ('creative genius') which informs debate ('is it art?', 'is this particular work of art an "original"?', etc.), it is quite conceivable that either now or at some stage in the future Duchamp will turn out to have never had anything to do with Dadaism. We tend to experience art (or politics, or science, or love) only in terms of an account, built up from opinion, although paradoxically something of its originality remains open to knowledge. Finally, this openness is what Badiou names generic. Each and every truth has a finite generic part which can be subtracted from knowledge. For Badiou, this subtraction is the 'subject' of philosophy. In spite of equivocations the subject rallies selflessly to the support of truth and emerges from within the situation where truth is dismissed as being impossible. Or rather truths plural, since the subject of philosophy always occupies a *'conjuncture'* – a 'thinkable conjunction' – where truths coexist (MP, 19). Badiou names this conjuncture the 'compossibility of truths'. Meaning is now suspended by the power of an abstract impression, a conceptual apparatus, a revolutionary slogan, an amorous glance. The subject accedes to the infinite horizon of multiplicity under the conditions of art, science, politics and love.

The fact that truth is suspended in the future anterior of a situation is the proof of truth's eternity. The subject subsists momentarily in the vicinity of truth, although the moment in question is infinitely variable (roughly five years for the French Revolution; a lifetime for a couple in love; 10^{66} years for the evaporation of solar mass black holes[28]). Clearly the subject *makes history* in this sense, carving out a phase or timescale in the void monotony of the universe. At this heightened stage of humanity, death is irrelevant. But what of the actual passage *into* the future? The suspicion may remain – a metaphysical suspicion which occasionally shatters our faith in science – that the subject of history is tragic and therefore carries with it certain potentially disastrous implications. The subject who supports the future anterior of a situation is one who acts in the confidence that what it is doing is right, a subjective confidence which truth invariably shatters after the event. Acting with the benefit of hindsight can we not say that the subject is a *casualty* of truth?

There is perhaps no better symptom of tragedy than in the strains of Rousseau's text on freedom. We need to return to the impasse of the dictatorship mentioned at the end of the previous section. There it was noted that the power and authority of the dictator are set aside for those rare instances where the rule of law is suspended. Even in accepting that such key historical moments create a space or time for the subject to seize, informed reflection alerts us to the dangers of freedom which is without grounds. A particularly pertinent example is surely the Chinese Communist Party's Hundred Flowers Campaign, officially inaugurated by Mao in February 1957 under the pretence of generating intellectual debate, but which gained notoriety as a false ploy for weeding out counter-revolutionaries. In a situation where it is possible for a dictator to decide that the general will is frustrated, the people, in Rousseau's infamous words, 'will be forced to be free'.[29]

The suspicion that the subject bears the hidden consequences of impending disaster is an ethical question to which we shall return in the final chapter. Suffice to say in the meantime that such questions are not deemed axiomatic in *Being and the Event*. For Badiou, force – or what he calls 'forcing' – is 'the relation implied in the fundamental law of the subject' (EE, 441). It must not be mistaken for an exterior constraint. Instead, forcing is what guarantees the subject's otherwise random trajectory. Furthermore, force is the historical power of *producing* something new, or of forcing truth to *be* true (truthful), in a new situation. Of course, this degree of consistency comes at a price and invariably at the expense of transforming – or, better still, *deforming* – the elements of the original situation in the process.

Forcing is the mathematical theorem which Badiou borrows from the set theorist Paul J. Cohen. Needless to say it involves a rather complex set of mathematical proofs, although Badiou summarises the concept neatly as follows: 'veridicality in a generic extension is controllable *in the situation* by the relation of forcing' (EE, 468). More precisely:

A term forces a statement [*énoncé*] if its positive connection to the event forces the statement to be truthful in the new situation (the situation supplemented by an indiscernible truth). Forcing is a relation *verifiable by knowledge*, since it brings about a term of the situation (which is therefore presented, and named in the language of the situation) and a statement of the subject-language (whose names are 'makeshift' with the multiples of the situation). (EE, 441)

As an example, the statement 'Let a hundred flowers bloom, let a hundred schools of thought contend' is forced to be truthful on condition that the petty bourgeois intelligentsia adopts the correct line in its criticism of Chinese cultural austerity which avoids straying into counter-revolutionary propaganda. Truth is said to be controllable under such conditions. Here a revolutionary subject will retain *a priori* knowledge that what it is doing is consistent with the language of the situation. However, the strength of such a conviction carries forward risks, and indeed can only be upheld at the expense of subtracting truth from the language of the situation to come. In such circumstances the language of opinion gradually gives way to the universal subject-language, which at first appears to fly in the face of all common sense. Gradually the risks multiply, since a language which strictly corresponds to the life of the subject rather than the community of interests tends to bring with it a total reordering of the cultural landscape. For example, Mao's subsequent 'exploitation' of the Hundred Flowers Campaign as a means of weeding out undesirable elements may appear (for us) to rely on wholly unfounded suspicions about the true extent of counter-revolutionary activity in Chinese society. Such an observation (on the part of outsiders) is perfectly – and perhaps even 'objectively' – justified. For a generic truth is, after all, one which is wholly lacking in definable qualities, and therefore must be generated from the void (of sense). However, in terms of the subject's actual experience of the singularity of a truth the apparent randomness of Mao's intervention *makes* sense, i.e. it structures the very conditions under which terms like 'cultural austerity', 'counter-revolutionary', and 'blooming and contending' (a key phrase during the Hundred Flowers Campaign) acquire their meaning. In the wake of the actual event the Chinese intelligentsia succeeds in adopting the correct line in the Hundred Flowers Campaign on condition that it manages to resist the consequences of its own counter-revolutionary impulse. With forcing, then, the truth of such an event would have been universally realised, albeit in a new subject-language which retroactively transforms the terms of reference of the original situation.

The concept of forcing marks the culmination of *Being and the Event* in advancing an ontological theory of the subject. In conclusion, let us draw some general lessons regarding this subject.

1. The subject serves no particular interests, and so must be distinguished from all objective criteria. In the global sense, 'things

change': capitalism becomes other, annihilating the vested interests of the dominant class; while for Mao, the universal law of
contradiction holds that things turn into their opposites.
Globally, everything is foreseeable. The difference lies in the
locally indiscernible trajectory which the subject carves out in
reaching truth. The subject serves truth regardless of how discon-
certing the latter might turn out to be for the community of
interests. The subject has a finite status to this end: a wholly
exhaustible capacity to reach the very end of what it can do, and
to make the situation where it is endure for all time.

2. The subject's 'point of application is precisely the errancy of the
   statist excess' (EE, 468). The subject is not the one counted for by
   the state; it is not re-presented. Instead, the subject is that singular
   multiple which escapes counting, and whose local trajectory is
   therefore 'strictly unassignable'. The fact that the state always
   counts at least one multiple which doesn't belong to the situation
   means that the state is quantitatively larger, and hence different
   from, the situation which it counts. However, we must avoid the
   common misconception that the subject is simply dominated by
   the State as the totalitarian fiction suggests. Adopting Althusser's
   terminology, the subject is what induces the State to *guarantee* the
   power of its own ideological apparatus (ordinarily indifferent to
   individuals), and to hold inquests into truth whenever 'misrecognition' occurs; whenever subjects threaten to escape the system.

3. Leading on directly from this, an impasse or formal limit emerges
   at a certain axiomatic point, where the state's integrity is subjec-
   tively called into question: is the state different from the situation
   which it ordinarily represents? Is the state 'more than' the individuals which comprise it? The answer is something of a wager,
   since an intervention is the condition of finding out, by which
   stage the question will have already been transformed. We therefore say that this impasse is undecidable.[30] The undecidability of
   state control *is* the subject itself in the making.

4. Finally, the subject, as undecidable, supports truth in the future
   anterior of a situation, not in terms of what is true, but of what
   would have been true under a hypothetical set of conditions.
   However, this 'would have been', although a retroactive judgement, is also indiscernible (generic) in the new situation which
   the subject now stands on the brink of entering into. In this sense
   a truth, while not yet true, can always be *forced* to be truthful
   under certain *a priori* conditions. Assuming that the petty bour-

geois intelligentsia follows the correct line there is nothing preventing the successful implementation of a slogan which alters, perhaps irrevocably, the very fabric of common sense. Providing Marcel Duchamp enters fully into the spirit of art as ready-made his work will lose nothing of its power to affect us 'by chance'. And as long as Albert Lautman adheres to the principle of dissymmetry concerning mathematical structures our attention is drawn to a universe composed, not of atoms and molecules, but of 'a multiplicity of bodies and their alteration in a single place in the world of sensation'.[31]

But isn't this all in the end a bit too *dogmatic?* Doesn't it rely on the prior negation of scientific fact – or simple common sense – for the sake of reasoning by the absurd? The political militant, artist, scientist or lover is not in a position to reflect on the conditions of his or her own discipline. Moreover, ethical considerations apart, we are strongly inclined to admit the paradoxical sense of Badiou's argument that the subject, in being 'in the capacity of indiscernment', must be forced to take a decision in relation to truth (EE, 469). Historically there was, is, and will be no path to progress other than by thinking and acting in the spirit of this 'dogmatism'.

5
The Cult of Deleuze

With *Deleuze: The Clamour of Being* (1997), published nearly ten years after *Being and the Event*, Badiou enters into a long overdue encounter with the one philosopher whose work most resembles his own. Despite his association with the postmodern turn, Deleuze is arguably the most 'consistent' philosopher of modern times, the one whose thought displays the most irrepressible singularity, and who therefore, as Badiou says, 'constitutes a polarity *to himself alone'*. Clearly Deleuze has exerted more than a formative influence on Badiou despite the fact that throughout the 550 or so pages of *Being and the Event* Deleuze's name appears only in a minor footnote. Their respective works – which mark a relationship, Badiou notes, which despite spanning some 30 years ended without a single meeting (D, 10; *3*) – exhibit an unmistakable overlap of shared scholarly concerns, and it is clearly the nature of this non-relationship which accounts for the uneasy proximity which exists between the two thinkers.

In the book's preface Badiou briefly recalls the correspondence between Deleuze and himself which took place towards the end of Deleuze's life, a correspondence which would have formed the groundwork, under less tragic circumstances, for a collaboration. As it turned out such an enterprise was ruled out, and what Badiou presents us with instead is, in style and method, not a work of theoretical discussion at all, but an attempted philosophical *intervention*. Politically, as Badiou admits, there was a world of difference between Deleuze and the events that shaped Badiou's own militant history. Then, in 1982, during what was to become a phase of theoretical transition for Badiou – one which, with the publication of *Theory of the Subject*, he sutured to 'the political givens of the time' – a 'new period' brought about the right conditions for a proper philosophical engagement with Deleuze (D, 9–13; *3–5*). According to Badiou, henceforth the political antagonisms which had previously driven a wedge between Deleuze and himself were – in theory at least – now dissolved. The fact that the 1980s were to mark Badiou's new period

– politics having given way to ontology – dictates the entire nature of this encounter, its terms of reference and choice of texts. In what follows, then, as well as examining Badiou's reading of Deleuze, we will need to consider the extent to which this reading is indeed one based on valid philosophical considerations.

(Non-)relations

Badiou's first task is to rule out completely the popular impression of Deleuze as the prophet of 'anarcho-desire'. As far as Badiou is concerned Deleuze and Guattari's most famous work, the *Anti-Oedipus*, belongs to a superseded political conjuncture. Furthermore, he argues, in stripping away the layers of Deleuze's diverse philosophical creations in fields ranging from modern literature to cinema, painting, mathematics and natural science one discovers the same ontological proposition, which Badiou retrieves from the pages of Deleuze's *Difference and Repetition*:

> There has only ever been one ontological proposition: being is univocal. There has only ever been one ontology, that of Duns Scotus, which gave being a single voice. (D, 153; *105*, citing *Difference and Repetition*, 35)

It would be an error, Badiou says, to regard the 'common image' of Deleuze as 'liberation of the anarchic multiple of desires and errant flows' as the real one. Indeed, the assemblage of 'multiple/multiplicities' which operates at the heart of Deleuze's work only serves to mask a 'renewed concept of the One' which Deleuze himself names the 'One-all'. 'The fundamental problem for Deleuze,' Badiou insists, 'is certainly not to liberate the multiple, but to fold thought to a renewed concept of the One' (D, 19–20; *10–11*).

Clearly this is an audacious move on Badiou's part. To claim that Deleuze's thought not only has a 'destination', but that this destination is 'the One', seems to contradict flatly the anarchic spirit of his work and its attachment to the vitalist generation of Spinoza, Nietzsche and Bergson. Initial reservations aside, however, how amenable is Deleuze to such a re-reading?

First of all, Deleuze must be read as a philosopher of *pre-individual* modes of existence, and Badiou's initial task is to rid Deleuze of the subjectivist misinterpretations that have plagued his work ever since Deleuze and Guattari's invention of the 'desiring machines'. If a metaphor will do then it is the 'purified automaton' rather than the 'bearded sixty-eighters' that best sums up the Deleuzian image of thought. However, Badiou refuses to let things rest there. Not content to affirm the 'purification' and 'sobriety' of Deleuze, he then goes on to propose somewhat controversially that his thought is 'profoundly aristocratic' (D, 22; *12*). 'The use of the word "anarchy",' Badiou explains, 'in order to designate the nomadism of singularities, must not delude us. For Deleuze specifies: "crowned anarchy", and it is crucial to think as well, to think above all, the crown' (D, 23; *13*). Although Deleuze is unquestionably the thinker of heterogeneity and difference, he is also the thinker of hierarchy and power, and the key to understanding and appropriating his thought lies in the way in which heterogeneity and difference manage to transcend and temporally supplant this hierarchy. 'Thought only exists in a hierarchical space', Badiou writes. Moreover:

> [I]n order that an individual comes to the point where he is transfixed by his pre-individual determination, and therefore by the power [*puissance*] of the One-all – of which he is at the outset only a poor local configuration – it is necessary that he surpasses his limit, that he endures as his actuality is paralysed and defeated by the infinite virtuality which is true being [*l'être véritable*] of actuality. (D, 22–23; *12–13*)

Here Badiou recognises, in his own way, the Deleuzian concept of becoming. Univocal being *becomes* identical, different, other, woman. With Deleuze the categories of existence are not given, they must be made. Moreover, the power, as '*puissance*', that the individual summons in making itself (identical, different, other, woman) is immanent, i.e. it rests within the individual's own degree of power to make it. One is not born a king, a subject, a citizen, but in a key sense one becomes one. Of course, needless to say it is crucial not to confuse the act of becoming with any degree of rational 'choice'. A pauper does not choose to be a king any more than a king chooses to be a pauper. Instead, what makes the individual what he is is the '*hubris*' that compels him to face his own destiny, which is nothing less than the limit (as '*peras*') of his own desire. In this case being is no longer the illusion of choice, it is the reality of being chosen on the basis of what he or she, the individual, existing at the extreme limit of his or her powers, actually is. Ultimately the acquisition of thought is dependent upon the individual's most intimate relation to self or, what will amount to the same thing, a direct confrontation with the outside, 'since to think is to come ascetically to the point where the individual is paralysed by impersonal exteriority, which is also equally his or her authentic being' (D, 24; *13*).

Far from ruining the 'democratic' tendencies in Deleuze's work, then, the aristocratic realm or hierarchy is in reality the very assurance of its arrival. The established order of things – e.g. the existing class structure in a given society – is always the constraint *against which* individuals have to think, the 'force' (another key concept in Deleuze's work) which levers thought *into* the system, thereby resulting in a real shift in power, e.g. the toppling of a monarchy or State. It is furthermore important to note that thought for Deleuze is always 'impersonal', it sets out from a 'case' and not a principle, and, crucially, is '"no more abstract than its object"' (D, 28; *16*). The initial case or circumstance, whether a 'concrete' historical conjuncture or else an 'abstract' theory (cf. Deleuze's work on the cinema), is only a kind of initial springboard for thought, which relates itself to other concepts rather than to concrete things. 'Concepts,' Badiou writes, '... never being concepts-of, connect themselves to the initial concrete case *only in their movement*, and not in what they give to thought' (D, 29; *16*). Thought, both despite, and indeed because of, the multiplicity of the concrete (cases), *thinks itself*. Multiplicity therefore exists as an indivisible mode of thought, which is ultimately guaranteed by the sovereign power of the One.

The power of the One must not be mistaken for that of a single and same Being which distributes beings to specific locations (a time or a place). This is the ancient view of philosophy from Plato to Hegel where the One falls under the reign of the absolute Idea (D, 49; *31*). Here, Being is analogous to a genus, and beings to individual species where each one is classified under a unitary category. The One does not express itself, as Aristotle would have said, in 'several senses'. Instead, the One, which for Deleuze is the One-all, or singularity, expresses itself in one sense for all its forms. 'Or again: the immanent attributes of Being,' Badiou says, 'which express its infinite power of One, "are *formally* distinct, but all equal and *ontologically* one"' (D, 40; *25*, citing *Difference and Repetition*, 303).

In *Difference and Repetition* Deleuze embarks on his project of 'overturning Platonism' which involves 'denying the primacy of original over copy, of model over image' and instead 'glorifying the reign of simulacra and reflections'.[1] In Deleuze's view it is clearly misguided to make believe, as is the penchant of the avant-garde, that the simulacrum is a superficial variety or mere copy of an original. However, as Badiou points out, to claim, as Deleuze does, that there is no hierarchy in Being hardly establishes an 'overturning' in the order of priority between original and copy. Instead, Badiou notes that such a move may even be regarded as decidedly Platonist in 'affirming the right of simulacra which joyously attest to the univocal power of Being' (D, 42; *26*). 'I am not so certain,' Badiou remarks, 'that Plato is so remote from [Deleuze's] recognition of beings, even sensible beings, as immanent differentiations of the intelligible, and positivities of the simulacrum' (D, 43; *27*). In Badiou's estimation, then, rather than overturning Plato, Deleuze has in fact returned to the ancient problem, handed down throughout the history of philosophy, of identity and difference.

What are we to make of Badiou's interpretation of Deleuze's work so far? Clearly by choosing to situate Deleuze in relation to the classical tradition of philosophy from Plato to Hegel, Badiou's reading denies Deleuze's work its usual ambivalence, nay hostility, in respect of this tradition. We might say that Badiou is aiming to rescue Deleuze from the cult of postmodernism which has built up around his work, and which so often afforded Deleuze, in life, the strategic advantage of not adopting any one philosophical position. There is, however, I believe, something else going on here in Badiou's interpretation, and before we can properly make it out we will need to venture a bit further along the path of his exposition.

The main potential area of dispute between Deleuze and Badiou is summarised by the term 'dialectic', which Deleuze reads as a pure (anti-Hegelian) philosophy of difference. Deleuze never relented on his outright rejection of mediation. As Badiou puts it:

It is why [his method] is essentially anti-dialectical. Mediation is exemplarily a category. It pretends to pass from one being to another 'under' a relation which is internal to at least one of them. For Hegel, for example, this internalised relation is the negative. But it will not be possible to have the negative, for univocal being is affirmation through and through. (D, 51; *32*)

At first sight many Deleuzian concepts would appear to be divided along dialectical lines, apparently shoring up Hegelian logic ('deterritorialization/reterritotialization', 'sense/nonsense', etc.). But such an impression would be misguided. The first thing to recognise is that, with Deleuze, the terms of any pair are nominal, i.e. they are only *names* for the one Being. As Deleuze himself recalls with 'the celebrated examples: morning star–evening star, Israel–Jacob, *p*lan–*b*lanc',[2] there are alternate ways of saying the same thing. However, what is crucial to bear in mind is that these alternate ways, although real, are neither numerical nor ontologically distinct (D, 44; *28*). The advance of Deleuze is to maintain that there is no division in a pair, since each term, as one, merely expresses univocal Being, which entertains no division. We might respond immediately by using this insight to reinforce the allegation often levelled at the French anti-Hegelians, Deleuze at their head, that any break with Hegel only ever amounts to the renewal or reinstallation of the dialectic under an alternative name ('difference', 'deconstruction', 'overdetermination', etc.). And yet with Deleuze there is no break to be had – not because the labyrinthine logic of the dialectic is simply insurmountable for opponents, but because, according to Deleuze, any 'break-with' involves no opposition at all.

For Deleuze the way round, or rather through, the dialectic does not lie in opposing it, but in *subverting* it, in turning its own dialectical logic against it. Deleuze calls his method, this anti-logic, the 'disjunctive synthesis' (the 'and-or-neither'[3]) whose operation reveals its very own nonsense. According to Deleuze what thought as being forces itself towards, by way of an intuition which the classical tradition from Plato to Hegel via Descartes and Kant fails to embrace fully, is *neutrality* (what Deleuze also calls 'extra-being'). Thought revels in an ungrounded universe even to the extent that to assume any *loss* of the faculties would itself be illusory. The idea that the faculties are today somehow lost or confused has become a standard proposition for the postmodernists, and often goes hand in hand with the fatalist view that society has entered a terminal phase in its history. Moreover, the impression that thought is illuminated in the 'natural light' of intuition can be found in Descartes and perfectly suits the idea of thought as somehow in need of revival. Wouldn't it be more appropriate in the circumstances, Deleuze asks, to regard thought as a case, or complex assemblage, of the 'clear-confused', rather than a clear and distinct idea which triumphs over obscurity? (D, 54–6; *34–5*) Badiou responds on Deleuze's behalf that 'between' Descartes and Deleuze, 'Intuition completely changes sense'. Thereafter:

> It is certain that [intuition] cannot proceed from a single fleeting glance. It must plunge into the clear intensity in order to seize the being-confused, and revive the 'dead' distinction of the being sepa-

rated from it by detecting the obscure part, the living immersion as its concealing isolation. This is why the Deleuzian intuition is not a fleeting glance of the soul, but an athletic course of thought; just as it is not a mental atom but an open multiplicity; and just as it is not a unilateral movement (a light pointed at the thing), but a complex construction that Deleuze very often calls 'perpetual relinking' ['*réenchaînement perpétuel*']. (D, 56; *35–6*)

There is always a 'double movement' of intuition which pursues thought, not as a clear and distinct idea, but as the 'pairing of the clear-confused and distinct-obscure'. The Deleuzian universe is populated by doubles, not as mediations of independent entities, but as immediate essences in a constant state of flux. Deleuze invites us to imagine a '*philosophically* bearded Hegel, a *philosophically* clean-shaven Marx',[4] leading us to believe that the two of them are one and the same individual. Elsewhere we discover the case of Alice in Carroll's *Through the Looking-Glass* who all of a sudden grows simultaneously larger and smaller.[5] Apparent paradoxes, then, which in fact exist as the very essence of things. For Deleuze, the paradox assumes no false dichotomy and demands no resolution or re-inversion of sense. What is more, since the event, like the temporality of *Aion*, only ever occupies the plane or surface of a situation, it disturbs nothing in depth, and therefore causes no *actual* inversion in the established hierarchy of things. Lest we forget Marx's failed attempt to stand Hegel right side up![6]

What Deleuze's method aims to achieve is not, as countless commentators have claimed, the deliberate loss of sense or the pretension of chaos. Instead, for Deleuze it is a question of forcing a paradox or problematic to its logical extremes, to the point where its implicit nonsense is finally exposed as the very foundation of sense. According to Badiou, however, this is not to be taken as an anti-Hegelian strategy *per se*. With Deleuze we might say that the challenge – if there is one in relation to Hegel – is rather to pursue logic relentlessly in order to outwit it to the point where the dialectic is finally rendered comical.[7] It is the same tactic found in the pages of *Capital* where Marx strives to expose the reified nature of social relations, such as the patent absurdity of linen 'recognising' its value in a coat, and a coat attaining its value in the quality of the linen.[8] For Deleuze such absurdities amount to the intuitive construction of thought itself, which runs 'from A to B, then from B to A' 'ideally, at infinite speed'. As Badiou puts it:

We must intuit that 'every object is double, without the halves resembling themselves'. (*Difference and Repetition*, 209, translation modified) Thought ends when, constrained by a case, it has unfolded until the end the duplicity of the being [*l'étant*], duplicity that is only the formal expression of what the univocity expresses as equivocity. (D, 57; *36*)

Positions

In Badiou's reading Deleuze emerges as the hardened scholar of singularity (the 'One-all') where multiplicity, rather than being non-totalisable, remains immanent to the One. As we have noted, such a reading is far removed from the usual interpretations of Deleuze as the philosopher of infinitely differential differences. For his part Badiou concedes that he has introduced an image of Deleuze that the latter would certainly not have tolerated. What, then, is the source of this potential dispute?

In Badiou's estimation the reason for the disagreement is found in their respective conceptions of the term 'multiple'. As we have seen, for Badiou the pure multiple is, following Cantor's theory of sets, the multiple-*without*-one, or multiple of multiples. According to Badiou the multiple is never 'multiple of Ones' since there is no 'All' (*Tout*), which means that the sole foundation or 'end point of the multiple' is 'the multiple of nothing: the null set' (D, 70; *46*). For Deleuze, however, this scientific and thus axiomatic conception of the multiple is to misconstrue the real (whose true nature is 'virtual') multiplicity, along with its 'chaotic form', its 'primordial Inconsistency' (D, 70; *46*). Put simply in other words, the dispute between Badiou and Deleuze is that which exists, in principle, between an ordered conception of chaos, one which is mathematically definable, and a chaotic conception of order, one which is philosophically intuitive.

We might permit this paradigmatic distinction to rest there. However, Badiou then proceeds to use it as the basis for a reappraisal of Deleuze's principal formulas. Thus we have: 'the virtual and the actual (doctrine of the event); time and truth (doctrine of knowledge); chance and the eternal return (doctrine of action); the fold and the outside (doctrine of the subject)' (D, 46; *29*). In the case of the first of these formulas, Badiou notes how Deleuze resists confusing the virtual and the possible. Philosophy has tended to treat the possible as a category of Platonism, where 'that which exists must resemble a concept', whereas for Deleuze, 'the virtual actualises itself in the being [*l'étant*] as immanent power [*puissance*], and subtracts itself from all resemblance to its actualisations' (D, 73; *48*). There is nothing secondary or derived about the virtual, it isn't an image of a simple essence. Instead, its virtuality, which is thoroughly real, is wholly determined.

In *Difference and Repetition* Deleuze draws on the work of the French mathematician Albert Lautman in an attempt to illustrate the true idea of the virtual. In Lautman's work, problems, as ideas, do not cry out for solutions. 'On the contrary,' Deleuze states, '"solvability" must depend upon an internal characteristic: it must be determined by the conditions of the problem, engendered in and by the problem along with the real solutions.'[9] A solution is not the logical outcome of a particular problem, but an integral part of an expanding series of problems which involve 'only events and affections', and which ultimately cannot be separated from *the* Problem as Idea. For example, consider the Marxist 'problematic' as found in Althusser. Here we have a problem as a 'differential virtuality' of the economy, whose economic conditions 'determine or give rise to the manner in which it finds a solution within the framework of the real relations of the society'. Significantly with Althusser there is no transitive solution to economic social relations, even under communism. Instead of being solved the (economic) problem is merely allocated to specific 'fields of resolvability' which, in Althusser's case, amount to political, economic, scientific or ideological forms of practice.[10] The real (virtual) nature of the problem, in other words, is always *masked* by its eventual (actual) solution.

It is at this stage that Badiou seizes on an apparent hurdle in Deleuze's theory of the virtual. Deleuze treats problems as virtual expressions of the actual world, immanent although irreducible to their solutions – so where, *effectively speaking*, is the problem? Is it really worth pursuing a 'problem' that merely turns out to be a further variety of itself, the Same one? And what type of tactical significance could this idea of a virtual problem possibly give rise to as a result? Badiou reverses the priority of terms in the Deleuzian virtual/actual formula, conceiving problems as *actual* multiplicities and maintaining that the One-virtual 'does not exist' (D, 69; *46*). Deleuze's virtual totality admits no problems grounded in actual situations. Instead, problems tend to assume transcendence in Deleuze – a tendency, we might add, which he inherits from Nietzsche (*Beyond Good and Evil*) and also from Freud (*Beyond the*

Pleasure Principle). According to Badiou, then, it is the virtual realm of univocity which best defines Deleuze's system, and which Badiou names, rather provocatively, a 'Platonism of the virtual'.

Deleuze is not renowned for his Platonism. Quite the reverse in fact, since throughout his work Deleuze has repeatedly led calls to overturn Plato. However, Badiou advises us to 'look twice before believing that we have finished with the foundation, or that we have "overturned" Plato'. The same is true of Marx, Badiou adds, whose famous 'overturning' of Hegel only ever amounted to 'the support for a long perpetuation' (D, 68; *45*). Platonism, in some form or another, is indispensable to philosophy, for even in *denying* 'the primacy of an original over a copy' and 'glorifying the reign of simulacra' one still invokes a form of Being – as the Idea or as negation – despite the anarchy of its beings. It is a principle, Badiou notes, which also escapes Deleuze in his theory of time.

Deleuze replaces the common sense view of time as the succession of distinct moments with a time of pure duration (*la durée pure*). For Deleuze, who is a follower of Bergson, time is *non*-chronological and beyond movement, its 'truth' is 'immobile'. Thus we envisage an essential coexistence between the present and the past. The Deleuzian past is 'a positive production of time. Far from characterising a loss of being, or an annihilation of the precariousness of becoming, it is a growth, a supplement of being, an incorporation in change of the One (but the One is its own change)' (D, 92–3; *61–2*).

In considering Deleuze's theory of time the question we must pose, Badiou argues, is whether this virtual time – time as 'superficial mobility' – is really so far away from Plato's conception of time as the '"mobile *image* of eternity"'[11] (D, 92; *61*). What propels the Deleuzian theory of time is the concept of truth, which 'is absolutely formulated under the restricted motif of the model (and the copy)' (D, 86; *57*). However, Deleuze characteristically abhors truth and, drawing on his Nietzschean roots, replaces the concept with what he prefers to call the 'power of the false' (Nietzsche's 'will to power'). Assuming this power has access to the virtual must mean that, far from relating itself to actual beings in time, truth consists in the proper form of eternity. For Deleuze, 'time *is* truth itself', a proposition which leads him to consign truth to the memory of the 'absolute past' (D, 97; *64*). With Deleuze, then, the question of time demands an emptying out of all the faculties of sense, of which truth is the prime embodiment, to the benefit of a perpetual present where simulacra show up as pure events and relations. These are the *plays* of truth which creatively expand and curtail all attempts to be grounded in truth. And yet for Badiou this self-defeating form of truth where time has all but evaporated can still be said to harbour a set of relations, albeit an empty (void) one. Furthermore, it is precisely in the 'abolition of time' that the 'eternity of truths' is established (D, 97; *65*).

What distinguishes Deleuze from the dominant classical tradition of philosophy is not his ability to destroy, in any definitive or absolute sense, its 'global setting'. Rather the great strength of Deleuze lies in the originality of his *method* – expressive rather than negative, intuitive rather than dialectical – along with the 'free indirect style' which he brings to the (re)creation of concepts *from within the vicinity of* the classical tradition (D, 96; *64*). As far as over-turning Platonism is concerned Deleuze stands at the forefront of a line of great modern thinkers, from Nietzsche through Heidegger, who not so much overturn Platonism – since 'it has, from the very beginning, been overturned' – as overturn *anti*-Platonism, or Platonism as the 'great fallacious construction of modernity and postmodernity alike'. Against this popular current Deleuze exhibits 'the most generous anti-Platonism, the most open to contemporary creations, the least destinal, the most progressive' (D, 149–50; *101–2*). Otherwise put, Deleuzianism is Platonism in new form.

Badiou's critique of Deleuze's work is grounded in six of the latter's 'classic' texts.[12] It establishes an 'object' of his philosophy – singularity or 'One-all' – and, in identifying Deleuze's method, aims to reappraise his principal 'doctrines'. This arguably amounts to a reductionist account of Deleuze's work. Underlining the generic difference between their respective enterprises Badiou then proceeds to utilise such difference as the true measure of what, conceptually speaking, can be held in common for both. Of course, by Badiou's own admission the difficulty emerges in the one-sided nature of the 'debate', which founders on the question of multiplicity. For Badiou, multiplicity is a question of the 'actual-multiple'. For Deleuze, the 'virtual-One'. This aspect of the 'controversy' between Deleuze and Badiou, the latter explains, never managed to reach 'a synthesis' (D, 72; *48*). However, this doesn't prevent Badiou from correcting Deleuze when his silence on a point of principle threatens to undermine the consistency of the argument.

Badiou's study marks an important intervention in Deleuze scholarship which forces us to rethink the 'sets' of relations between

Deleuze and the classical tradition which we often uncritically assume he breaks with. We must not forget that Deleuze is a philosopher who, despite appearing to us in several different guises, is no less part of the classical generation where spectres and doubles are to be expected; a generation which has, for all time, never ceased to inspire the sophist. Given this crucial assessment it would clearly be pointless to ask whether Badiou's reading is the true one, for there is always plenty of room for another Deleuze. Instead, the question I want to pose is whether classical philosophy can really have the last word here, an impression which Deleuze, for all his scholarly brilliance, never lost sight of.

Which One?

'I am convinced of the existence of principles', declares Badiou in his introduction (D, 30; *17*). The same could hardly be said of Deleuze. Indeed, his work would appear to resist any straightforward categorisation or critique – or at least, by virtue of its bold eclecticism, it makes such encounters more problematic than they first appear. Deleuze is a thinker whose thought parades itself in *colours, sounds, sensations, intensities*. His aesthetic sensibility is renowned for ground-breaking studies of literature and the cinema, and revives a myriad of 'minor' themes from what can only rather inadequately be described as the history of ideas. From Baroque architecture to geology, from semiotics to military strategy, and from all things avant-garde to his intense appetite for popular culture, Deleuze's 'work' (if there is one) is *anti-schematic*. What this means is that, instead of adhering to a preferred method of exposition which facilitates our understanding of an argument (as exemplified by Badiou in *Being and the Event*, where mathematical expressions are supported by demonstrations), Deleuze proceeds by slogans. He uses strings of independent clauses and conjunctions in constructing an argument, constantly reworking hypotheses and shelving conclusions along the way, while attacking every theoretical position including his own. Moreover, if Deleuze 'has' a philosophical system then this system is *to take over* Kant, Hume, Spinoza … It is not, first and foremost, a question of establishing relations on the road to truth.[13] For Deleuze, philosophy is a never-ending *construction*. To this end (or never-ending beginning) Deleuze hijacks all manner of material from the arts and sciences, at times forcing the most unlikely of 'philosophical' bedfellows to do battle with one another. The result, if and when it arrives, is not the revelation of a *generic* category (art *or* science *or* politics ...). In Deleuze's scheme of things philosophy is 'bricolage' (but what is philosophy?) which never ceases to collapse the boundaries between science and technology, macro- and micro-politics, philosophy and art, etc. In this sense the classical wisdom which teaches us that philosophy's original site is Greek is far too inhibited to allow free reign to thought. What thought demands instead for the production of concepts is an apparatus approaching the concrete reality of a war machine capable of deterritorialising the earth. 'Descendants of the Scythians, the Amazons spring forth like lightning, "between" the two States, the Greek and the Trojan. They sweep away everything in their path.'[14] Philosophy is nomadology: the construction of habitat.

Truth tends to take a battering in Deleuze's hands. In spite of Badiou's point that Deleuze conceives truth as the 'power of the false', where '*truth is defeat, or defection, of the object whose truth it is*' (D, 94; *63*), the concept of power rarely escapes Deleuze's hypercrit-ical gaze, and certainly doesn't underscore any so-called 'defeat'. Power is simply synonymous with the lives of bodies, their fluxes and machinations. All that power demands is obedience. Furthermore, as in the case of speech acts, power is redundant outside the context in which it gains its sense: 'We see this in police or government announcements, which often have little plausibility or truthfulness, but say very clearly what should be observed and retained.' Truth therefore involves whatever the 'collective assem-blage' happens to judge as appropriate to guarantee order in the circumstances (although, of course, the circumstances in question are never the same for all). What we might call the *passage* of truth Deleuze and Guattari liken to a game of Chinese whispers played out between a teacher and a student where questions and answers are distorted, first in one direction, then in the other, along a chain of communication.[15]

Deleuze's Nietzschean thought is indispensable when it comes to the question of truth, although not in the way Badiou would like. For Nietzsche the question of truth is not one which navigates between the 'undecidable alternatives' of true and false (D, 87; *58*). Instead, the question of truth is first and foremost to *desire* the truth, the 'will to truth': *who wants truth?* That truth is never abstract, and remains inseparable from he who asks the question, is to recognise that philosophy can only ever hope to '[relate] truth to a concrete will of its own, to a type of forces, to a quality of the will to power'.[16]

With Nietzsche, truth is always inescapably shot through with the pious wishes and agendas of the self-righteous. And, of course, when virtue is finally exhausted there is always the resort to science:

> It is disturbing that truth conceived as an abstract universal, thought conceived as pure science, has never hurt anyone. In fact the established order and current values constantly find their best support in truth conceived in this way. 'The "truth" … is an easy-going and pleasant creature, who is continually assuring the powers that be that no one need fear any trouble from its quarter: for, after all, it is only pure science.'[17]

How naïve we must be, Nietzsche goads us, to fall for such rubbish!

When it comes to science it is certainly not the discovery of truths which motivates Deleuze, who employs all manner of minor tactics in order to evade positivism. Deleuze doesn't limit himself to a particular scientific paradigm. Indeed, he even relies on some quite controversial scientific theories (e.g. chaos theory) in an attempt to outwit more conventional wisdom in science. For example, in *What is Philosophy?*, Deleuze and Guattari liken chaos to 'an infinite speed of birth and disappearance' wherein thought, like particles of light, struggles for consistency. It is only by introducing a 'plane of reference' for scientific propositions that absolute limits are set in our understanding of the Universe (the Big Bang, the Kelvin scale, the speed of light), although, in reality, such limits are merely 'coextensive' with its 'whole development'.[18] For Deleuze and Guattari it is clearly not the case that such coextensivity – this 'whole development' of physical reality – is reducible to 'the unitary vocation of science'.

> In fact, each limit on its own account generates irreducible, heterogeneous systems of coordinates and imposes thresholds of discontinuity depending on the proximity or distance of the variable (for example, the distance of the galaxies). Science is haunted not by its own unity but by the plane of reference constituted by all the limits or borders through which it confronts chaos.[19]

Science confronts a multiplicity of limits and borders which form branches or 'cuts' of chaos. Moreover, the nature of the confrontation is relative to the way in which these cuts function in a given locale. It is in such locales that scientific theories tend to become established. But any locale whatever is a mere 'aleatory point' – i.e. a disjunctive synthesis of incorporeal processes and connections in a state of disequilibrium – and the scientific theories distributed by these points remain irreducible to one another. We might regard these theories as discrete regions of a universal problematic of scientific understanding which hold together or 'set' our 'holes in knowledge', i.e. the accolades of as yet unconquered realms of science. But to attempt to conceive this problematic from a single point or perspective gives us no real sense of the positive multiplicity of what the Universe is, even in part.

It is here that Badiou's conception of ontology enters the phase of its dispute with Deleuze, since for the latter the definition of science takes in all of *natural* science rather than the 'pure science' of mathematical ontology. Although Badiou hails Deleuze as the philosopher of univocity, such a definition clearly relies on the strict application of Badiou's system and his support for ontology as mathematical science. However, for Deleuze the distinction between philosophy and science must be qualified and does not, at any rate, mark an original separation.

Deleuze and Guattari argue consistently along these lines in *What Is Philosophy?* In a brief example they observe how the schematic method of *Being and the Event*, which ascends from the lower order of being to the higher order of the event, means that philosophy attains its true conditions (politics, art ...) as *functions* of science. For Deleuze and Guattari, this privileging of science over philosophy, function over concept, is 'ruinous' for philosophy, since 'it makes science the concept par excellence, which is expressed in the scientific proposition'.[20] Moreover, mathematical science is not unassailable when it comes to conceptualising 'any multiplicity whatever', since 'even mathematics', they remark, 'has had enough of set-theoreticism'.[21]

We have reached the crux of the matter. As Deleuze never tires of saying, there are two types of multiplicity – or 'multiplicit*ies*': the *qualitative* multiplicity which we associate with philosophy and which involves differences in kind, and the *quantitative* multiplicity which we associate with science and which concerns differences in degree. As we have seen, this distinction is one which Badiou does not permit, since for him multiplicity is not numerical in the standard sense, but the ontological structure which composes/ presents, or counts, any set of multiple elements. But is the distinction sufficiently avoidable? We know that the multiple is not numerical in the everyday sense of the word – e.g. a value which is counted on a scale of measure – since Badiou's idea of the multiple is 'without one', radically multiple of multiples. However, it *is* unquestionably the case that multiplicity *aspires* to differences in value, to the ordinal and cardinal limits of Cantor, and to the *counting* as one that conditions being as being.

In set theory we manipulate elements on the basis of a theorem which informs us *a priori* that the elements in question *are* (i.e. can be counted as) *elements*. In other words the multiple is always generically defined regardless of what the multiple is multiple of ('trees', 'philosophers', 'natural numbers'). For Deleuze, this mathematical reading of multiplicity is immune to the precise *nature* of the elements being counted, or what he calls, drawing on Bergson, their differences in kind.[22] Can we really compare the multiplicity of bodies, the exhilaration of being in a certain place in the world at a certain time, with the laborious tasks which the 'same' individual carries out the very next day? How might we go about constructing the assemblage of the tick, its inclination towards the light, and its falling off a branch onto the back of a passing mammal?[23] In Deleuze's scheme of things there are as many conceptual frameworks for posing such questions as there are objects in the world, whose infinite variety will more often than not turn out to be conventionally unscientific (in which case we can always drop things and start the investigation again from a different perspective). The problem would appear to crop up with every one of Deleuze's books in the sense that, with each of them, we enter into a new dynamic, a new regime of thinking is opened up which shifts (what we believed to be) the philosopher's original position. With Deleuze, philosophy is not a system, but a nomadic existence which pitches its tent in any field it can. In the light of all this we might have cause to wonder *which* Deleuze – which *'one'* – Badiou manages to single out, since Deleuzian ontology generates many ontological frameworks – many 'possible worlds' – each time we try to pin it down.

There is no more fascinating exploration of this conceptual schizophrenia – this schizophrenic attention to detail – than Deleuze's book *The Fold: Leibniz and the Baroque*. As the foreword advises, we approach this book as a kind of manual for rethinking the dimensionality of territory – 'population, habitat, displacement, geocide'[24] – which leads to a 'way out', perhaps, of our monstrously overcrowded megalopolises. Needless to say, for Deleuze it is not a question of conventional architecture. With the Baroque – which is a *sensibility* rather than a school – we discover the inspiration for new relations between 'the fluidity of matter, the elasticity of bodies, and motivating spirit as a mechanism'.[25] But the relations are not relations as parts, not in the set theoretical sense. Instead, the 'parts' 'form a fold, such that they are not separated into parts of parts but are rather divided to infinity in smaller and smaller folds that always retain a certain cohesion'. The world, and within the world the universe, is a fold. 'The model for the sciences of matter is the "origami", as the Japanese philosopher might say, or the art of folding paper.'[26]

Is Deleuze advancing a solution in response to competition for an ever-shrinking human habit which makes the individual reflect within herself on worlds infinitely small? Such an interpretation is clearly possible, but completely misses the tenor of Deleuze's argument. The concept of fold is folding, unfolding, enfolding to the extent that a new way of tying our selves to the predicate of a proposition is called for. For Deleuze the predicates of being and non-being, inherited from classical philosophy, no longer provide sufficient reason to found – to *unfold* – the real multiplicity of a proposition. Against essentialism, Deleuze revives the 'incorporeal' or virtual predicate favoured by the Stoics – a 'Stoic mannerism' which re-emerges with the Baroque. 'The coupling *basis-manners*,' Deleuze explains, 'disenfranchises form or essence.' Borrowing his example, the proposition 'The tree *is* green' now reads 'The tree *greens.*' With mannerism the predicate or verb becomes the event itself, 'passing endlessly from one thought to another'.[27] In *The Fold* Deleuze introduces us to a world, not of being, but of manners – of style, performance, posture, display ... – whose meticulous detail is ingrained in each and every human soul. The Leibnizian subject or 'monad' is a world, each one programmed by God in a slightly different way. Does this mean that the possible worlds of Leibniz are without event,[28] eternities without creation? Not at all, since each monad masks an 'indiscernible' harmony with all the others. Unlike Badiou, for whom the indiscernible is actually void, Deleuze pursues the truly Baroque riddle of a real indiscernible: how can something (rather than nothing) happen if there is no actual limit to the universe? For Deleuze, the answer would appear to rest with the discordant harmony or inertia which brings as many worlds as possible into close proximity while at the same time maintaining the utmost (infinite) variety within each one: a question of 'pure variability'.[29] The event unfolds itself along several series of intrinsic properties (of height, colour, sound ...), each one acquired in the act of perception. However, perception is not a pure act, since each property comprises the 'data' of prehension (the event as public spectacle) and the prehended 'datum' (the event as private reflection). Prehension itself has three qualities: 1) folding, or the impression which the event makes on the subject; 2) unfolding, or the subject's passage between prehensions; and 3) enfolding, or the joy which the event inspires in the subject. Finally, an 'eternal Object' (e.g. a famous monument such as 'The Great Pyramid') ingrains itself into the event – as 'quality', 'figure', or 'thing' – and so refolds itself into a prehension.[30]

The Baroque is an infinite play of the world(s) in which *nothing ever dies*, and where matter endures at variable speeds and across different zones of intensity in its passage between different metastable states. In scientific terms the Baroque is the aesthetic realisation of the first law of thermodynamics according to which matter, in the form of pure energy, can neither be created nor destroyed. Matter constantly unfolds the architecture of bodies, their different fabrics, textures and pleats. It is a process without end: 'The problem is not how to finish a fold, but how to continue it, to have it go through the ceiling, how to bring it to infinity.'[31] For Deleuze, the Baroque is the perfect allegory, not just for art, but for politics as well. A politics of the (neo-)Baroque has all the spontaneous creativity of nature at its disposal, thus providing us with the resources to reconstruct social reality outside the macro-political. The Green movement's campaign for clean energy, sustainable agriculture, and its general promotion of 'environmental consciousness' is an example of one such attempt to re-imagine the relationship between human beings and nature. It is one *possible* model, since nature in the Deleuzian sense is anti-essentialist (the depletion of the earth's 'natural' resources is no barrier to capitalism's 'deterritorialization' of new ones). Indeed, for Deleuze it is more a question of natures plural rather than nature singular, which politically might involve a multiplicity of communities (molecular assemblages), each one living in blind proximity (discordant harmony) to the next. However, with Deleuze the relations between molecules and assemblage are *qualitative* – not numerical – which crucially allows for the subject's ethical constitution in the practice of everyday life. Politics, as *praxis*, is not limited to the exercise of a communist, or conventionally egalitarian, principle. As Deleuze's communist collaborator

Félix Guattari also believed, it is quite conceivable that capitalism's 'ecological crisis' could, in cultivating the right balance of molecular forces, bring about 'the reinvention of the environment and the enrichment of modes of life and sensibility'.[32] For Deleuze, the Baroque provides one possible means for such hidden potential to find expression.

Deleuzianism is a strange cult, a 'practical philosophy' whose theoretical boundaries extend beyond the sufficient reason of classical philosophy. For all its strength of originality, Badiou's critique is clearly an attempt to *outradicalise* Deleuze with the aid of dialectics. But Deleuze departs from the classical device in his writings, perverting the dialectic beyond all rational sense with his own brand of metaphysical intuition. Badiou's claim that 'univocity' is the cornerstone of Deleuzianism can only be maintained by discounting or ignoring the positive ambivalence of Deleuze – emanating from his total repudiation of negation – which is arguably his most formidable philosophical weapon. Deleuze will not conform, and resists being labelled or forced into any one position which would conveniently suit the interests of a rival. And yet such ambivalence – as opposed to what is 'undecidable' in axiomatic terms – is, as we have seen, precisely what the scientist in Badiou cannot bring himself to accept.

6
The Ethics of Philosophy

Badiou's philosophy would not immediately appear to be compatible with an ethical standpoint. The 'principles' which he prioritises in his work are of the scientific kind (mathematical axioms) rather than models for behaviour; conditions for being rather than codes for conduct. However, Badiou's meticulously rationalist system cannot escape ethics, and in the 1990s Badiou begins to incorporate broadly ethical themes into his work, as well as for the first time actively distinguishing between good and bad – or Good and Evil – events. In this chapter I want to focus on this shift in emphasis as a means of developing the observation I made at the end of the previous chapter. There I highlighted the problem of ambivalence as it appears in Deleuze, and here I want to extend this theme in relation to Badiou's more recent work. The question remains as to why a people, despite having satisfied the conditions for a politics of truth, satisfy the conditions of justice at the same time. For there is ample evidence in the history of mass uprisings, and in the calamitous leaderships which mass movements spawned throughout the twentieth century, that politics is no guarantee of justice.

In light of the polemic which Badiou launched against 'revisionists' at the height of Maoism, can we assume that Badiou's turn to ethics marks a self-critical phase in the development of his thought? Not at all. In fact, my hypothesis in this chapter will be exactly the opposite: namely, that Badiou's ethics is first and foremost a way of safeguarding the autonomy of thought from the moral injunctions of the new philosophers;[1] it is a method for combating the often wilful confusion of philosophy with the history of philosophy, and all the potential disasters such confusion brings.

'The end of the End'

In his essay 'The (re)turn of philosophy *itself*' in *Conditions* (1992), Badiou sets out in five theses the measure of philosophy's destitution in the present, along with the future conditions of its recovery. According to Badiou's initial thesis, '*philosophy is today paralysed by the relation to its own history*' (C, 57). There is broad agreement among contemporary philosophers that the history of philosophy has reached its 'closure', and that philosophy as such, caught between 'historiography' and 'delocalisation', 'no longer knows if it has a proper place'. This pessimistic and nostalgic vision, where philosophy constantly confronts its 'glorious metaphysical past', comes to us from Heidegger, and, as we noted in Chapter 3, provides the theoretical resources for Badiou's concept of the event. In Heidegger, however, the event takes the form of historicism and is envisaged romantically as a temporal being, a being in time, whereas Badiou's concept of the event resists temporalisation. For Badiou, a past event is completely foreclosed from being, and cannot be accessed via some forgotten venue, e.g. a written text (Derrida). What is past is void, irredeemably finished forever. The task for philosophy is therefore to break with historicism – this 'museum' of philosophy – in order to acquire thought in the realm of its 'autonomous legitimation' (C, 59).

To break with historicism does not mean to break with history. Badiou is not endorsing the postmodernist acceptance of the 'end of history'. After all, such thoughtless declarations always revert to a tragic or profound sense of history, i.e. another form of historicism. There is no way of finishing with what Hegel called the 'ruse of reason'. 'Philosophy must assume the axioms of thought and draw the consequences. It is only then, and starting from its immanent determination, that [philosophy] will convene its history' (C, 59). The only end we can speak of in relation to history is the end of its (assumed) End. Philosophy takes on this task – 'from within itself' – not by simply distinguishing itself from what it is not, but from what it has, in the history of philosophy, more often than not appeared to be. For Badiou, *sophistry* is the 'implacable twin of philosophy', an idealist version of the rational kernel of (materialist) philosophy itself. Suppose that for each of the great philosophers of antiquity one substitutes a sophist, a pretender to his throne (a Gorgias for Plato, a Protagoras for Aristotle), and one then gains a good impression of the scant enterprises of the modern philosophers (C, 60). Between the linguistic determinism of Wittgenstein ('the limits of my language are the limits of my world') and the rhetorical flair of Lyotard's assault on grand narratives, philosophy is no longer defined by the concept of truth. Instead, philosophy admits 'only conventions, rules, genres of discourse and plays of language' (C,

62). Quite inadvertently, however, in their retreat from historical considerations, these philosophers cannot help but expose the means of their own downfall and are thus confronted, in arrears as it were, by the truth of their own discourse. According to Badiou, one finds no better demonstration of this 'intraphilosophical status' of truth than in the three 'intellectual endeavours' which define the history of the twentieth century: namely, Stalinist Marxism, Heidegger's seduction by German Fascism, and, partly under the influence of the latter two, the Western 'democratic' appeal of Anglo-Saxon philosophy (C, 62–3). The decline of each, Badiou argues, can be gauged in the course of their respective antagonisms towards 'the Platonic foundation of metaphysics'. In none of the three cases did the will to overcome Platonism meet with the desired effects; nor for that matter did the task end with philosophy.

Anti-Platonism, rather than Platonism itself, has today surpassed itself in marking the closure of modern philosophy. However, we should resist the temptation to believe that any philosophy opposed to Platonism (implicitly or explicitly) can be deployed in anticipation of its own collapse. For wouldn't this all too soon and all too easily lead – as in the case of the apologists of Heidegger's flirtation with Fascism – to a situation where the aberrations of a once great thinker are accepted on the grounds of a minor indiscretion (the cult of the flawed genius)?[2] Badiou is wise to this ethical perversion which would seek to make philosophy a closed enterprise outside the realm of history. For Badiou, *philosophy begins here, at the very moment when its historical and universal enterprise of truth is declared impossible.* For example, consider the question of the Jewish Holocaust, which for Lyotard stands 'as an event beyond the resources of Hegel's philosophy'.[3] Today, the idea that 'Auschwitz' is the name of an event somehow beyond the experience of human suffering, and as such one which cannot be adequately spoken about or understood, has become a cliché of modern journalism which invariably succeeds in blinding onlookers to the fact that the Holocaust was *a politically motivated act*. The consequences of this cliché are multiple, but virtually all are politically disastrous. For there is little difference between claiming, as Lyotard does, that only a moment of sublime silence could testify to the victims of the Holocaust, and the equally esoteric and somewhat grotesque proposition that the Holocaust, as such, never actually happened. The silence of philosophy does not in this case mark a just silence. It is a silence which proves instead that in a certain set of historical circumstances philosophy did not act.

'Before philosophy, in a "before" which is not temporal, there are *truths*.' 'Philosophy is a construction of thought where one proclaims, *against sophistry*, that there are truths. But this central proclamation supposes a properly philosophical category, which is that of *the* Truth' (C, 65). For the postmodernists the suspicion surrounding definitions like these is that Truth is too universal to be a well-founded category, and that the intervention of Truth into a community is always an imposition which destroys the autonomy and legitimacy of local norms and values. However, 'Truth designates simultaneously a plural state of things (there are heterogeneous truths) *and* the unity of thought.' Firstly, it is not the case that the first state of affairs precludes the second. The variety of truths are perfectly 'compossible'. Secondly, Truth 'with a capital T' 'is by itself void. It operates, but presents nothing' (C, 66). Badiou warns us not to confuse this logical Truth – the one 'where philosophy operates on truths which are exterior to it' – with the ontological Truth where what 'is' true acquires sacred importance with the passage of time.

In respect of the category of Truth, Badiou identifies two essential operations for philosophy. Either philosophy operates on the basis of a 'rhetoric of succession' which dispenses a *'fiction of knowledge'*, as found in Descartes or in the *'more geometrico'* of Spinoza; or else it relies on an artistic procedure where Truth becomes at a certain point suspended (C, 67). Taken together these two operations form a pair of 'pliers' of Truth which, 'connecting and sublime, has for office to seize *truths'*.

> The relation of Truth (philosophical) to truths (scientific, political, artistic or amorous) is a relation of *seizure*. In 'seizure', we understand capture, hold, and also sudden chill, surprise. Philosophy is this place of thought where (non-philosophical) truths are seizures as such, and seizing us. (C, 68)

It is clearly the case, then, according to this definition, that philosophy cannot choose the time of its vacation from the political scene, nor can it proclaim that it, philosophy, no longer has the power to act. Badiou's Hegelian logic dictates that the non-relation always in fact marks a deeper relation than the relation itself. By virtue of being supposedly absent or 'outside truth' one invariably provides cause for even greater suspicion, and, in the case of renegade philosophers, the promise that in the end Truth will find them out.

It is nevertheless as axiomatic as it is essential that the philosophy of Truth is 'polarised by a specific adversary, who is the sophist' (C, 69). As we have seen previously, as with those revisionists targeted by Badiou during his Maoist phase, the sophist provides the momentum to struggle against.

But there is a paradox at work here, perhaps an aporia, and a potentially dangerous one at that, since what seizes by chance and without warning can all too easily be taken up by the State and enacted as the rule of law. In such circumstances where philosophy is elevated to the heights of ethical responsibility ('the philosopher-king named by Plato') disaster looms. 'Disaster in philosophical thought is the order of the day when philosophy presents itself as being, not a seizure of truths, but a *situation of truth*' (C, 70). There we encounter the jump from logic to ontology. As we will recall from our earlier chapters, the situation is the set of circumstances, infinitely multiple, which is interrupted and named 'after the event'. In light of what we have also said above, the situation is seized from the outside before being 'sutured' to politics, art, science or love as one of the four conditions of its truth. The 'suture' is a concept derived from Lacan, and Badiou employs it to define the tendency of philosophy to '*delegate* its functions to such or such of its conditions' at times when its intellectual circuit becomes 'blocked' (MP, 41). In the nineteenth century for example, 'between Hegel and Nietzsche', we mainly encounter the positivist suture, which pretends to be able to manage time scientifically, thereby playing into the hands of the 'diffuse religiosity' of capitalist industry. There is also, in the same epoch, the suture of philosophy to politics, where we discover Marx's commitment to philosophy as the practical means to change the world. And of course, what has overtaken both science and Marxism in the twentieth century – largely as a result of Heidegger's influence, although continued in the philosophy of Blanchot, Derrida and Deleuze – is the suture of philosophy to art: the 'age of the poets' (MP, 42–58).

The suture always brings about a reduction of thought – synonymous with a 'heightening of the void' – which turns out to have a 'triple effect': truth is made 1) ecstatic, 2) sacred and 3) terroristic (C, 71–2). Taken together, these three aspects add up to the concept of disaster. Although the latter pertains primarily to thought, disaster finds expression in empirical effects, while 'Reciprocally, every real disaster, in particular historical, contains a philosopheme which joins together ecstasy, the sacred and terror.' The destiny of the German people to establish a new world order, for example, and

Stalinist Marxism in its claims over the future course of history both combine a terroristic element (the persecution of 'traitors'), an ecstatic element (a romantic sense of 'place' or community, e.g. German *Heimat*) and a sacred name ('Führer') (C, 73). Can we assume, therefore, that every philosophy must navigate this perilous path on the brink, or at least within the vicinity of disaster? For Badiou, the answer to this question is yes, since disaster is always internal to the conflict between philosophy and sophistry. 'Philosophy must never abandon itself to anti-sophistic extremism. It loses its way when it feeds the dark desire to finish with the sophist *once and for all*' (C, 73). The sophist, it would seem, serves the ends of Good in setting the philosopher a worthy target, a good enemy as Nietzsche says. Evil is not the practice of the sophist, but is made possible whenever the philosopher arrogantly denies that sophistry does not exist. The sophist is the measure of Evil, the means of holding Evil within our sights. 'The ethics of philosophy,' Badiou says, 'is at heart to maintain the sophist as an adversary, to preserve the *polemos*, the dialectical conflict' (C, 74–5).

The Stakes of Evil

For Badiou, philosophy is made possible, and must be made to begin, at the moment where the sophists and their perverse social and cultural side-effects (journalists and critics, the public relations industry, capital-parliamentarism in general) would appear to have thought locked in a stranglehold. But what are the actual discourses of Evil? In Badiou's short work *Ethics* (1993) – which he lends the subtitle *Essay on the Understanding of Evil* – we find the author in characteristically militant mode, embarking on another one of his balance-sheet assessments, this time of a set of negative consequences for the practice of modern ethics. For Badiou ethics has become far too thoughtless in its definitions and discredited in its field of application, a victim of too many journalistic platitudes to defend effectively the universal rights of man. Badiou rejects outright the doctrine of universal or natural human rights – which he regards as having resulted largely from the failure of the revolutionary project of Marxism – and its replacement by the ideology of liberal humanitarianism and the law of the global market (E, 7). The intellectual scene reflects the failure. Today, in the realm of philosophy as in politics, it is as if Foucault's announcement of the 'death of man', or Althusser's 'process without a subject', or Lacan's split with the Ego-ideal, had never actually happened. It is a strange and bitter irony that these once revolutionary ideas attacking the notion of the human essence are today widely regarded as having emerged in a period of intense ideology, or as evidence of their authors' remote indifference to the pragmatics[4] of Western democracy (E, 8–10). From Badiou's perspective, in order to escape this misrepresentation and return ethics to its proper ground philosophy must once again be made to seize the event of the militant act; theory must be reunited with practice.

It is from Kant that we inherit the founding principles of ethics as human rights. And yet what we overlook in accepting Kant's categorical imperative, according to which human beings act with some ideal notion of human conduct in mind,[5] is the extent to which this doctrine *makes man a victim*. The human being is not an end in itself. It is a negative dialectic which seeks to make man alternate between saviour and victim of human suffering and injustice. Here, right is forced to lead the fight against Evil, a fight with little understanding of what constitutes Good. Today public opinion has never been more confident in its ability to identify *in*justice, and to mount calls for the universal condemnation of 'criminal acts'. But where justice itself is concerned the ethical parameters are far from clear (AM, 109). Is this uncertainty a symptom of the public's inability to acquire an ethical conscience, let alone actually adopt one for Good? Badiou strikes a strong chord here. At every level of public life the rules binding individuals into various pseudo-social contracts of mutual rights and responsibilities (consumer rights, workplace rights, parental rights, animal rights) threaten to trivialise our collective humanity. *Law*, along with the booming legal industry which supports it, rather than right, more than ever dictates the path of ethics as 'ethical policy', a policy which, at the limit, is nothing more than the capacity of a constitutional government to keep its subjects in order (along with any 'outsiders' it deems worthy of attention beyond its immediate jurisdiction).

Against this paltry vision of man as a 'mortal animal' who requires constant supervision by the laws of the State, Badiou heralds 'the rights of the Immortal, asserting for themselves, or the rights of the Infinite exercising their sovereignty over the contingency of suffering and death' (E, 14). Being-for-death, *ressentiment*, bad conscience ... these are the names for the pathetic victimhood which eats away at humankind to the point where even the most modest stand for progressive social change is automatically met with universal derision. The same moral conservatism is voiced in all manner of postmodern discourses. From the 'respect for the other' to the 'ethics of difference', culturalism belies the basic fact that despite the multitude of differences between communities the world over there is no specific difference (E, 26). If everyone is different then it must follow that such difference simply adds up to the same thing. In nature, as in culture it seems, nothing *is* the same. But how on this evidence can a true ethics be advanced – one which must, after all, be capable of distinguishing between good and bad forms of behaviour? Inhabitants of an indifferent world, how can we adequately account for the alleged differences in attitudes, actions, identities, etc. between the one and the other? We are seemingly back on the terrain of being and the event.

Badiou acknowledges that the most intricate logic is not the logic of difference, but the logic of the same. And the one and only logic of the same which is capable of affirming differences for what they are is truth (E, 27). But if *a* truth is *'indifferent to differences'* and *'the same for all'*, then isn't it the case that truth returns the subject to the same old hierarchy of differences, thus limiting his or her potential to become other than what society would ordinarily prefer him or her to be? The suspicion is certainly strong that Badiou's faith in a redemptive side to humanity, presumably in need of 'something rather than nothing', might just as well be the cause, rather than the effect, of nihilism. However, let us accept that humanity is capable of inhabiting, from time to time, the 'best' of both worlds: the world of cultural relativism with its ethics of difference and infinite respect for the other on the one hand, and Badiou's ethics of truths (political, scientific, artistic and amorous) on the other. We must also aim to distinguish the latter from the ethics of economic necessity (consumer politics), along with a far more sinister effect of nihilism: 'bio-ethics'.

The campaigners for euthanasia aim to attain legal recognition for the right to a 'dignified end' to the lives of terminally ill patients. However, as Badiou notes, this campaign is highly dubious in employing categories of human dignity in order to define suffering, as well as disastrous in seeking to enshrine the right to life in laws which would ultimately rest in the hands of the State. It was, after all, the Nazis who last legislated, with horrific consequences, for the health of the nation to be protected from the unnecessary suffering said to emanate from the *un*dignified presence of other races (E, 33–6).

The Good Life

Clearly, then, these *subtractions* from ethics exclude all the usual founding assumptions about the human being as the possessor of certain inalienable rights. Any such rights merely amount to the right *not to be* (offended, mistreated, threatened, tortured, etc.). With Badiou, this standard conception of right is clearly nothing of the kind, and depends rather on the *lack* of an infinite set of particular rights. Ethics must therefore begin, not with abstractions which would seek to distinguish between primary and secondary rights, but from the concrete demands of any given situation. Following the Hegelian and Maoist models, then: from the particular to the universal. There is also a debt to Spinoza in Badiou's approach to ethics, since if the 'human animal' is 'convened by circumstances to *become* subject', 'to enter into the composition of a subject' (E, 37), then it also enters the realm of freedom (*libera*) and necessity where a thing acts according to the force of its very own reason.[6] However, for Badiou the circumstances of becoming are not ultimately the circumstances of the ordinary, everyday world (what Spinoza calls 'nature'). The subject – which ordinarily is not – in order to surpass itself (its indifferent nature) in becoming what it is, must harness the historical supplement of the truth-event (E, 38). Henceforth, for the duration of its existence (in this new realm of being), the subject is compelled to think or act (it's the same thing now) in a way which is *unique* to the (new) situation where it finds itself. As we have already seen, this procedure where, in a set of historical circumstances, the subject manages to rally selflessly to the enterprise of truth is called 'fidelity'. Singularity, therefore, is where ethics must begin, since ethics always involves the new emergence of a subject (E, 38–40). Finally, the consensus surrounding what is or is not, does or does not involve ethics, can have no part of and gain no access to truth. Ethics is a construction, must be constructed, in the here and now. It is not concerned with founding a universal law of human conduct, and so takes no account of the possible negative consequences that a given set of principles may inadvertently unleash.

But we must be wary here. For if humanity is ordinarily indifferent to this seemingly higher project and simply makes do with 'what goes on' in the world, then couldn't it all too easily be claimed that Evil, when and where it occurs, is simply a *natural consequence* of ethics? Badiou anticipates the problem, responding that Evil is itself 'a possible dimension of truths', not their absence. Evil 'arises as the *(possible) effect of Good itself* (E, 54). There are, as we have already seen, historical events which rely upon the absolute transcendence of a given social reality. The Nazi State's extermination of the Jews provides us with an illustration of what Badiou names 'radical Evil' in this regard. However, as Badiou is equally quick to point out, this radical Evil, in being transcendent, is only an approximate indication (void in itself) of the Nazi exterminations, and as such one which has led down the years to a host of misleading comparisons from politicians and media-mongers alike (Hitler periodically reincarnated as Nasser of Egypt, Saddam Hussein, Slobodan Milosevic ...) (E, 56). But the equation is in fact far more complex. Evil must be *understood* ethically, i.e. as a singular historical construction, rather than as the perennial return of something which is naturally bad. It was, after all, arguably the insidious and blind appeal of Nazi ideology during the war which succeeded in representing its doctrine of mass extermination in terms of essentialism, i.e. as a 'necessary' Evil. Not only does such a consensual approach to Evil threaten to elevate a historical event to the Absolute, it also threatens to make us immune to Evil's singular ability to transform itself anew, perhaps in appearing to be something other than what it was in the past.

So-called 'radical evil' does not exist (E, 57). What we must accept instead is that human beings, in the course of pursuing their natural interests, are sometimes seduced by circumstances which appear to be true, *formally* obeying all the protocols of the truth-event, but which in the end turn out to have been based on deception. This is straightforward enough and all very well. However, it provides no account whatsoever of how to avoid the practical indifference of a community towards Evil and its passive participation in disaster.

Badiou sketches out his theory of ethical practice as follows. Firstly, every event is historically punctuated by the void, which fastens the event to its past. In the case of Marx's politics the name 'proletariat' performs this axial and invariant function, around which all the political struggles of the time circulate, and whose effective mobilisation depends upon the ability of the name to spring a subject into action. Secondly, in terms of fidelity, we must bear in mind that *the attachment of a subject to its name is never inevitable* (E, 62). Badiou remarks that the genuine militant displays a 'disinterested-interest'[7] in truth. The genuine militant, whose pursuit of truth is uncertain at every stage, is one who manages to avoid converting belief into a religion. Even atheism, in the hands of

Hitler most notoriously, eventually becomes a religious dogma with a potentially terrifying set of rites and rituals. The goal of the genuine militant, therefore, is actively *not* to surrender to any particular desire. Finally there is the question of how, during the course of the fidelity procedure, truth is able to inform the subject's progress. For Badiou, truth is opposed to opinions and communicates nothing. However, *a* truth can be *forced* to be truthful by compelling the subject to subtract truth from the future anterior of a situation to come, thereby rearranging the very fabric of common sense. This is what sometimes takes the form of 'progress' (E, 62).

Here, then, we have the Evil variants of Good, understood as the dialectical momentum of the process of truth itself, in three stages: 1) the *event* which denies the void and tends towards 'terror' or 'simulacrum'; 2) the *fidelity* which passively yields to its desire in an act of 'betrayal'; and 3) the totalitarian accession of *truth* to the point of 'disaster' (E, 63). For the militant practitioner of ethics (and for Badiou there can be no other kind), given the fact that Evil remains immanent to Good – a simulacrum as it were – Good must not be regarded as the mere avoidance of Evil. The only means of truly avoiding Evil, so to speak – particularly given the fact that every truth, as well as being undecidable, is also indiscernible and unnameable – is to (attempt to) appreciate the perils of not standing up to it. The act of the informed decision (or perception) is naturally perilous here and risks regression (although of course there are always risks ...). For given the ethical practitioner's uncertain attachment to the event, we might say that the subject is forced to find out for itself, *this side of* (rather than beyond) Good and Evil, what ethics is (E, 75). In this sense, finally, 'The Good is Good only inasmuch as it doesn't pretend to render the world good.' The notebooks on ethics are not a bible, nor must they be read as one.

In highlighting the constitutive political dimension to ethics, Badiou's *Ethics* avoids lapsing into the kind of abstract moral reasoning which tends – in the 'analytic' tradition – to distort the field of enquiry. No longer is it a question of what the individual would do in some ideal world with adequate time for reflection. Instead, for Badiou ethics becomes a question of being catapulted into the here and now, and of following through the consequences of a decision – which is always already decided – to the limit, as far as the ethical practitioner has it within his or her power to go. Politics in this sense intervenes in a situation, thereby transforming the very object of the enquiry, before facing up to the consequences of its actions. Ethics, from this militant standpoint, cannot take an effective back seat when it comes to determining what is right (unlike the journalist who claims to enable the facts to 'speak for themselves'). Of course, the question which we have been dealing with here all along involves the *ambivalence* which returns to afflict the ethical practitioner in the service of truth, in any one of its four realms, although politics is the one which will continue to interest us for the remainder of this book.

The Police

There can be little doubting the virtuosity of Badiou's ethico-political impulse. However, we must acknowledge the problem which threatens to undermine this militant project. The problem with politics today would appear to involve the precise *meaning* of popular dissent and whether what passes under the banner of 'politics' can be generically defined. Unquestionably devalued in the popular imagination, what does 'politics' actually mean today? To begin with, the rather abstract question of 'meaning' is not one which features so prominently in Badiou's work (it doesn't really feature at all). Can we assume, therefore, that when Badiou speaks about politics he is, in a certain sense, counting for its absence, ruminating on its loss, or at least its virtual ineffectiveness in the present? Moreover, is there a sense here in which the politics of truth is not only inescapably idealist, precisely given the political impoverishment which Badiou describes, but also *non-democratic*, since it rests on certain axiomatic assumptions about a (non-)community (e.g. the 'disinterested-interest' of the militant) which satisfy the interests of 'no One', the unrepresentable? We accept that truth is anti-statist. However, it remains less clear why the people's disenchantment with the prevailing affairs of State would make them want to affirm any precarious situation which threatens the status quo and merely prolongs its uncertainty.

Here I have provided a summary account of the hypothesis of the former Althusserian, Jacques Rancière (most famous in English for *The Lesson of Althusser* (1974)), which appears in his book *La Mésentente* (*Dissension*) (1995). Although not aimed at Badiou by name, he is clearly the implied target of Rancière's critique, still unjustifiably Platonist, and responsible in Rancière's estimation for upholding a misplaced distinction between philosophy and politics which is untenable. For Rancière the key distinction instead lies between 'real politics', or politics as it actually exists, and politics as defined by philosophers like Badiou, which is politics as philosophy prefers to imagine it (politics as the democratic illusion of the Greek *polis*).[8] For Rancière, politics actually concerns inequality or injustice, and raises the cry, not of right, but of a situation which is fundamentally 'wrong'.[9] Politics exists, or will be set to work, at the moment when the gulf 'appears' which marks the inequality between the haves and have-nots. For Badiou the generic part of society which voices this claim for universal equality was, in a preceding epoch, named 'proletariat'. Today, the fact that this name no longer functions as the rallying point for a set of political demands signals 'the cessation of politics tied to this name' (AM, 130). But it also marks the cessation of something altogether more decisive. If we assume that the name is the *transitional* bearer of a political project, then why should we assume that it performs anything more than a socially (re)integrative function? From ancient Greece to the present day, history is overcrowded with political movements which the State or state of the situation (Rancière prefers the term 'police') could not count as one. These are the parts without a whole, or 'parts of no part' as Rancière prefers to call them, which do not advance a rival political manifesto, but which demand inclusion *within* the existing (albeit imaginary) status quo. In these terms, the law of the State is not so much punctuated by revolutionary uprisings which threaten its legitimacy as by demands for more effective representation on behalf of marginalised groups. Far less a case, then, of calls for radical change than of calls for things to return to normal.

Here, right does not stand for justice, since justice in its militant exercise depends on the militant hole-piercing of consensus, and a real split in the fabric of common sense. Indeed, we can go further, it seems, and propose that right has today become synonymous with a movement to raise the stakes of consensus, to accelerate the 'constantly moving equilibrium' of social hegemony, which is by no means guaranteed to distinguish right from wrong. On the stage of capital-parliamentarism right is simply a situation which must, at any price, be 'put right'. And whatever the objective merits of a particular call for social justice (from direct action against racism to the anti-fuel-tax lobby), order (which is always ruled by the police) is the only universal condition.

The invariants of social justice would no longer appear to be able to operate in the way they used to, since the frequency of social 'crises' and the ubiquity of injustice now make politics amenable to the interests of everyone and no one. Politics is today 'without name'. Rancière illustrates this fact by noting the replacement in French political discourse of the word 'proletarian' with that of 'immigrant', and the National Front's accompanying seizure of the ethico-political ground from the PCF. According to Rancière, this perverse development puts an end to any lingering hope of a politics of emancipation. The name is no longer the badge of a revolutionary struggle in the making as it once was, but simply the measure of widespread political disenfranchisement. However, Badiou remains largely unimpressed by the tone of Rancière's critique, highlighting his confusion over the true relation between philosophy and real politics. Real politics, Badiou argues, cannot be accurately gauged in the 'political philosophy' of intellectuals. Instead, the relation is reversed: it is real politics which *conditions* philosophy (AM, 134). The myth of the philosopher-king as some remote pioneer of thought who hands down directives to activists from on high is a familiar one. However, such a cliché ignores the degree to which philosophy is itself a political 'work'. Accepting that real politics is unadjusted to the capital-parliamentary settlement and its moral guardians (several liberal intellectuals spring to mind here[10]) permits us to recover the principle of the philosopher-militant: namely, that politics always crops up where the State 'is not', at the point where a norm collapses.

Elsewhere Badiou elaborates this thesis further, suggesting in the light of the so-called 'death of communism' that 'If there is no event, it's a question of the history of States, and in no way of the history of politics' (DO, 21). The suture of communism to the Soviet experience gave communism a bad name, or rather continues to deprive it of a (new) name in the present. However, despite this fact, the living proof of communism's vitality is found in the huge and ongoing efforts of States to defend the 'free world' against the return of this untimely spectre (this project extends considerably further back in history than McCarthyism, and is as ancient as communism itself). What more evidence is required of communism's living potential than the appropriation (rather than the defeat which Rancière imagines) of its politics of emancipation towards all manner of reactionary ends (nationalism, the rights of the sovereign State, globalisation, etc.). There is an abject normality to politics today. But this is nothing more than the temporary suspension of the historical process, where cries of wrong are predictably interpreted as calls for justice. What is crucial to recognise in the meantime, however, is that the mistaken idea of democracy in the present is merely the non-being of all democracy to come.

Aporias

Can we regard the 'historical repression' of the communist impulse, as described above, as evidence of what is historically repressed, i.e. actually existing communism? Or does this 'repressive' history instead imply a far more ambivalent future for communism? Badiou's philosophy is founded on the concept of separation, and specifically the original separation of philosophy and mathematical ontology. As we have seen, Badiou develops an ontological theory of the State where democracy is realised in a historical moment where the rule of law becomes suspended by the will of the people. This is, we might add now, an antithetical theory of society where power is vested in the State's authority to count as one its citizens, which it exerts against the threatened overthrow of this authority. The suspicion remains, however, that this dialectic of State/non-State fails to account adequately for the historical repression of a natural impulse among the people (for democracy, say), but invokes instead the *contradictory desires of the masses*, desires which are merely synonymous with their own essential vitality. We should already be aware that Badiou's concept of the event is ambivalent in the sense that its subjects are never in a position to decide whether an event actually happened (in the way they would have planned) or not. What we need to explore further in this case is the degree to which such (in)decision promotes a host of other uncertainties about the constitution of a people, none of which can be resolved historically.

The idea that history is bound up with – rather than intervening in – the life of the State is an idea drawn, thanks to several expert readings, from the writings of Spinoza. Of these, Étienne Balibar follows a particular trend in reading Spinoza's three core texts – the *Ethics*, the *Tractatus Politicus*, and the *Tractatus Theologico-Politicus* – together as one work. Balibar's contention is that any move to interpret these works in isolation, or as distinct phases in Spinoza's thought, would be to negate the historical and political conjuncture in which they were first conceived, and whose concrete dilemmas they continue to reflect. According to Balibar we can formulate three 'problems' in and around Spinoza's anthropology, which distinguish his work from that of his successors: sociability, obedience and communication. What has also been referred to as the 'savage anomaly' of Spinoza's thought[11] we detect in the stark singularity of a thinker who remains out of step with the history of philosophy. What Spinoza attempts to bring together is philosophy and politics as eternal expressions of human nature. But how does Spinoza manage to succeed in bringing about such an antagonistic synthesis?

In the case of sociability, Balibar notes that the antithetical form of social institutions versus human nature relies on two alternative demonstrations of Spinoza's founding principle of the City.[12] On the one hand, man acquires freedom through the rational means of friendship and association with other men; while on the other, man is subject to certain passions which vary these relations and threaten to drive men apart. The key is not to view these alternative demonstrations as proof of an antithetical rivalry between the State of reason and the State of nature, but rather to view them as two means of securing the same social bond. In other words it follows that we might just as well arrive at the (State) foundation of Good and Evil through fear as through reason.[13] In the case of obedience, Spinoza demonstrates the extent to which our 'conventional' way of viewing the supposed constraints imposed on human freedom is, in any given context, governed by the 'affective complex' (love and hate, fear and hope, etc.) of individuality.[14] We could highlight in this respect the prevailing ideology at work in Western liberal democracies as one which views the State as an excessive authority whose power over private rights and freedoms must be constantly held in check. However, this 'democratic' ideal, itself responsible for a host of 'revolutionary' political alternatives (Marxism among them), might equally turn out to be founded on entirely imaginary conceptions of the common good. Indeed, one could argue in this sense that Western liberal ideology consistently underestimates the need for laws to regulate civil obedience, which in turn (today at least) guarantee private rights and freedoms.

Balibar draws the lesson from Spinoza's texts that democracy is ambivalent in terms of its relation towards Good and Evil. Clearly this disputes the idea of a natural impulse (e.g. for equality) which struggles for expression in the people. Instead, Balibar introduces the notion of 'equaliberty' in order to cover both equality as well as the far more problematic idea of freedom which, in his view, unite in every struggle over democracy.[15] In support of his thesis, Balibar sets to work what he regards as Spinoza's highly ambiguous concept of the masses (*multitudo*). Social struggles convened in this context will have the task of constructing a viable civic space where their competing agendas can be articulated. The overriding concept here is communication, although it is, on closer inspection, profoundly aporetic. For:

> How can one produce a *consensus*, not just in the sense of the communication of pre-existing opinions, but above all as the condition of the creation of *communicable opinions* (that is, opinions which are not mutually exclusive)?[16]

The masses provide the very medium of communication, although this does not rest on a principle of democracy *a priori* (none could be drawn up in advance), but on a *process of democratisation* (a 'becoming-democratic' so to speak). A rational form of communication, one which is more likely to expand the 'publicity' of the State, is one where an ever-increasing diversity of opinion becomes possible, while at the same time limiting the potential for any distortion of views.[17] Although Spinoza's concept of the masses is aporetic, Balibar uses the aporia to propose a form of consensus-based democracy where the greatest number of opinions have the potential to become actualised, based not on the assumption that the greatest number are more likely to be 'right', but that they pose the least threat of ever being 'wrong'. The Internet and its accompanying communications media are clearly the most striking candidates for this huge executive power. What Balibar provides us with here, then, is a theory of communication and a theory of State security (or hegemony) rolled into one. Since the masses are historically prone to inspire fear in their leaders, as well as fearing themselves in relation to what, as a body, they are capable of doing, the solution would appear to lie in bringing the two (a purely imaginary distinction, although no less effective in this sense) into ever greater proximity.

How does Balibar's theory of the State constitution stand alongside Badiou's, and can we find any key areas of mutual agreement between these two ex-'Althusserians'? The most general area of difference involves Balibar's 'aporetic' approach to the question of the masses. Balibar refuses to see any principle underlying the masses' conduct, since the latter are synonymous with the power of the State. Badiou, on the other hand, regards the masses (ideally) as the bearers of the category of justice, to which the State remains indifferent (AM, 114). Two divergent theories of the State, then, each of which is placed in the service of a distinctive ethics. With Balibar we have an ethics – or 'ethic' in the sense of *praxis* – of communication which encourages a dynamic and expanding equilibrium of desires where every opinion has an equal chance of counting in the democratic sphere. With Badiou we have an ethics of truths which hunts down those exceptional political statements in order to subtract from them their egalitarian core, thereby striking a blow for justice against the passive democracy of the State. Overall we might say that the general area of agreement lies in the fact that, in each case, 'democracy' remains a rational possibility. In particular, for both Balibar and Badiou, it is *love* as an amorous feeling towards or encounter with one's fellow man – a recognition that the fraternal part that is held in common between human beings is somehow 'greater' than the whole of their differences – which forges the social bond. However, on the precise nature of the ratio of this bond their respective paths diverge somewhat. In Balibar's case we are dealing with an *objective illusion* wherein one *imagines* that the love one feels for an object (an abstract egalitarian ideal, say) is shared by others. Crucially, love in this sense is wholly ambivalent, wildly vacillating between itself and its inherent opposite, hate.[18] On this evidence we might say that a 'communist' peace would be really indistinct from a 'fascist' one. Therefore, the challenge for Balibar is to construct a prescriptive political framework capable of operating without repression in a utilitarian public sphere where the free exchange of opinions is more likely than not to result in the self-limitation of extreme views.

In Badiou's case what we are dealing with, on the other hand – and what we have been dealing with more or less consistently throughout this book – is a *subjective reality*. The social contract is forever being conditioned, worked on practically from within by the political militants, in readiness for the occurrence of the truth-event. This is the unforeseen moment of an 'amorous encounter' between two natural adversaries (a group of students mounting a boycott of university fees, for instance) which retrieves the latent communist axiom of equality from within the social process. Here we have a particular call for social justice ('free education for all!') which strikes a chord with the whole people (students and non-students alike). Crucially, love in this sense is *infinite*, de-finite, in seizing back (at least a part of) the State power directly into the hands of the people. Moreover, in this encounter between students and the university authorities there is an invariant connection (of communist hope) which is shared by all, and where any difference of opinion is purely incidental. Momentarily, at least.

For Badiou, the challenge is to develop and deepen an ethical practice, not in any utilitarian or communitarian sense – since the latter would merely risk 'forcing' a political manifesto prematurely, perhaps giving rise to various brands of State-sponsored populism[19] – but in the sense of a politics capable of *combating repression*; a politics which, in its extreme singularity, holds itself open to seizure by Truth.

Appendix
Some Basic Principles
of Set Theory

I remarked in the Introduction that the reader need not be put off by the fact that Badiou's philosophy is raised on mathematical foundations. The information which follows should therefore not be regarded as essential reading, but rather as a useful supplement to the main text, in particular Chapters 2, 3 and 4 on *Being and the Event*. My aim here is to familiarise the reader with the *problematic* of set theory, its axioms and symbols, rather than take the reader through a series of rigorous exercises and complex mathematical proofs. That being said, I would recommend the next few pages to those readers who wish to get the most out of the main text.

The history of set theory can be divided, somewhat simplistically for our purposes, into two phases. First there was the founding research of Georg Cantor *et al.*, followed by set theory's 'post-Cantorian' axiomatisation. The Zermelo-Fraenkel axioms, devised by Ernst Zermelo and Abraham Fraenkel, present the formal system (ZF) which comprises modern set theory. There are eight (or nine; see below) axioms in all, and together they allow for the construction of the ordinal and cardinal number systems. Of course, the idea that these systems need to be 'constructed' often strikes non-mathematicians as rather odd. Surely numbers just exist!

A useful analogy is provided by the young child in the initial stages of learning to count. At first unsure of the ordering principle which dictates that 1 is the first ordinal number, 2 the second, etc., in time he manages to abstract the concept of what makes an ordinal number, and is able to apply it in basic arithmetic. Set theory, like the rules which govern the child's counting, is the foundation of mathematics. It enables us to put the concept of number on a sure and sound footing.

What Makes a Set?

Intuitively we can say that a set is any collection of objects. What the objects are is immaterial. All that matters is that their overall classification, or 'counting as one', results in a distinct entity, i.e. *a* set.

For example, suppose we wish to indicate that the object α is a member (or 'element' in Badiou's jargon) of the set β. In this case we employ the symbol $\in$ in order to express the set membership, or belonging, of α to β. Thus,

$$\alpha \in \beta$$

which reads 'α belongs to β'.

Where α does not belong to β we may write

$$\alpha \notin \beta$$

although there are many different ways of expressing the same relation in symbols.

The fundamental point to bear in mind here is that the relation of belonging, or set membership, is the only legitimate ontological relation in set theory (apart from the relation of equality ($=$)). It is an object's belonging (or not as the case may be) to a set which provides the foundations of the entire lexicon of mathematics, including Badiou's ontology. It is crucial not to confuse belonging itself ($\in$), the founding relation of ontology, with the logical symbols which enable us to perform operations on sets, such as $\rightarrow$ (implication), $\neg$ (negation), and $\leftrightarrow$ (equivalence). (This is not meant as an exhaustive list.) Armed with the concepts of *set*, *relation*, *symbol* and *operation* we can now go about constructing more sophisticated principles (I will not say axioms at this stage).

For instance, suppose we have two sets γ and η. These two sets will be identical if all the objects of γ also belong to η. Otherwise put, γ will equal η if and only if the objects in γ are equivalent to the objects in η.

This may be written thus,

$$\gamma = \eta \leftrightarrow (x \in \gamma) \leftrightarrow (x \in \eta).$$

Given also the fact that the identity of x, which stands for the objects of γ and η, will determine whether or not γ and η are equal, we can further modify the above equation with the aid of the universal quantifier, the symbol $\forall$, thus,

$$\gamma = \eta \leftrightarrow \forall x \, [(x \in \gamma) \leftrightarrow (x \in \eta)].$$

With the introduction of this new symbol our equation now reads 'γ equals η if and only if for every x its membership of γ is equivalent to its membership of η'. Here we can see the disparity between equality and equivalence, for it soon becomes clear that the two sets γ and η need not be equal in order to be equivalent, since the individual identities of their objects is irrelevant to their membership of sets γ and η. Where two sets are not equal but share certain elements in common we say that a given set is a subset of another, which is written with the aid of the symbol $\subset$, thus,

$$\gamma \subset \eta.$$

By now at least two things should be clear. First of all, as was noted at the beginning, the identity of the objects which comprise a set is irrelevant in set theory. The only condition is that these 'objects' can be counted and ordered into sets, i.e. collections which can be counted as one. However, that being the case it must follow that a given set of objects could also include a set of sets, since sets are simply *collections* with no immediate relation to the individual identities of the objects they supposedly contain. This leads to our second inference, which is that set theory can just as easily build sets from its own axioms as it can from independently existing objects, and this is indeed what set theory does. One of the 'objects' of set theory is set theory itself, along with the presentation of its axiomatic framework. The notion of set always has to be *made*.

If the existence of all sets – and hence all sets of numbers – depends on the speculative possibility of being able to construct a single set, then, as abstract as this idea may appear at first, we can at least begin from 'nothing', which in set theory terms is the empty or null set, ϕ. The existence of the empty set is crucial for set theory. Like the invention of the mathematical zero in arithmetic, the empty set enables us to construct the ordinal number system. For example, let the null set ϕ equal the first ordinal thus,

$$\phi = 0.$$

We can denote the second ordinal as follows

$$\{\phi\} = 1.$$

and the third

$$\{\phi, \{\phi\}\} = 2$$

and the fourth

$$\{\phi, \{\phi\}, \{\{\phi\}\}\} = 3$$

and so on.

However, we must pause for a moment in order to consider what this type of operation tells us about the ordinal number system. Let us assume that each set on the above 'scale' is a subset of its immediate successor, thus,

$$\phi \subset \{\phi\} \subset \{\phi, \{\phi\}\} \subset \{\phi, \{\phi\}, \{\{\phi\}\}\}...$$

or in equivalent terms,

$$\phi < \{\phi\} < \{\phi, \{\phi\}\} < \{\phi, \{\phi\}, \{\{\phi\}\}\}...$$

It follows from this that in order to denote a well-ordered system of ordinals we must be able to determine a greatest element, or 'limit ordinal', at some point on the scale. At the precise point where our determination succeeds we would have a system of *finite* ordinals. Note, however, that our ability to count out the ordinals from 0 will hinge on the determination of a set which is 'less than' the last (limit) ordinal on the scale. This is what set theorists refer to as the 'power set', and Badiou as the 'set of subsets', and is written $p(\alpha)$.

But what if, having tracked down a limit ordinal, such a finite scale of measure is in fact established? We are drawing ever nearer to the heart of Cantor's conjecture. Assuming we can prove the existence of a limit ordinal, ω, it then becomes possible to find its successor, $\omega + 1$, which logically must turn out to be the first infinite number or cardinal (Badiou writes this as ω_0). From here it is hypothetically possible to generate and add together infinite *sequences* of infinite numbers, or 'transfinite' numbers: $\aleph_0, \aleph_1, \aleph_2,$ etc.

Zermelo-Fraenkel Set Theory (ZF)

But what *is* an infinite number? And doesn't the above operation inevitably result in the relegation of the question of infinity *per se* to the level of a logical puzzle with pre-established rules governing the manipulation of set theory symbols? This familiar prejudice is based on the somewhat naïve assumption that infinity is somehow 'definable'. In countering this prejudice we must remind ourselves that Cantor's initial hypothesis is speculative in the sense that it confronts an ancient problem from the history of the philosophy (i.e. the nature of infinity), and wagers on being able to solve it in spite of the widely conflicting definitions and approaches to the problem which this history has produced. Not only is there no possibility of the 'nature of infinity' being solved in any definitive sense of the term, but any 'solution' already presumes the existence of a unitary and self-consistent language which is capable of solving it.

The axiomatisation of set theory as conducted by Zermelo and Fraenkel brings to an end any hope of solving the continuum problem, of bringing consistency to the unsolvable. On the contrary, it seeks to present the *in*consistency of the notion of infinity, and push back the limits of sense where the notion of a 'cumulative hierarchy of sets' is concerned. This is, at any rate, all that infinity could ever mean for a set theorist. For this purpose there are initially eight, and eventually nine, axioms, some of which we have been working with already. My aim here is simply to state them as simply as possible, occasionally adding examples and referring the reader to the appropriate chapter of the main text. Hopefully he or she will also begin to recognise their wider philosophical significance. The axioms are listed in alphabetical order.

The Axiom of Extensionality

By far the most basic axiom, the axiom of extensionality, states that two sets are equal if they have the same elements:

$$\alpha = \beta \leftrightarrow \forall x\,[(x \in \alpha) \leftrightarrow (x \in \beta)].$$

See Chapter 4.

The Axiom of Foundation

If α is a non-empty set then this set possesses an element x whose intersection ($\cap$) with that same set is void:

$(x \in \alpha) \leftrightarrow (x \cap \alpha = \phi).$

This axiom prohibits thought of the event, which can only be approached on the edge of the void.

See Chapter 3.

The Axiom of Infinity

This axiom facilitates the leap into the transfinite. There is a set α to which nothing belongs which implies the existence of a limit ordinal. Since the axiom of infinity affirms the existence of at least one set, i.e. the null set, we can take that set as the first infinite number:

$(\phi \in \alpha \rightarrow \{\phi\}) \leftrightarrow \omega.$

See Chapter 4.

The Axiom of Replacement

If α is a set then every element of α can be replaced thereby generating a new set α'.

The Axiom of Separation (The Axiom of Subset Selection)

Let α be a given set, and let $\phi(\beta)$ be a given formula in which the elements of α express themselves. It follows that there is a part of α consisting of elements which are separated by the formula ϕ.

As Badiou notes, 'This axiom indicates that being is anterior to language' (EE, 538). Since being must be presented or articulated as such, its being resides in the act of being 'separated' from itself.

See Chapter 2.

The Axiom of Subsets or Parts (The Power Set Axiom)

If α is a set then there exists a set $p(\alpha)$ which consists of all the subsets or parts of α.

See Chapter 4.

The Axiom of Union

If α is a set then there exists a set $\cup\alpha$ which consists of all the elements of elements of α.

The Axiom of the Void (The Null Set Axiom)

There is a set ϕ which has no elements.

See Chapter 3.

ZF with The Axiom of Choice (AC)

Where the axiom of choice is added to ZF we get ZFC. It is beyond the scope of this text to treat this axiom in any great detail. We need only be content with the fact that AC enables us to prove that every set can be well ordered. AC is thereby also needed in order to prove the existence of a cardinal set.

For every set α there exists a choice function f which chooses elements from this set thereby forming another set β. The latter is called a choice set for α, since its existence depends on its elements being chosen:

$$(\forall \alpha)\, (\exists f)\, [(\beta \in \alpha) \to f(\beta) \in \beta],$$

where $\exists$ is the existential quantifier.

In general, however, where α is infinite the existence of the choice set cannot be proved. It is this 'illegality' and 'anonymity', as Badiou puts it, that makes AC stand apart from all the other axioms of set theory, for unlike them AC affirms the *existence* of a set without being able to characterise any previously defined properties it may have had. Nevertheless, we assume that AC and the principle of well-ordered sets are equivalent, not least because there is no possibility of proving $\neg$ AC from ZF.

Notes and References

Introduction: The Unnameable

1. François Dosse, *History of Structuralism*, vol. 2, p. 112.
2. Under Althusser's direction the Philosophy Course for Scientists at the École Normale Supérieure lasted from November 1967 to May 1968. Some of the work from the course in various branches of Marxist philosophy was published in Althusser's *Théorie* series. Badiou's contribution, *The Concept of Model*, eventually appeared in 1969. See the following chapter.
3. See Badiou, *Contribution au problème de la construction d'un parti marxiste-léniniste de type nouveau*. This pamphlet lays out the preconditions for the foundation of the UCFML, exploring as it does the problem of legitimately laying claim to the title of 'party' – even 'union' – in the absence of a mass base.
4. See Michel Debeauvais (ed.), *L'Université ouverte*, pp. 271–2.
5. Badiou was by no means the sole adversary of the new philosophers. See for example Gilles Deleuze, 'Gilles Deleuze contre les nouveaux "philosophes"'.
6. Gilles Deleuze, *Spinoza et le problème de l'expression* (1968); Alexandre Matheron, *Individu et communauté chez Spinoza* (1969) and *Le Christ et le salut des ignorants chez Spinoza* (1971); Pierre Macherey, *Hegel ou Spinoza* (1979). Of these only the book by Deleuze has been translated into English, as *Expressionism in Philosophy: Spinoza* (1990).
7. A question which Nietzsche had responded to with a resounding 'No' in the previous century (in Book Three of *The Gay Science*). It is interesting to note in passing that Heidegger regarded Nietzsche as the last metaphysician – although still as 'a prisoner of metaphysics'; all the better, we might add, to characterise himself as the first authentic anti-metaphysician. See Joseph Vande Wiele, 'Heidegger et Nietzsche. Le problème de la métaphysique'.
8. Jacques Derrida, *Of Grammatology*, p. 4.
9. See Christopher Norris, 'On the Limits of "Undecidability": Quantum Physics, Deconstruction, and Anti-realism'.
10. For Lyotard, the postmodern condition is essentially a stage of capitalist society where the technocratic legitimation of knowledge paralyses any

wider emancipatory potential such knowledge may otherwise have. Lyotard, *The Postmodern Condition: A Report on Knowledge.*

11. Badiou admits four conditions of philosophy: art, politics, science and love.

12. Plato, *Republic*, 596a.

13. Hegel, *The Science of Logic*, p. 166.

14. A key term in Deleuze's philosophical vocabulary, adopted from Stoicism, used to describe time as the realm of the virtual present and of 'surface effects', opposed to *Chronos* as the order of the variable present and of the 'effects of bodies'. See Gilles Deleuze, *The Logic of Sense.*

15. Ibid., p. 165.

16. Badiou, 'Being by Numbers'.

17. Althusser, *Lenin and Philosophy and Other Essays*, p. 56.

18. Badiou, EE, 229: 'There are no heroes of the event.'

19. On the problem of 'purity' in Badiou see Juliette Simont, 'Le pur et l'impur'.

20. Ernesto Laclau and Chantal Mouffe, *Hegemony and Socialist Strategy: Toward a Radical Democratic Politics*, p. 176.

21. I have therefore adopted the capital letter when referring to the Lacanian 'Real'. See Chapter 2, note 3, for a fuller explanation of this Lacanian distinction.

22. '"Thinking and being are the same thing."' EE, 49.

23. As far as English philosophy of science is concerned Badiou would no doubt find support for such a position in the work of Michael Dummett. See Dummett, *Truth and Other Enigmas.*

24. The consistent axiomatic *presentation* of mathematical discourse – the 'presentation of presentation' – rather than the definitive resolution of the continuum hypothesis is Badiou's task in *Being and the Event.* In set theoretical terms we say that '[The continuum hypothesis] is a statement in the language of ZF about sets which can be proved to exist from the axioms of ZF.' Mary Tiles, *The Philosophy of Set Theory*, p. 136. For Badiou's statement of the necessity of the axiomatisation of set theory in the language of ZF see EE, 49–59.

25. See Kurt Gödel, 'What is Cantor's Continuum Problem?' in Benacerraf and Putnam (eds), *Philosophy of Mathematics*, p. 263.

26. See Gödel, ibid., not only for an indispensable account of Cantor's original hypothesis, but for a useful summary of subsequent research of the hypothesis up until 1964.

27. I have erred on the side of extreme caution, and invariably risked extreme oversimplification, when discussing mathematical definitions of the generic sets as they relate to the work of P. J. Cohen. In Cohen's terms a generic set is a set which is *not* constructible according to a given model of ZF, but nevertheless contains a finite amount of information which can be extended ('forced'), and therefore interpreted, in ZF. See Mary Tiles, *The Philosophy of Set Theory*, pp. 185–91.

28.   Here I take 'shorthand' very simply to mean a criteria-based under-standing of set theory axioms rather than an understanding based on their logical manipulation.

1. Maoist Beginnings

1.   *For Marx* and *Reading Capital* were originally published in 1965; *Reading Capital* as two volumes, the first co-authored by Louis Althusser, Jacques Rancière and Pierre Macherey, and the second by Althusser, Étienne Balibar and Roger Establet. 'Matérialisme historique et matérialisme dialectique' appeared in 1966 in *Cahiers marxistes-léninistes*, no. 11.
2.   Louis Althusser, 'What Must Change in the Party', p. 35.
3.   Although the phrase is attributable to Althusser, economic determina-tion 'in the last instance' is in actual fact drawn from Engels' letter to Bloch of 21 September 1890. See Althusser, *For Marx*, pp. 111–13.
4.   See Althusser, *Reading Capital*, pp. 183–4.
5.   This is the argument in Sartre's *Critique of Dialectical Reason*, vol. II. Needless to say the metaphor lacks the subtlety of Althusser's concept of an overdetermined historical conjuncture, where exploitation is a complex unity of economic, ideological, political and theoretical prac-tices articulated together.
6.   Richard Harland has observed more recently that Althusser's dispute with Hegel in fact amounts to a dispute with 'Sartre's slewed and selec-tive interpretation [of Hegel]'. Richard Harland, *Superstructuralism*, p. 93. As we shall see, Badiou stands virtually alone among contemporary French philosophers in permitting no significant break with the philos-ophy of Hegel.
7.   Althusser, *Lenin and Philosophy*, p. 18. Althusser's formulation of 'the class struggle in theory' today remains far from exhausted as a mani-festo in political philosophy. See Badiou, AM, 67–76.
8.   See in this respect Michèle Barrett, 'Althusser's Marx, Althusser's Lacan' in E. Ann Kaplan and Michael Sprinker (eds), *The Althusserian Legacy*.
9.   The point here is not that Althusser's famous essay was not political, or failed to register a political impact. It seems fair to say, however, that the essay's significance was and today remains somewhat 'overdeter-mined' by Althusser's subsequent self-criticisms and 'autobiographical' reflections, which are clearly symptomatic of more than just 'Marxist politics'.
10.   André Glucksmann, *La Cuisinière et le mangeur d'hommes* (1975).
11.   The term 'revisionism' is one which has attracted a host of supplemen-tary meanings and associations down the years, although in this context it is to be understood as any deviation from the true interpre-tation of the writings of Marx and Lenin.
12.   For an excellent account of Mao's 'guerrilla tactics' during the Cultural Revolution see Philip Short, *Mao: A Life*, esp. Chapter 15.

13. The translation of the French word *raison* causes problems here, since it conveys both the philosophical faculty of 'reason' as well as the more mundane sense of simply 'having reason' or, in English, 'being right'. Any Kantian application of 'reason' is strenuously opposed by Badiou at all times. However, the problem of rendering *raison* as 'right' is equally problematic due to Badiou's opposition to any philosophy of right in the Hegelian sense. As such I have rendered *raison* as 'correct' in this chapter, adhering to the Maoist sense in which a revolutionary subject must follow the correct party line.

14. Mao Tse-tung, 'On Contradiction' in *Selected Works*, vol. II.

15. See Althusser, *For Marx*, p. 94n. In fairness to Althusser the Chinese Cultural Revolution began the following year in 1966. See Althusser's essay of the same year, 'Sur la révolution culturelle'.

16. Such a reading is clearly based on comments made by Mao in 'On Contradiction' regarding the 'The metaphysical world outlook or the world outlook of vulgar evolutionism', p. 14. This is a disputable reading of metaphysics to say the least, particularly in light of more recent Marxist applications of metaphysics. See for instance Antonio Negri, *The Savage Anomaly: The Power of Spinoza's Metaphysics and Politics*.

17. Althusser, *Lenin and Philosophy*, p. 123.

18. Jacques Derrida, *Writing and Difference*; *Of Grammatology*; and *Speech and Phenomena*.

19. The term tends to be misleading as it was not used in France at the time, and conflates some quite diverse French philosophers and philosophies.

20. François Dosse, *History of Structuralism*, vol. 2, p. 22.

21. For a brief explanation of the new philosophers see the Introduction.

22. For a clear statement of Badiou's anti-syndicalism see Badiou, *Le mouvement ouvrier révolutionnaire contre le syndicalisme*.

23. See for instance André Glucksmann, *Les Maîtres Penseurs*.

24. For an impression of the type of cultural interventions pursued by Le Groupe Foudre, or 'Lightening Group', at the University of Vincennes see the chapter by Georges Lapassade in Michel Debeauvais (ed.), *L'Université ouverte*.

25. Michel Foucault, *Discipline and Punish. The Birth of the Prison*, especially parts three and four in this respect.

26. Michel Foucault, *The History of Sexuality*, vol. I.

27. We can agree on Foucault's behalf that the politicisation of human sexuality, or what for Deleuze and Guattari is the immediate investment of the socius with physic drives ('desire'), is accompanied by political effects which are in themselves ambivalent.

28. For a detailed historical account of Münzer see also Ernst Bloch, *The Principle of Hope*, vol. I.

29. Marx and Engels, 'Manifesto of the Communist Party' in *Selected Works*, pp. 60–1: 'The Communists fight for the attainment of the immediate

aims, for the enforcement of the monetary interests of the working class; but in the movement of the present, they also represent and take care of the future of that movement. In France the Communists ally themselves with the Social-Democrats, against the conservative and radical bourgeoisie ... In Switzerland they support the Radicals, without losing sight of the fact that this party consists of antagonistic elements ... In Poland they support the party that insists on an agrarian revolution ...', etc.

30. J. Hampden Jackson, *Marx, Proudhon and European Socialism*, pp. 75–7.
31. Sartre's famous historical example of a boxing match between *working class opponents* where the bourgeois audience is actually embroiled in the violent *spectacle* taking place in the ring can be found in Book III of *Critique of Dialectical Reason*, vol. II.
32. Badiou would, however, write a short pamphlet (*Jean-Paul Sartre*) as a tribute, which was published in 1980, the year of Sartre's death.
33. For more detailed historical background on Lin Biao and the Ninth Congress see Philip Short, *Mao: A Life*, Chapter 16.
34. The example is taken from Hegel's *Lectures on the History of Philosophy*.
35. Gilles Deleuze, *Difference and Repetition*, p. 8.

2. The Science of Being

1. See Félix Guattari, *Les Années d'hiver: 1980–1985*.
2. We must mention in passing Badiou's involvement, since 1984, with L'Organisation politique, a group which he co-founded with Sylvain Lazarus as a contribution to a new post-Leninist phase of political activism under the guiding principle of 'politics without party'. For a slightly more detailed account see Badiou, 'Philosophy and Politics'.
3. On this point I am being faithful to the distinction which Lacan makes between 'reality' and 'real', the former being 'perfectly knowable', the latter being the 'foreclosed element, which may be approached, but never grasped'. Lacan, *Écrits*, p. x. It is a key distinction which I have tried to observe in the main, although it is often glossed over by Lacanians, most notably in the work of Mikkel Borch-Jacobsen.
4. The question is from Leibniz, 'Principles of Nature and of Grace, Based on Reason' sec. 7, quoted in Nicholas Rescher, *G. W. Leibniz's Monadology*, p. 116.
5. John D. Barrow and Frank J. Tipler, *The Anthropic Cosmological Principle*, p. 32.
6. Martin Heidegger, *The Question Concerning Technology and Other Essays*, p. 165.
7. Friedrich Nietzsche, quoted in 'Introduction', *Thus Spoke Zarathustra*, p. 15.
8. It seems appropriate to mention Democritus as the main influence here. See Badiou, TS, 76–8. However, we must bear in mind first of all that

Badiou's atomism identifies the atoms as compositions *of* the void, rather than bodies which collide *in* the void. Furthermore, whereas with Democritus atoms (*a-toma*) were indivisible, with Badiou an atom can be split, as even the most rudimentary understanding of atomic physics will confirm. The infinite divisibility of atoms is also wholly consistent with Aristotle's predictions in the *Physics*. The decisive break comes with the arrival of Cantor. Following the latter, Badiou's theoretical physics holds that since atoms are merely compositions of the void, the void itself can also, in principle, be infinitely divided.

9. A status which Badiou certainly does *not* claim for his work, pointing out in his introduction to *Being and the Event* that the world is a 'phantasm'. It is science as discourse, rather than science devoted to unravelling the mysteries of the cosmos, which interests Badiou. EE, 14.

10. From a subjective point of view we say that presentation is always 'retroactively apprehended'. EE, 33. See also my Appendix on the axiom of separation.

11. Badiou will insist on subtracting the purely *material* status of a variable from its *nominal* status which, like 'Gustave Eiffel', is always mathematically reducible to a set of elementary constituent parts.

12. Whereas Saussure makes 'value' the conceptual component of signification, for Badiou a concept is thought without in any way 'defining the signification'. Cf. Saussure, *Course in General Linguistics*, p. 114; Badiou, EE, 95.

13. Benacerraf and Putnam (eds), *Philosophy of Mathematics*, p. 15. Also quoted in Badiou, CT, 95.

14. This is by no means the only possible interpretation, although favoured by Badiou. It seems fair to speculate that Badiou would certainly view the state of *aporia* induced in the slave-boy as a positive stage in the process of *anamnesis* ... For an excellent commentary on a wide range of interpretations of the *Meno* see also John E. Thomas, *Musings on the Meno*.

15. Unlike Chomsky's contention that the subject is divided between (inner or 'deep') *logical* and (outer or 'surface') *syntactic* structures of language. See also John E. Thomas in ibid., pp. 139–44.

16. That 'mathematical ideas' can be generalised to include both the geometrical structures that we find under discussion in the *Meno*, *and* numbers, is taken for granted by Badiou, since set theory makes no distinction between the various different types of mathematical objects.

17. See Stephen Hawking, *A Brief History of Time*.

18. Paul Bernays, 'On Platonism in Mathematics' in *Philosophy of Mathematics*, p. 284. Bernays does, however, qualify his point by saying that 'the duality of these two tendencies ... is not a perfect symmetry'.

19. Plato, *Parmenides*, 129c–d.

20. Ibid., 133.

21. Ibid., 141e.

22. Ibid., 160e–161.

23. Compare the concept of determination in this respect with Spinoza (*omnis determinatio est negatio*). See Badiou, CT, 73–93.

24. Mikkel Borch-Jacobsen, *Lacan. The Absolute Master*, p. 225.

25. Badiou regards Rousseau as a key philosophical antecedent of Lacan.

26. Borch-Jacobsen, *Lacan. The Absolute Master*, p. 105.

27. Unlike Lacan, for Badiou there is no question of a transcendental subject negating itself in order to affirm what it lacks. See Lacan, *Écrits*, pp. 164–5. Instead, the subject participates in truth during the course of what Badiou names a 'generic fidelity procedure'. The subject is a fragment of truth, or part of truth's essential fabric. See EE, 432–4.

28. Adopting the language of set theory we shall say that the subject is a finite part of a generic subset.

29. Kurt Gödel, 'What is Cantor's Continuum Problem?', p. 259.

30. The proof rests with the 'axiom of choice'. See Appendix.

31. That Cantor's continuum problem is, in Gödel's mind, in all likelihood 'undecidable' results from the fact that 'the difficulties of the problem are probably not purely mathematical'. Gödel, 'What is Cantor's Continuum Problem?', p. 263.

32. The Löwenheim-Skolem-Tarski theorem 'almost' succeeds in proving that a finite set of axioms will be absolutely true for all of ZFC (Zermelo-Fraenkel set theory), although significantly this cannot be proved completely in the language of ZFC. 'We do not actually have a formula of set theory which says of the set, M, that M is a model for ZFC.' We can verify this in turn with reference to Gödel's Incompleteness Theorem which enables us to prove the construction of a set M which satisfies 'all of ZFC', although 'this platonistic argument cannot be formulated within ZFC'. Kenneth Kunen, *Set Theory. An Introduction to Independence Proofs*, p. 134.

33. Badiou employs the generic doctrine of sets in order to overcome finitism. As we shall see, he wants to prove that truth is immanent to the situation, which means that the situation will, in principle, be infinite. See Chapter 4 for an explanation of how the generic, along with the mathematical idea of 'forcing', function together in EE.

34. See note 31.

35. An epistemological break of the type envisaged by Bachelard and famously adopted by Althusser would no doubt count as what Badiou names 'event'.

3. The Event of Non-Being

1. Cf. Deleuze and Guattari, *A Thousand Plateaus*, pp. 20–1: 'Arrive at the magic formula we all seek – PLURALISM = MONISM – via all the dualisms that are the enemy ...'; and Badiou, *Theory of the Subject*, p. 23: 'It is the Two which gives its concept to the One, not the inverse.'

2. Deleuze wonders whether the dialectic, as 'a genuine philosophy of difference', is 'simultaneously the measure of both Platonism and the possibility of overturning Platonism?' *Difference and Repetition*, p. 59.

3. Along with some important set theoretical qualifications regarding nature and infinity; EE, 161–79. See below.

4. At least two books which span the period in question – Deleuze's *Expressionism*, originally published in 1968, and Pierre Macherey's *Hegel ou Spinoza* (1979) – chart the range of re-evaluations of Spinoza's relation to Hegel which were under way in French philosophy at the time.

5. Engels, 'Feuerbach and the End of Classical German Philosophy' in Marx and Engels, *Selected Works*, p. 569.

6. Ibid., p. 587.

7. Ibid., p. 568.

8. See Louis Althusser, 'Contradiction and Overdetermination' in *For Marx*.

9. See *The Althusserian Legacy* for an account of the widespread influence of 'Althusserianism'.

10. Althusser's definition of philosophy was subsequently modified in *Lenin and Philosophy*, becoming 'the class struggle in theory'.

11. A fact which inclines Badiou in *Of Ideology* to label Althusser a 'revisionist'. An inspection of 'Contradiction and Overdetermination' in *For Marx* reveals numerous references to the '*simple concept* of contradiction' in Hegel, a 'simplicity', Althusser suggests – no doubt by way of excusing his own simplistic definition – which has 'answered to certain subjective necessities of the mobilization of the masses'; pp. 103–4.

12. Althusser, *For Marx*, p. 9.

13. Ibid., p. 145.

14. Ibid., p. 68.

15. See Badiou, 'Althusser: the subjective without subject' in AM.

16. See Althusser, 'Lenin before Hegel' in *Lenin and Philosophy*.

17. On this point Badiou draws attention to the declaration of Parmenides: '"Thinking and being are the same thing."' EE, 49.

18. Althusser and Balibar, *Reading Capital*, p. 42.

19. Nevertheless we should neither forget nor underestimate Althusser's lectures on science, *Philosophy and the Spontaneous Philosophy of the Scientists*, which were delivered in 1967 and published in the same *Théorie* series as Badiou's *The Concept of Model*.

20. Cf. *Reading Capital*, p. 40: 'the *difference* of the *concept* of object must be produced ...'; and Deleuze and Guattari, *What Is Philosophy?*, p. 2: 'philosophy is the art of forming, inventing, and fabricating concepts'. However, for Althusser there is nothing artistic about such production, since philosophy is the theory of scientific practice.

21. Althusser and Balibar, *Reading Capital*, p. 42.

22. Ibid., p. 47.

23. We recall Mao's comments on the universality of contradiction who, quoting Lenin, observes the 'mutually exclusive, opposite tendencies in all phenomena', which extends to the mathematical operations of '+ and –; differential and integral'. Mao Tse-tung, *Selected Works*, vol. II, p. 20.

24. Engels in Marx and Engels, *Selected Works*, p. 563.

25. Mao Tse-tung, *Selected Works*, p. 19.

26. Ibid., p. 25.

27. Tony Bennett, *Formalism and Marxism*, p. 70.

28. See Badiou, AM, 67: '... "Marxism" is the (void) name of an absolutely inconsistent set, since one submits it – as one must do – to the history of political singularities'.

29. Engels, 'Introduction to *Dialectics of Nature*' in Marx and Engels, *Selected Works*, p. 332.

30. In *Les mots et les choses* (1966) Foucault had already argued that man was the humanised product of modern scientific ('epistemic') knowledge.

31. Mikkel Borch-Jacobsen, *Lacan. The Absolute Master*, p. 182.

32. The idea that in order to name an event we must somehow cross the bar of being, or enter into the void of sense ('the defect of established significations'), can equally inspire an exercise no less poetic than mathematical, as we discover in the work of Mallarmé and Celan. See Badiou, 'Philosophy's appeal to the poem' in C, 100.

33. Cf. Heidegger, who raises the question of the ontological foundations of negation in *Being and Time*: 'Has anyone ever made a problem of the *ontological source* of notness, or, *prior to that*, even sought the mere *conditions* on the basis of which the problem of the "not" and its notness and the possibility of that notness can be raised?' 285–6. That nullity – void – requires a basis, even if 'this Being-the-basis is itself null' is *the* ontological proposition for Badiou.

34. Marx, *The Poverty of Philosophy*, p. 119.

35. Althusser, *Lenin and Philosophy*, p. 181.

36. Deleuze and Guattari, *A Thousand Plateaus*, pp. 431–2.

37. This is a summary account of Badiou's position in PP.

38. I am drawing here on Louis Althusser's reading of Lenin's 'theory' of the weakest link, which Althusser makes extensive use of in *For Marx*. It is worth quoting him at length. According to Althusser, politics in a given historical conjuncture (the '1917 Revolution') exists in a 'practical state', 'without feeling the need to make the theory of its own practice, the Theory of its "method". It may exist, survive and even progress without it; just like any other practice – until the moment in which its object (the existing world of the society that it is transforming) opposes enough resistance to it to *force* it to fill in this gap, to question and think its own method ... so as to produce ... the *new knowledges* corresponding to the content of the new "stages" of its development.' *For Marx*,

pp. 175–6. Empirical research of the type conducted by Lenin in essays and diary extracts on the course of the Russian Revolution can therefore be read, according to Althusser and – evidently following his lead – Badiou, as the experimental proofs of the underlying principles of science itself, whose *scientific* (not social!) reality such proofs support.

39. The context for Balibar's book *On the Dictatorship of the Proletariat* was the 22nd Congress of the French Communist Party which in 1976 declared that it was abandoning the principle of the dictatorship of the proletariat and would be removing the phrase from its constitution.

40. Étienne Balibar, *On the Dictatorship of the Proletariat*, p. 66, quoting Lenin.

41. When it comes to politics, Badiou had already refuted the idea of the class in-itself, having declared that 'if the process of the politics of emancipation has as its sole condition to be open from the point of the event, it is submitted to no predicative condition as to situations. "Worker" and "popular" are the traces of the old social substantialism, which pretended to deduce the politics of organisation from class society'. PP, 80.

42. Cf. Badiou, PP, 88, in which he admits no 'great taste for the proofs of the existence of the proletariat'. For Badiou, epistemological anti-realist that he is, it is politics as the principle of a 'heterogeneous political capacity', rather than as a fact of life, which is at stake.

43. Lenin, *The State and Revolution*, p. 103.

44. Badiou regularly remarks how he is 'inclined to think that the idea of the world is itself in the final analysis a phantasy'. 'Being by Numbers', p. 85.

45. Pascal, *Pensées*, VI, 110.

4. The Politics of Truth

1. Deleuze and Guattari, *What is Philosophy?*, p. 85.

2. See Appendix.

3. The concept of *'glissement'* was first introduced by Lacan to account for the floating signifier which, like the subject of the unconscious, has become unanchored from its signified meaning. See Lacan, 'The subversion of the subject and the dialectic of desire in the Freudian unconscious' in *Écrits*.

4. Pascal, *Pensées*, 418.

5. Barrow and Tipler, *The Anthropic Cosmological Principle*, pp. 444–9.

6. See Gödel, 'What is Cantor's Continuum Problem?', especially note 15.

7. Harold J. Laski, *Communism: 1381–1927*, p. 13.

8. 'Defiant' since as far as Cantor's continuum hypothesis is concerned, any 'contradiction' cannot ultimately be proved. This despite the fact that the work of Gödel establishes that CH cannot be disproved, and is

furthermore inherently undecidable according to ZFC axioms. On this point see also Devlin, *The Joy of Sets*, p. 93.

9. Voltaire's novel *Candide* is the most famous caricature of Leibniz's supposedly anti-empiricist world-view. However, the detail of Leibniz's life tells a rather different story. See Ishiguro, *Leibniz's Philosophy of Logic and Language*, especially the introduction to his life and times.

10. The three principal inheritors of Leibniz's project are Frege, Peano and Russell. See Kurt Gödel, 'Russell's Mathematical Logic' in *Philosophy of Mathematics*.

11. Ishiguro, *Leibniz's Philosophy*, pp. 37–9.

12. Ibid., p. 24.

13. For Badiou the difference between two terms is actually indiscernible, although not inexpressible. However, since there is no difference which cannot be expressed, the *true* identity of the terms in question cannot be decided by linguistic convention, but rather appears as whatever manages to subtract itself from language. With Leibniz, on the other hand, difference cannot be subtracted from language, since with him 'we are not absolutely constrained to decide between the state p and the state non-p, between which exist an infinity of intermediary states' CT, 132.

14. See Badiou, 'Being by Numbers', pp. 118, 123, for a passing comparison between his philosophy and Foucault's. In short, Badiou's absolutist definition of truth is opposed to Foucault's relativist approach to knowledge. Badiou, a Marxist, retains a largely undiluted faith in the idea of transition between situations which Foucault rejects.

15. Compare Badiou's criticisms of Leibniz on the question of limit to the presumed 'difference' on the same question between Leibniz and the French mathematician Antoine Cauchy: 'We have seen that Leibniz denied that infinitesimals were fixed magnitudes, and claimed that we were asserting the existence of variable finite magnitudes that we could choose as small as we wished. We could say that Cauchy claimed that limits existed whereas Leibniz wanted to say that they were a well-founded fiction. But is there a substantial difference between their claims? Very little, it seems to me. For both, the existence of a limit follows from the internal properties of the sequence itself.' Ishiguro, *Leibniz's Philosophy*, p. 92.

16. This is certainly the view of Deleuze, *The Fold: Leibniz and the Baroque*.

17. Mikkel Borch-Jacobsen, *Lacan. The Absolute Master*, p. 7.

18. Ibid., p. 136.

19. Ibid., p. 91.

20. Hegel, *The Phenomenology of Spirit*, §§772–4.

21. The fact that time is always the time of politics, art, science, and love during which time philosophy is *sutured* to its historical conditions of truth, amounts to a phase of subjective fulfilment – the 'pregnancy of sutures' – rather than one of lack. See Badiou, MP, 41–8.

22. Marshall Berman, citing Rousseau, in *All That Is Solid Melts Into Air*, p. 17. The book remains indispensable reading for any study of modernism.

23. Badiou avoids reference to 'political philosophy', preferring the term 'metapolitics'. Whereas political philosophy rests on the side of 'inactive judgement' and reflection among political commentators, Badiou regards metapolitics as the retention, in thought, of the pure political act.

24. Rousseau, *The Social Contract*, IV, ii.

25. Berman, *All That Is Solid Melts Into Air*, p. 19.

26. Rousseau, *The Social Contract*, IV, vi.

27. Cf. Badiou, 'On a Finally Objectless Subject' in Eduardo Cadava *et al.* (eds), *Who Comes After the Subject?*

28. Barrow and Tipler, *The Anthropic Cosmological Principle*, p. 652.

29. Rousseau, *The Social Contract*, I, vii.

30. For Badiou, the undecidable is any term which neither can or cannot be deduced from set theoretical axioms. Cantor's continuum hypothesis would on this basis be undecidable. See Badiou, EE, 548. See also Kurt Gödel, 'What is Cantor's Continuum Problem?', p. 263.

31. Albert Lautman, 'Symmetry and Dissymmetry in Mathematics and Physics' in F. Le Lionnais (ed.), *Great Currents of Mathematical Thought*, vol. I, p. 46.

5. The Cult of Deleuze

1. Deleuze, *Difference and Repetition*, p. 66.

2. Ibid., p. 35.

3. For Badiou's account of the 'and-or-neither' of Deleuze, see Badiou, CT, 61–72.

4. Deleuze, *Difference and Repetition*, p. xxi.

5. Deleuze, *Logic of Sense*.

6. Louis Althusser makes exactly the same point regarding the 'sense' of Marx's supposed 'inversion' of the Hegelian dialectic: 'But such an inversion in sense would in fact leave the dialectic untouched.' Louis Althusser, 'Contradiction and Overdetermination' in *For Marx*, p. 91.

7. Deleuze, *Logic of Sense*, p. 9: '... with the Stoics, humor found its dialectics, its dialectical principle or its natural place and its pure philosophical concept'.

8. Marx quoted in Francis Wheen, *Karl Marx*, p. 307.

9. Deleuze, *Difference and Repetition*, p. 162.

10. Ibid., p. 186.

11. See Deleuze, *Cinema 1: The Movement Image*.

12. The six texts are: *Difference and Repetition*; *Foucault*; *Cinema 1: The Movement Image*; *Cinema 2: The Time Image*; *Logic of Sense*; *The Fold*.

13. In *Being and the Event* the encounter, or 'Two', which takes place between the point of intervention and the operation of fidelity consists

in a generic procedure of truth. For Deleuze, truth cannot occur without the exertion of power, and any act of faith would certainly not remain 'disinterested' in upholding truth as Badiou believes. See below.

14. Deleuze and Guattari, *A Thousand Plateaus*, p. 355.
15. Ibid., p. 76.
16. Deleuze, *Nietzsche and Philosophy*, p. 95.
17. Deleuze, citing Nietzsche's *Untimely Meditations* in *Nietzsche and Philosophy*, p. 104.
18. Deleuze and Guattari, *What is Philosophy?*, pp. 118–19.
19. Ibid., p. 119.
20. Ibid., p. 150.
21. Ibid., p. 152.
22. Deleuze, *Bergsonism*, pp. 18ff.
23. Deleuze and Guattari, *A Thousand Plateaus*, p. 257.
24. Deleuze, *The Fold*, p. xvi.
25. Ibid., p. 4.
26. Ibid., p. 6.
27. Ibid., p. 53.
28. For Badiou's encounter with Leibniz on this question, see the previous chapter.
29. Deleuze, *The Fold*, p. 65.
30. Ibid., pp. 77–9.
31. Ibid., p. 34.
32. Félix Guattari, *The Three Ecologies*, p. 28. Guattari goes on to recommend the construction of a 'mental ecology' to accompany the social ecology which when brought together will have the potential to 'resingularize' the lives of subjugated groups; pp. 60–1.

6. The Ethics of Philosophy

1. André Glucksmann's *The Cook and the Maneater* (1975) was one of the first in a series of books published in France which announced a complete break with Marxism on the grounds that the latter had provided the totalitarian logic for the creation of the Nazi and Stalinist concentration camps. The book was illustrative of a wider return to ethics in French metaphysical philosophy during the 1970s which sought to recast the question of freedom and democracy in terms of individual self-understanding rather than in terms of the extension of the theoretical anti-humanism of Althusser's Marxist rationalism. As we have seen, Badiou can safely be regarded as the inheritor of the latter tradition. See also Dominique Lecourt, *The Mediocracy*.

2. Philippe Lacoue-Labarthe falls squarely into this category in attempting to separate the philosophical from the political aspects of Heidegger's alleged Nazism. His conclusion is that this must be posed in terms of '"Heidegger's thought"', since 'We are not talking about any old person

being politically compromised, about some teacher or other or party member so and so ... We are talking about the greatest thinker of our age.' Lacoue-Labarthe, *Heidegger, Art and Politics*, p. 135.

3. James Williams, *Lyotard. Towards a Postmodern Philosophy*, p. 119.
4. The liberal pragmatist's approach to ethics, which veers between deconstructive foundationalism and anti-foundationalism, is explored in Simon Critchley, Jacques Derrida, Ernesto Laclau and Richard Rorty, *Deconstruction and Pragmatism*.
5. See John Hospers' discussion of the categorical imperative in *An Introduction to Philosophical Analysis*, pp. 598–600.
6. Spinoza, *Ethics*, ID7.
7. What Rousseau also refers to as 'restrained action'. Cf. Badiou, AM, 118.
8. 'Modernity does not only put "subjective" rights in place of the objective rule of law. It invents right as *philosophical* principle of the *political* community [i.e. as the 'spirit of the law']. And this invention goes hand in hand with the story of origin, the story of the relation of individuals to the whole, told in order to liquidate the contentious relation of parts [which for Rancière are the 'parts of no part'].' Jacques Rancière, *La Mésentente*, p. 115.
9. 'For, in politics, it is not right which is founding but wrong, and that which can differentiate [*différencier*] a politics of the moderns from a politics of the ancients is a different structure of wrong.' Ibid.
10. Among them Richard Rorty and Anthony Giddens stand out. Rorty's liberal politics holds that calls for social justice, and acts of injustice, emerge from within a 'contingent community' of social interests where 'liberal hope and private irony' do battle for publicity. He is, in this respect, remarkably close to Rancière, especially when he writes that 'One can substitute for this [i.e. 'the idea that those who are alienated are people who are protesting in the name of humanity against arbitrary and inhuman social restrictions'] the idea that the poet and the revolutionary are protesting in the name of the society itself against those aspects of the society which are unfaithful to its own self-image.' *Contingency, Irony and Solidarity*, p. 60. For Giddens we might say that real politics has no place in the 'third way' pantheon of modernisation (essentially the capital regeneration) of civil society. For a short and decisive critique of Giddens, see Gregory Elliott, 'Via dollarosa. On the "Third Way"', pp. 2–5.
11. See Antonio Negri, *The Savage Anomaly*.
12. Étienne Balibar, *Spinoza and Politics*, pp. 80–3.
13. Ibid., p. 82.
14. Ibid., p. 91.
15. See Étienne Balibar, *Masses, Classes, Ideas*, pp. 39–59.
16. Balibar, *Spinoza and Politics*, p. 119.
17. Ibid., p. 121.
18. Ibid., p. 111.

19.   The concept of forcing and the question of its ethical application would appear to mark a dilemma for Badiou – one which he inherits from Rousseau – of how to direct a democratic movement when the will of the people is suspended. Its resolution involves the dialectic of Good/Evil, where the militant, on the brink of the void, polices the border of the event site, so preventing the descent into disaster. See also Badiou, E, 71–7.

Bibliography

Badiou's major writings are usually arranged by the author in chronological order under the following headings. Unless otherwise stated all references are to first editions. I have also included a further list of articles, interviews and reviews by Badiou which were also consulted during the writing of this book. I should point out that this second list is indicative only, and not exhaustive of available material.

1. Books by Alain Badiou
(* indicates shorter work or pamphlet)

Philosophy:

Le Concept de modèle (Paris: Maspero, 1969).
*Jean-Paul Sartre (Marseille: Potemkine, 1980).
Théorie du Sujet (Paris: Seuil, 1982).
Peut-on penser la politique? (Paris: Seuil, 1985).
L'Être et l'événement (Paris: Seuil, 1988).
Manifeste pour la philosophie (Paris: Seuil, 1989).
Le Nombre et les nombres (Paris: Seuil, 1990).
Conditions (Paris: Seuil, 1992).
L'Éthique (Paris: Hatier, 1993).
Deleuze. La clameur de l'être (Paris: Hachette, 1997).
Saint Paul. La fondation de l'universalisme (Paris: Presses Universitaires de France, 1997).
Abrégé de métapolitique (Paris: Seuil, 1998).
Petit manuel d'inesthétique (Paris: Seuil, 1998).
Court traité d'ontologie transitoire (Paris: Seuil, 1998).

Critical Essays:

Rhapsodie pour le théâtre (Paris: Imprimerie nationale, 1990).
Beckett. L'increvable désir (Paris: Hachette, 1995).

Literature and Theatre:

Almagestes (prose) (Paris: Seuil, 1964).
Portulans (novel) (Paris: Seuil, 1967).
L'écharpe rouge (opera) (Paris: Maspero, 1979).
Ahmed le subtil (farce) (Arles: Actes-Sud, 1994).
Ahmed philosophe, followed by *Ahmed se fâche* (theatre) (Arles: Actes-Sud, 1995).
Les Citrouilles (comedy) (Arles: Actes-Sud, 1995).
Calme bloc ici-bas (novel) (Paris: POL, 1997).

Political Essays:

*Contribution au problème de la construction d'un parti marxiste-leniniste de type nouveau in collaboration with H. Jancovici, D. Ménétrey and E. Terray (Paris: Maspero, 1969).
Théorie de la contradiction (Paris: Maspero, 1975).
De l'idéologie in collaboration with F. Balmès (Paris: Maspero, 1976).
*Le Mouvement ouvrier révolutionnaire contre le syndicalisme (Marseille: Potemkine, 1976).
Le Noyau rationnel de la dialectique hégélienne in collaboration with L. Mossot and J. Bellassen (Paris: Maspero, 1978).
*La 'contestation' dans le PCF (Marseille: Potemkine, 1978).
D'un désastre obscur (La Tour-d'Aigues: L'aube, 1998) (originally published in 1991).

English Translations to date:

Manifesto for Philosophy, trans. N. Madarasz (New York: SUNY, 1999).
Deleuze: The Clamor of Being, trans. L. Burchill (Minneapolis: University of Minnesota Press, 1999).
Ethics. An Essay on the Understanding of Evil, trans. P. Hallward (London: Verso, 2001).

2. Selected Articles, Interviews and Reviews by Alain Badiou

'L'autonomie du processus esthétique' in *Cahiers marxistes-léninistes*, no. 12/13 (1966), pp. 77–89.
'Le (re)commencement du matérialisme dialectique' in *Critique*, no. 240 (1967), pp. 438–67. (Review of Althusser, *For Marx* and *Reading Capital*.)
'Marque et manque: à propos du zéro' in *Cahiers pour l'analyse*, no. 10 (1969), pp. 150–73.

'Custos, quid noctis?' in *Critique*, no. 450 (1984), pp. 851–63. (Review of Lyotard, *The Differend*.)

'L'entretien de Bruxelles' in *Les Temps modernes*, no. 526 (1990), pp. 1–26.

'Saisissement, dessaisie, fidélité' in *Les Temps modernes*, no. 531, special edition on Jean-Paul Sartre (1990), pp. 14–22.

'On a Finally Objectless Subject', trans. B. Fink in Cadava *et al.* (eds) *Who Comes After the Subject?* (New York: Routledge, 1991), pp. 24–32.

'Being by numbers', interview with L. Sedofsky in *Artforum* (October 1994), pp. 84–7, 118, 123–4.

'Politics and philosophy', interview with P. Hallward in *Angelaki: Journal of the Theoretical Humanities*, 3:3 (1998), pp. 113–33.

'Metaphysics and the Critique of Metaphysics', trans. A. Toscano in *Pli*, vol. 10 (2000), pp. 174–90.

Other Books and Articles Consulted (Alphabetical by Author)

(**indicates secondary material on Badiou)

Althusser, L. *Essays in Self-Criticism*, trans. G. Lock (London: NLB, 1976).

_____, *For Marx*, trans. B. Brewster (London: Verso, 1996).

_____, *Lenin and Philosophy and Other Essays*, trans. B. Brewster (London: New Left Books, 1971).

_____, *Philosophy and the Spontaneous Philosophy of the Scientists and Other Essays*, trans. B. Brewster *et al.* (London: Verso, 1990).

_____, 'What Must Change in the Party' in *New Left Review*, no. 109, pp. 19–45.

Althusser, L. and Balibar, É. *Reading Capital*, trans. B. Brewster (London: Verso, 1979).

Anonymous, 'Sur la révolution culturelle' in *Cahiers marxistes-léninistes*, no. 14 (1966), pp. 5–16. (The author is clearly Louis Althusser).

Balibar, É. *Masses, Classes, Ideas*, trans. J. Swenson (London: Routledge, 1994).

_____, *On the Dictatorship of the Proletariat*, trans. G. Lock (London: New Left Books, 1977).

_____, *The Philosophy of Marx*, trans. C. Turner (London: Verso, 1995).

_____, *Spinoza and Politics*, trans. P. Snowdon (London: Verso, 1998).

Barber, B. R. *Superman and Common Men. Freedom, Anarchy and the Revolution* (Harmondsworth: Penguin, 1972).

Barrow, J. D. and Tipler, F. J. *The Anthropic Cosmological Principle* (Oxford: Oxford University Press, 1988).

Benacerraf, P. and Putnam, H. (eds) *Philosophy of Mathematics. Selected Readings* (Oxford: Basil Blackwell, 1964).

Bennett, T. *Formalism and Marxism* (London: Routledge 1979).

Berman, M. *All That Is Solid Melts Into Air* (London: Verso, 1983).

Bloch, E. *The Principle of Hope* (three volumes), trans. N. Plaice *et al.* (Oxford: Basil Blackwell, 1986).

Bogue, R. *Deleuze and Guattari* (London: Routledge, 1989).

Borch-Jacobsen, M. *Lacan: The Absolute Master*, trans. D. Brick (Stanford: Stanford University Press, 1991).

**Brasier, R. 'Stellar Void or Cosmic Animal? Badiou and Deleuze on the Dice-Throw', in *Pli*, vol. 10 (2000), pp. 200–16.

Cadava, E., Connor, P. and Nancy, J-L. (eds) *Who Comes After the Subject?* (New York: Routledge, 1991).

Cantor, G. *Contributions to the Founding of the Theory of Transfinite Numbers*, trans. P. E. B. Jourdain (New York: Dover, 1955).

Chomsky, N. *Language and Mind*, enlarged edition (London: Harcourt Brace Jovanovich, 1968).

Cohen, P. J. *Set Theory and the Continuum Hypothesis* (New York: W. A. Benjamin, 1966).

Critchley, S., Derrida, J., Laclau, E. and Rorty, R. *Deconstruction and Pragmatism*, C. Mouffe (ed.) (London: Routledge, 1996).

Debeauvais, M. (ed.) *L'Université ouverte: les dossiers de Vincennes* (Grenoble: Presses Universitaires de Grenoble, 1976).

Deleuze, G. *Bergsonism*, trans. H. Tomlinson and B. Habberjam (New York: Zone Books, 1988).

_____, *Cinema 1. The Movement Image*, trans. H. Tomlinson and B. Habberjam (London: Athlone, 1986).

_____, *Difference and Repetition*, trans. P. Patton (London: Athlone, 1994).

_____, *Expressionism in Philosophy: Spinoza*, trans. M. Joughin (New York: Zone Books, 1990).

_____, *The Fold. Leibniz and the Baroque*, trans. T. Conley (London: Athlone, 1993).

_____, *Foucault*, trans. S. Hand (London: Athlone, 1988).

_____, 'Gilles Deleuze contre les "nouveaux philosophes"' in *Le Monde*, 19–20 June 1977.

_____, *The Logic of Sense*, trans. M. Lester with C. Stivale (New York: Columbia University Press, 1990).

_____, *Nietzsche and Philosophy*, trans. H. Tomlinson (London: Athlone, 1983).

_____, *Spinoza. Practical Philosophy*, trans. R. Hurley (San Francisco: City Lights, 1988).

Deleuze, G. and Guattari, F. *Anti-Oedipus*, trans. R. Hurley, M. Seem and H. R. Lane (Minneapolis: University of Minnesota Press, 1983).

_____, *A Thousand Plateaus*, trans. B. Massumi (London: Athlone, 1988).

_____, *What is Philosophy?*, trans. G. Burchell and H. Tomlinson (London: Verso, 1994).

Deleuze, G. and Parnet, C. *Dialogues*, trans. H. Tomlinson and B. Habberjam (London: Athlone, 1987).

Derrida, J. *Of Grammatology*, trans. G. C. Spivak (Baltimore: Johns Hopkins University Press, 1976).

_____, *Writing and Difference*, trans. A. Bass (London: Routledge, 1978).

Devlin, K. *The Joy of Sets. Fundamentals of Contemporary Set Theory*, second edition (New York: Springer-Verlag, 1993).

Dosse, F. *History of Structuralism* (two volumes) trans. D. Glassman (Minneapolis: University of Minnesota Press, 1998).

Dummett, M. *Truth and Other Enigmas* (London: Duckworth, 1978).

Elliott, G. (ed.) *Althusser: A Critical Reader* (Oxford: Blackwell, 1994).

_____, 'Via dollarosa. On the "Third Way"' in *Radical Philosophy*, no. 94 (1999), pp. 2–5.

Foucault, M. *The Archaeology of Knowledge*, trans. A. M. Sheridan Smith (London: Routledge, 1989).

_____, *Discipline and Punish. The Birth of the Prison*, trans. A. Sheridan (London: Penguin, 1991).

_____, *Histoire de la Sexualité*, tome I: *La volonté de savoir* (Paris: Gallimard, 1976).

_____, *The Order of Things*, trans. A. Sheridan (London: Tavistock, 1970).

Fraenkel, A. A. and Bar-Hillel, Y. *Foundations of Set Theory*, second edition (Amsterdam: North-Holland, 1973).

Glucksmann, A. *La cuisinière et le mangeur d'hommes. Essai sur les rapports entre l'État, le marxisme et les camps de concentration* (Paris: Seuil, 1975).

_____, *Les maîtres penseurs* (Paris: Bernard Grasset, 1977).

Golinski, J. *Making Natural Knowledge. Constructivism and the History of Science* (Cambridge: Cambridge University Press, 1998).

Guattari, F. *Les Années d'hiver: 1980–1985* (Paris: Barrault, 1986).

_____, *Molecular Revolution. Psychiatry and Politics*, trans. R. Sheed and introduced by D. Cooper (London: Penguin, 1984).

_____, *The Three Ecologies*, trans. I. Pindar and P. Sutton (London: Athlone, 2000).

Guattari, F. and Negri, T. *Communists Like Us*, trans. M. Ryan (New York: Semiotext(e), 1990).

**Hallward, P. 'Ethics Without Others: A Reply to Simon Critchley', in *Radical Philosophy*, no. 102 (2000), pp. 27–31.

**_____, 'Generic Sovereignty. The Philosophy of Alain Badiou' in *Angelaki: Journal of the Theoretical Humanities*, 3:3 (1998), pp. 87–111.

**_____, *Subject to Truth* (draft extracts from unpublished manuscript) (Minneapolis: University of Minnesota Press).

Hampden Jackson, J. *Marx, Proudhon and European Socialism* (London: The English Universities Press, 1957).

Hare, R. M. *Plato* (Oxford: Oxford University Press, 1982).

Harland, R. *Superstructuralism* (London: Routledge, 1987).

Hawking, S. *A Brief History of Time. From the Big Bang to Black Holes* (London: Bantam, 1988).

Hegel, G. W. F. *The Phenomenology of Spirit*, trans. A. V. Miller (Oxford: Oxford University Press, 1977).

_____, *The Science of Logic*, trans. A. V. Miller (London: George Allen & Unwin, 1969).

Heidegger, M. *Being and Time*, trans. J. Macquarrie and E. Robinson (Oxford: Blackwell, 1962).

_____, *The Question Concerning Technology and Other Essays*, trans. W. Lovitt (New York: Harper and Row, 1977).

Herrnstein Smith, B. and Plotinsky, A. (eds) *The South Atlantic Quarterly*, 94:2, special issue on 'Mathematics, Science, and Postclassical Theory' (1995).

**Hindess, B. 'Materialist Mathematics' in *Theoretical Practice*, issue 3/4 (Autumn 1971), pp. 82–95.

Hospers, J. *An Introduction to Philosophical Analysis*, revised edition (London: Routledge, 1989).

Hsiung, J. C. (ed.) *The Logic of 'Maoism'* (London: Praeger, 1974).

Inwood, M. *Heidegger* (Oxford: Oxford University Press, 1997).

Ishiguro, H. *Leibniz's Philosophy of Logic and Language*, second edition (Cambridge: Cambridge University Press, 1990).

Kant, I. *Prolegomena to any Future Metaphysics*, trans. P. G. Lucas (Manchester: Manchester University Press, 1953).

Kaplan, E. A. and Sprinker, M. (eds) *The Althusserian Legacy* (London: Verso, 1993).

Kunen, K. *Set Theory. An Introduction to Independence Proofs* (Amsterdam: North Holland, 1980).

Lacan, J. *Écrits. A Selection*, trans. A. Sheridan (London: Routledge, 1977).

Laclau, E. and Mouffe, C. *Hegemony and Socialist Strategy: Toward a Radical Democratic Politics* (London: Verso, 1985).

Lacoue-Labarthe , P. *Heidegger, Art and Politics. The Fiction of the Political*, trans. C. Turner (Oxford: Basil Blackwell, 1990).

Laski, H. J. *Communism: 1381–1927* (London: Thornton Butterworth, 1927).

**Lecercle, J. J. 'Cantor, Lacan, Mao, Beckett, *même combat*: The Philosophy of Alain Badiou' in *Radical Philosophy*, no. 93 (1999), pp. 6–13.

Lecourt, D. *The Mediocracy. French Philosophy Since the Mid-1970s*, trans. G. Elliott (London: Verso, 2001).

Le Lionnais, F. (ed.) *Great Currents of Mathematical Thought*, vol. 1, trans. R. A. Hall and H. G. Bergmann; vol. 2, trans. C. Pinter and H. Kline (New York: Dover Publications, 1971).

Lenin, V. I. *The State and Revolution* (London: The British Socialist Party, and Glasgow: The Socialist Labour Press, 1919).

Lyotard. J-F. *The Differend: Phrases in Dispute*, trans. G. Van Den Abeele (Manchester: Manchester University Press, 1988).

_____, *Libidinal Economy*, trans. I. Hamilton Grant (London: Athlone, 1993).

_____, *The Postmodern Condition: A Report on Knowledge*, trans. G. Bennington and B. Massumi (Manchester: Manchester University Press, 1984).

Macherey, P. *Hegel ou Spinoza* (Paris: Maspero, 1979).

Machover, M. *Set theory, logic and their limitations* (Cambridge: Cambridge University Press, 1996).

Mao Tse-tung, *Selected Works* (five volumes) (London: Lawrence and Wishart, 1954).

Marx, K. *The Poverty of Philosophy*, trans. H. Quelch with preface by Friedrich Engels (New York: Prometheus Books, 1995).

Marx, K. and Engels, F. *Selected Works* (London: Lawrence and Wishart, 1991).

Matheron, A. *Le Christ et le salut des ignorants chez Spinoza* (Paris: Aubier Montaigne, 1971).

_____, *Individu et communauté chez Spinoza* (Paris: Minuit, 1969).

McLellan, D. *The Thought of Karl Marx. An Introduction*, second edition (London: Macmillan, 1980).

Negri, A. *Marx Beyond Marx. Lessons on the Grundrisse*, trans. H. Cleaver, M. Ryan and M. Viano (London: Pluto Press, 1991).

_____, *The Savage Anomaly. The Power of Spinoza's Metaphysics and Politics*, trans. M. Hardt (Minneapolis: University of Minnesota Press, 1991).

Nietzsche, F. *The Gay Science*, trans. W. Kaufmann (New York: Vintage Books, 1974).

_____, *On the Genealogy of Morals*, trans. D. Smith (Oxford: Oxford University Press, 1996).

_____, *Thus Spoke Zarathustra*, trans. R. J. Hollingdale (Harmondsworth: Penguin, 1961).

Norris, C. *New Idols of the Cave. On the limits of anti-realism* (Manchester: Manchester University Press, 1997).

_____, 'On the Limits of "Undecidability": Quantum Physics, Deconstruction, and Anti-realism' in *The Yale Journal of Criticism*, 11:2 (1998), pp. 407–32.

_____, 'The Platonist Fix: why "nothing works" (according to Putnam) in philosophy of mathematics' (unpublished article, 2001).

_____, 'Putnam on realism, reference and truth: the problem with quantum mechanics' in *International Studies in the Philosophy of Science*, 15:1 (2001), pp. 65–91.

Oderberg, D. S. *Moral Theory. A Non-Consequentialist Approach* (Oxford: Blackwell, 2000).

Pascal, B. *Pensées*, trans. A. J. Krailsheimer, revised edition (London: Penguin, 1995).

_____, *The Provincial Letters*, J. De Soyres (ed.) (Cambridge: Deighton Bell and Co., 1880).

Pêcheux, M. *Les Vérités de la Palice. Linguistique, sémantique, philosophie* (Paris: Maspero, 1975).

Plato, *Parmenides*, trans. M. L. Gill and P. Ryan (Indianapolis: Hackett, 1996).

_____, *Republic*, trans. R. Waterfield (Oxford: Oxford University Press, 1993).

_____, *Sophist*, trans. N. P. White (Indianapolis: Hackett, 1993).

Queneau, R. *Zazie dans le métro* (Paris: Gallimard, 1959).

Rancière, J. *La leçon d'Althusser* (Paris: Gallimard, 1974).

_____, *La Mésentente. Politique et philosophie* (Paris: Galilée, 1995).

Rescher, N. *G.W. Leibniz's Monadology* (London: Routledge, 1991).

Rorty, R. *Contingency, Irony and Solidarity* (Cambridge: Cambridge University Press, 1989).

Rousseau, J. J. *The Social Contract and Discourses*, trans. G. D. H. Cole (London: Everyman, 1968).

Sartre, J-P. *Critique de la raison dialectique*, tome I (Paris: Gallimard, 1960).

_____, *Critique of Dialectical Reason*, vol. II (London: Verso, 1991).

Saussure, F. de. *Course in General Linguistics*, C. Bally and A. Sechehaye in collaboration with A. Riedlinger (eds), trans. W. Baskin (New York: The Philosophical Library, 1959).

Short, P. *Mao: A Life* (London: Hodder and Stoughton, 1999).

**Simont, J. 'Le pur et l'impur' in *Les Temps modernes*, no. 526 (1990), pp. 27–60.

Smart, B. (ed.) *Michel Foucault: Critical Assessments*, vol. 5 (London: Routledge, 1995).

Spinoza, *Ethics*, trans. A. Boyle, revised edition (London: Everyman, 1993).

Thomas, J. E. *Musings on the Meno* (The Hague: Martinus Nijhoff, 1980).

Tiles, M. *The Philosophy of Set Theory. An Introduction to Cantor's Paradise* (Oxford: Basil Blackwell, 1989).

UCFML, *Première Année d'existence d'une organisation maoïste* (Paris: Maspero, 1972).

Wheen, F. *Karl Marx* (London: Fourth Estate, 2000).

Wiele, J. V. 'Heidegger et Nietzsche. Le problème de la métaphysique' in *Revue Philosophique de Louvain*, tome 66, no. 91 (1968), pp. 435–86.

Williams, J. *Lyotard. Towards a Postmodern Philosophy* (Cambridge: Polity Press, 1998).

Wokler, R. *Rousseau* (Oxford: Oxford University Press, 1995).

**Zizek, S. *The Ticklish Subject. The Absent Centre of Political Ontology* (London: Verso, 1999).

Index

179

presentation, 43, 48, 49, 51, 52, 53,
54, 55, 56, 60, 64–5, 66, 67, 68,
69, 70, 71, 72, 79, 81, 84–5, 89,
91, 107, 109, 125–6, 133, 134,
151, 157n.24, 161n.10
of presentation, 43–6, 157n.24
see also set theory; situation
process without a subject
see Althusser, Louis
proletariat, 20–33, 70–4, 142–3,
165n.42
see also class; class struggle
Protagoras, 131
Proudhon, Pierre Joseph, 31, 32
PSU (United Socialist Party), 1
psychoanalysis, 41, 44, 52–3
see also Freud, Sigmund; Lacan,
Jacques
Putnam, Hilary, 4, 46
Pythagoras, 47

Queneau, Raymond, 46

Rancière, Jacques, 141–3, 158n.1,
169n.8, n.9, n.10
Real, 52–3
versus reality, 8, 41, 160n.3
see also Lacan, Jacques
Regnault, François, 13
relation(s)
see axioms of set theory;
ontology; set theory
replacement, axiom of
see axioms of set theory; set
theory
representation, 28, 30, 36–7, 67, 68,
70–3, 88, 89, 100–1, 104, 109,
142
see also set theory; state of the
situation
revolutionary working class
movement, 32, 33
see also class; class struggle
romanticism, 48, 49, 55
Rorty, Richard, 169n.10

Rousseau, Jean-Jacques, 5, 72,
98–105, 106–7, 170n.19
Russell, Bertrand, 48, 166n.10
Russian Revolution, 74, 84, 102, 105

Saint-Just, Louis de, 77, 84
Saint Paul, 84
same, the
see difference
Sartre, Jean-Paul, 13–18, 33, 34,
158n.5, n.6, 160n.31
Saussure, Ferdinand de, 65, 161n.12
science, 4, 5, 8–9, 13–18, 22, 24, 30,
39–58, 59–63, 70, 71, 97–8,
124–6, 128, 134, 161n.9
see also mathematics; ontology
Second World War, 13
sense, 108, 115–17, 120, 123,
164n.32, 167n.6
see also nonsense
separation, axiom of (axiom of
subset selection)
see axioms of set theory; set
theory
set(s), 17, 22, 23, 35, 56–8, 66, 67,
68, 83–4, 88, 89, 95, 96, 101–3,
107, 118, 121, 125, 149–55
see also axioms of set theory;
elements; set theory
set theory, 5, 6, 9–11, 55–8, 64,
66–70, 86–9, 125, 127, 149–55
Shiying, Zhang, 33, 34, 35, 37
simulacr(a)um, 24, 114–15, 120–1,
140
singularity, 63–4, 72, 111, 113, 114,
118, 121, 139
see also One-all
site
see event
situation, 44–6, 78–82, 84, 88, 89,
96, 97, 102, 103, 107–9, 117,
134, 140, 142
see also counting as one; set
theory
Socrates, 46–7, 49–52